Teacher's
Way

Anne D. Forester

Margaret Reinhard

PEGUIS PUBLISHERS

the Teacher's Way

The Role of the Teacher in Today's Classroom

Canadian Cataloguing in Publication Data

Forester, Anne D.

The teacher's way

Includes bibliographical references.

ISBN 1-895411-67-X

1. Education, Primary.
2. Teaching.
3. Curriculum change.
I. Reinhard, Margaret, 1931– II. Title.

LB1523.F67 1994 372.1
C94-920088-3

Book and cover design: Pat Stanton

Peguis Publishers Limited
100–318 McDermot Ave.
Winnipeg, Manitoba
Canada R3A 0A2

Printed and bound in Canada by Hignell Printing Limited

98 97 96 95 94   5 4 3 2 1

Editor's Note: One of the dilemmas facing today's editor is that of retaining clarity while ensuring gender balance. This relates specifically to the use of the personal pronouns he/she, him/her, himself/herself, and so on. Using both forms in all cases makes for particularly awkward reading. In this book we have chosen to use feminine pronouns in reference to teachers and masculine pronouns in reference to students. We assure the reader that no affront is intended in any way.

Contents

ACKNOWLEDGMENTS   **XV**

INTRODUCTION   **I**
   Keeping the tone positive   3
   Acknowledging that all teaching is multi-age   4

I.
EDUCATION FOR THE YEAR 2000   **5**

Shifting the focus from teaching to learning   6

Children are natural learners   7
   Linguistic research is valid in schools as well as out   7
   Active involvement shapes the brain   8
   Creating "inner maps"   9
   "Route memory" requires drill for skill   11

Meeting children's needs   15
   Children need a rich environment to be active learners   15
   Children need models that they can follow   19
   Children need to work at their own pace   20
   Children need to generate their own rules   21
   Children need to build on what they already know   22

The teacher as learner in the year 2000   23

2.

THE TEACHER'S ROLE 25

Celebrating the teacher's way 25

What teachers *do* to foster learning 26

Setting the climate 26

Providing learning materials 29

Organizing the learning activities 30

Providing information 32

Modeling learning behaviors 33

Working with parents 37

Being accountable 37

Observing learners – "kid watching" 40

Monitoring progress against the curriculum guidelines 42

Building on children's learning styles 44

Enhancing children's own sequence of learning 45

Applying knowledge of child development 46

Building on successes 46

Providing feedback that acknowledges and extends skills 48

Individualizing instruction 50

Fostering independence and responsibility 52

Collaborating to establish rules – maintaining discipline 54

Connecting learning to the world outside 54

Collaborating with helpers 56

Continuing to learn 57

Reaffirming the professional status of teachers 57

3.

CREATING A CONTEXT FOR INDEPENDENCE 59

Setting a climate for independence and responsibility 60

"You can do it yourself!" 62

Establishing routines allows for independence 65

Allowing children enough time 66

Developing independence in reading 67

Encouraging self-reliance in writing and spelling 69

Modeling helps to evolve independent report writing 72

Modeling webbing 73

Setting a climate of independence leads to creative thinking and
effective problem solving   77
   Independence leaves room for *all* levels of work 78
   The rewards of independence accrue to teacher and
   students alike 79

4.
WHO'S IN CHARGE HERE ANYWAY?   81

Sharing power – enhancing power   82
   What is power anyway? 83
   Discipline? Keep it positive 85

The *why* and *how* of sharing power   87
   Sharing power transforms energy 87
   Creativity shows itself in many ways 88
   Collaboration generates power 90
   Becoming a lead teacher 95
   Establishing routines diminishes the need for controls 95

The gains you make from sharing power   99

5.
CHILD WATCHING BECOMES A GUIDE TO
TEACHING/LEARNING   101
   Kid watching gives you answers to what, when, and how 103
   Start where the child is 103

What you already know about watching kids   105
   Freedom to move creates opportunities 106
   Your knowledge of child development guides you 107
   Observing the benefits of interaction 110
   Noting how fun enhances learning 111
   Recognizing individual patterns of learning 111
   Observations become your guides for stimulating learning 112

Watching the curriculum versus watching the kids   114

The *why* and *how* of watching learners   115
   Understanding and appreciating how children learn 115

Begin by learning to describe 116
Interpreting what you see 118
Expanding the art of listening 119
If the teacher listens attentively, so do the students 122
Setting the social climate by listening with care 123
Tapping the children's ability to "hear" 123
Taking feelings into account 124

The magic of observing the whole child   125
Recognizing learning behavior 126
Talents and interests build learning 126
Capturing teachable moments 127

Trusting the learners is the key   128

6.
A MULTI-AGE CLASSROOM IS NOT A "SPLIT CLASS" 129

Grouping children for multi-age learning 130
Teachers of multi-age classes are enthusiasts 131
There's really nothing new here 132
What multi-age grouping has to offer 133
Building a learning community 136
Learning together and from each other 137
No, you won't be teaching separate lessons for
each group! 137
Teaching becomes a matter of creating contexts
for learning 138

Why do we believe in multi-age classes?   139

7.
TO START THE YEAR—BEGIN AT THE BEGINNING   141

New parents' tea   142

Starting the new school year   144
Making grass-roots changes 146
Getting ready for the newcomers 147

The first and foremost job - setting the climate   150
Providing outlets for creativity 150

Using stories to draw children together and widen
their horizons 152
Talking and listening lead to news time and writing 153
Field trips and movement add pleasure and channel energy 155
The climate of delight shows itself in many ways 156
At the beginning of the year whole-group activities
predominate 158

Setting routines and guidelines   160

The teacher's way of setting the scene   161

8.
ACTIVITIES THAT INVOLVE ALL LEARNERS   **163**

Reading is for everyone   164
    Reading aloud 164
    Unison reading 164
    Reading workshop 165

Interest themes and projects draw students together   167
    Hands-on activities build learning for everyone 167
    Using literature to foster learning 172
    Making the reading/writing connection 174

Field trips are wonderful sources for learning   175

Writing serves many functions   176
    Composing and spelling are modeled in news time 177
    Writing workshop takes many forms 177

Center time is everyone's favorite   178

Math is for everyone   179
    Making math concrete in everyday work 179

What's left?   180

9.
STARTING THE FLOW OF LEARNING   **181**

Listening attentively gets activities started   182

Gathering information at the beginning of the day 182
Creating a flow of talk for general sharing and news time 184
Translating interests into actions 187

Drawing children to reading   189
The storybook road 191
Capturing the magic of reading 191
There are genuine lessons in all this reading 192
Unison, or choral, reading makes practice fun and easy 194
Books and reading inspire readers' theater 195
Adding nonfiction to the repertoire 197

Starting projects   198
Using books to launch a project 200
Outside influences can become triggers for projects 205
Starting long-term projects and all-school involvement 207

The teacher's personal interests get things rolling   208

10.
SPELLING DOES COUNT   **209**

The teacher's role in developing children's spelling   211
Making work with letters fun for emergent writers 211
Setting the scene with reading - building vocabulary 211
Showing the uses of spelling 213
Capturing the children's interest 213
Offering on-the-spot mini-lessons 214
Watching for progress then using it as a springboard for
further development 215
Modeling spelling during news time 215

The role of the teacher expands   218
Lessons teachers learn 219
Honoring the children's ways of learning 220

Writing provides both practice and feedback for spelling   221
Making children aware of the details of spelling 221
Encouraging self-reliance 224

Where do we go from here?   228

11.
A TYPICAL DAY IN CLASS 229

A day in Margaret's kindergarten-to-grade-two class 229
    Morning 229
    After recess 234
    Afternoon 235

Karen Abel's grade-two-three day 237
    Morning 237
    After recess 239
    Afternoon 240

The commonalities 242

12.
TO BE ACCOUNTABLE, TURN THE CURRICULUM UPSIDE DOWN 243

Where does the curriculum lead? 244
    Turning the curriculum upside down 245

Finding the fit between children's learning and the curriculum 247
    "Negotiating the curriculum" 247

Being accountable is as important as ever 249
    The "literacy continuum" 254
    Looking for "the basics" 256
    Finding "the foundation skills" in children's work 256
    Following broader curriculum goals 258
    Sources to help you assess progress 262

Finding the learner in the curriculum 262

13.
BUDDIES—POWER IN PARTNERSHIP 263

Getting started 265
    Selecting a partner for teaching 265
    Teachers explore possibilities 265

Setting the climate for students 266
Asking for student input 267

Making buddy work successful   268
Knowing the gains to be made 270
Selecting buddies 270
Starting out gently 273

From mundane materials favorite activities grow   274
Ikebana at the art gallery becomes the lead-in 275
Poetry sparks artwork and more 275
When young buddies build mansions 276
Giving thanks over a shared meal 278
Christmas offers many possibilities 279
Artwork blossoms in the spring 280
Sharing hands-on work teaches math 281
There are lessons even in feeding the ducks 282

Assuring there is closure   284

Closing the year – saying goodbye   285

14.
PARENTS AS CO-CREATORS OF LEARNING   287

Margaret's way of drawing parents into the circle of learning   288
Thoughts that guided me 289
Parents become facilitators of learning 290
Parent orientation in September 290
Scheduling helpers 291
Moving through the day with the children 294
Field trips 299
Special projects need extra help 301
Concerts 301
Parent appreciation 302
The cycle starts again with a new parents' tea 303

The benefits of positive parent involvement   304

15.
NETWORKING—TEACHERS' LIFELINE   307

The teacher–researcher connection 308

Teachers are networking with each other   310

Margaret's networking experience   310
The early days 311
A student teacher expands the network 311
The Wednesday Club 312
Networking within a school 314

Networking confirms and stimulates   317

16.
PULLING IT ALL TOGETHER   319

Celebrating successes   319

Looking back, looking ahead   320
Remembering high points and achievements 321
Turning memories into the class annual 322
Appreciating work well done 323
Visions of the year ahead 324
Appreciating the teacher 324
Reading expands and supports the year-end debriefing 325

Pulling it all together   327
A journey into the past - a vision of the future 327
Making it all worthwhile 328

BIBLIOGRAPHY   331
Professional references 331
Children's books 334
School-experience books 336
Books for chick-hatching project 336

FIGURES

Figure 1   Two Kinds of Learning – Natural Memory
            Versus Memorization   13

Figure 2   Methods of Research and Inquiry Used by Both
            Scientists Doing Research and Children Exploring
            Their World   17

Figure 3   Using a Management Model to Compare
            Teaching Styles   94

Figure 4   Individual Profile of Emergent Reading   250

Figure 5   Individual Profile of Reading Development   252

Figure 6   SCANS Report: What Work Requires of Schools   257

Acknowledgments

The journey back over our teaching years has been one of profound sharing. To express our appreciation to those who so willingly shared their own ongoing journeys, we wish to acknowledge their encouragement, help, and special input.

To Margaret's sister, Marilyn Galloway, goes the credit for the title of our book. As she listened to Margaret's son question his mother's ways of explaining something, Marilyn commented, "But, James, that's the teacher's way!", and there was our new book title.

To teachers who invited us into their classrooms, allowed us to take photographs, and freely shared their thoughts, materials, and ways of working with children, our deep gratitude. Those who worked most closely with us are Margaret's daughter, Anne Peterson, South Park teachers Karen Abel, Linda Picciotto, Marne St. Claire, Susan Gilberstad, and Elizabeth Hamblet (the teaching principal of South Park School). Special thanks to Margaret's partner-networkers Diane Cowden, Shelagh Levy, and June Domke, and to Judy Mainwaring who invited Margaret into her class to talk about and participate in implementing the learners' way. Their work continues to be both an inspiration and a joy to us, as each of them continues to search for better, more effective ways to work with children. Their classrooms are never the same but evolve from day to day to meet the needs of the children.

When working on "Spelling Does Count", we received special help and classroom tips not only from the classroom teachers but from special education teacher/librarian Barbara Beukema at South Park

School and from Mary Tarasoff, who made not only her expertise but several of her publications freely available to us. We are grateful for their generous help.

Special thanks also to Judy Norget who once again gave us her energy, patience, and expertise in editing our book.

But above all, our thanks go to the children. Without them there would be no teachers, no book. They have sustained us over the years and given us joy, fresh outlooks, and a deep appreciation of the power we all have to learn in natural ways.

Introduction

The Teacher's Way is a salute to all those primary teachers who constantly search for new and better ways of working with their students. It was at the suggestion of some of these teachers that we undertook writing this book. They made us aware that while our book *The Learners' Way*, with its focus on children's ways of learning, had filled a need, there was now a need to focus on teachers and *their* best ways of working.

Many teachers had the uneasy feeling that with the new global ways of teaching/learning and the abandonment of structured lessons, the teacher's role was becoming somewhat poorly defined - they felt they should not do any direct teaching for fear of interfering with children's ways of learning. Enthusiastic observers, a few less-than-perceptive researchers, and even some teachers promulgated the myth that learning "just happened" without teacher intervention when you allowed children free access to a wide variety of learning materials in the classroom and in the special settings provided through field trips.

While both views are, of course, extreme, there appears to be a need to take a close look at the role of teachers who work in learner-centered classrooms. To do so we looked back over Margaret's years of experience and also enlisted the aid of a number of other teachers whose work fosters learning in wonderfully productive ways.

Accordingly, what we offer in *The Teacher's Way* is a compendium of direct teaching experience that acknowledges the unique personal background each child brings to learning and the multi-age nature of every classroom in which children function at a wide range of levels of maturity and experience. The particular topics we address are based on questions teachers have asked us when they have visited Margaret's classroom or participated in our workshops. They observed the excitement, joy, and productivity that pervade when children are free to learn in their own best ways, and they wanted to know how to create that climate of delight.

Chapter 1 provides a firm foundation for the practical descriptions presented throughout this book. It includes concrete examples of brain-based learning, research into the natural functions of language acquisition, and the applications of cognitive research that affirm the effectiveness of child-directed learning. The expanded and changed role of teachers is defined in some detail in chapter 2. It emphasizes the fact that teachers do much more than dispense information. Chapters 3 and 4 address the importance of the classroom climate and describe how to help students become independent learners who share with the teacher the responsibility for their learning. In that context, the classroom empowers teacher and students alike.

The magic of using direct observation as a tool for day-to-day classroom decision making is the topic of chapter 5. It deals with keeping track of progress, building on strengths, finding ways to enhance learning, and discovering the special needs of students. Chapter 6 affirms that a multi-age classroom is not a split class that calls for separate lessons for different groups of children. It outlines the very solid benefits that both teachers and students derive from working in family groupings. Acknowledging the diversity of children calls for special ways of drawing them together into a learning community. Chapter 7 describes how to get the school year underway positively and effectively for everyone. How to involve all learners, even though they all function at their own unique levels, is discussed in chapter 8. It provides examples of whole-class activities that invite students to participate at their own levels of ability and interest. Chapter 9 discusses ways to draw learners into activities and to start the flow of learning. It suggests many positive ways to kick off projects and themes.

Spelling is still important, even in classrooms in which global ways of learning, rather than discrete skills, are stressed. Chapter 10 offers examples of how spelling is fostered in ways that build on the learners' ways of learning. Two capsule overviews of a day in class, one shaped by a kindergarten-to-grade-two teacher and the other by a grade-two-three teacher, are outlined in chapter 11. Finding the fit between children's learning and the curriculum is the topic of chapter 12. While it is important to know the curriculum, the chapter suggests that teachers turn the curriculum upside down to focus on its intended outcomes and to work on skills as they emerge in a global context.

Interpersonal, interactive work stands at the heart of working the learners' way. Chapters 13, 14, and 15 deal with ways of enhancing learning through interaction: bringing children from different grades together for buddy sessions; drawing parents into their children's learning, both in class and out; and forming a support network of like-minded teachers to compare notes, provide mutual support, and share the joys of positive teaching/learning. Just as we need to give thought to good beginnings, so we need to plan for closure. Chapter 16 describes year-end activities that keep energy high and see you and your students close the year on a high note - looking back with satisfaction and ahead with eager anticipation. That experience becomes a metaphor for your own ongoing learning.

The subject of assessment and evaluation is a large one, warranting more than a chapter in a book. Rather than dealing inadequately with the subject, we have chosen to weave comments about keeping track of student progress throughout the book - just as assessment is now interwoven with day-to-day teaching/learning.

KEEPING THE TONE POSITIVE

Throughout the book our approach is very positive and we focus on strengths rather than on difficulties. This attitude is a reflection of the way we interact with students, with parents, with our colleagues - and with each other. Over the years we have made a concerted effort to eliminate negative comments from our interactions and written communications. When preparing report cards, for example, Margaret will ask herself, "What good would it do if I made a negative comment about this child? Would it help the child's growth or be useful to the parents?" Invariably she decides to use positive comments and, if necessary, some remarks about skills or learning that could be enhanced by extra effort: "To help Mary improve her reading comprehension, I'm going to give her more individual attention and extra help. To improve her spelling, I'll consult with the learning assistance teacher to see if Mary would benefit from individualized work in spelling."

Little can be gained from bemoaning the mistakes of the past. Without ignoring what can be improved, we consciously choose to dwell on the joy, excitement, and satisfaction that accompany work that meets students' needs in positive ways. "Meeting the needs of students" is the guiding principle behind all our work.

In case you think that the positive tone sounds unrealistic or unattainable, we want to acknowledge that our own experience - on which we draw in this book - does not include working in inner-city schools, in classrooms in which only a third of the children speak English, or where violence is commonplace. We are well aware that teachers facing such challenges have much greater demands placed on their patience, courage, ingenuity, and stamina than we have had to face. But our own experience with difficult students, unreasonable parents, unresponsive authorities, and explosive incidents in class have taught us the value of maintaining our calm, positive attitude through thick and thin. In the long run, no matter how difficult it may be at times, staying positive and affirming your trust in students yield trust in return.

ACKNOWLEDGING THAT *ALL* TEACHING IS MULTI-AGE

Throughout the book, we write about working with children in multi-age settings because most of our own teaching experience has been with multi-age classes. We also believe that multi-age groupings are more effective for teaching/learning than single-grade classes. But whether you are working with a single-grade class or one that spans two or more grades, the considerations for meeting the needs of your students remain the same. So "think multi-age" whether you teach a single grade or a combination of several grades. As you are well aware, in either case the children in your care will have a wide range of needs, based not only on their chronological age, but on their physical maturation, personal experience, cultural background, health, and family support. They will also have different learning styles, talents, interests, and areas of difficulty. When there is open recognition that all the children in your class function at their own unique levels, then teaching/learning takes on new excitement, and anxieties about fixed deadlines or unrealistic goals are removed.

The suggestions and examples we offer in this book are just that – suggestions. Just as we see each child as unique, so we know you are unique and need to work in your own personal style. We provide examples of activities and ways of interacting as reference points only. And we invite you to adapt them to suit your own ways, to sort and select, and to discard whatever does not fit your style of teaching/ learning. Over the years we have found that watching the children and reflecting on their ways of learning and interacting rekindles our spontaneity, enthusiasm, and creativity. We hope that this book will become a spark for you. Enjoy creating your own climate of delight, one that fits your unique talents and needs as well as those of your students.

1.

Education for the Year 2000

All over North America, ministries and departments of education, school boards, and individual schools are producing documents that outline the requirements for education for the year 2000. Almost invariably the terms are broad, and the implied demands for teachers sweeping. Preparing students for the year 2000 means inculcating thinking and problem–solving skills, social responsibility, methods of inquiry, effective work habits, enthusiasm for learning, resourcefulness and creativity, aesthetic appreciation, decision–making and leadership qualities, not to mention factual information about history, geography, science, mathematics, and the language arts. Then there are the discussions of teaching methods and references to brain–based teaching; holistic, integrative ways of conveying information through reality–based projects; meeting the emotional needs of students; and focusing on process more than on product. Throughout there are references to the uniqueness of individual students and the importance of meeting their needs in flexible, open ways to promote growth that builds on their personal backgrounds and strengths. In short, what most of the documents acknowledge is that we need to return to education (drawing learning from within) and move away from too much teaching (focusing too strongly on instilling a closely circumscribed body of knowledge and facts).

The vision is sweeping and at the same time promising, because it draws on much of the best research on how the brain works, how natural learning takes place, and what motivates learners. It takes into account that community and workplace demands will continue to change and expand, and it acknowledges the complex human qualities of learners of all ages. With a focus on developing human potential rather than on monitoring exam scores and standard achievement tests, education for the year 2000 will be both a challenge and a promise – a challenge to teachers and curriculum planners to find new, more effective ways of fostering learning, and a promise of very exciting, rewarding ways of functioning in the classroom for students and teachers alike.

Shifting the focus from teaching to learning

Research and practice over the last two decades offer many practical suggestions and a very solid theoretical foundation to help teachers shift their focus from teaching to learning, from imparting facts and skills to fostering ways of inquiry and learning. Practical suggestions are provided throughout this book for shifting to a focus on learning. Here, however, we wish to present some of the research that supports the soundness of the practical work. The philosophy of learning that is emerging from these different strands of research acknowledges the natural ways of learning we all share and encourages teachers to draw on their knowledge and in-class observations of children to foster learning for *all* students – in *their* ways and at *their* pace. Since the mandates for teaching for the year 2000 are coming from those in authority, we have the strong hope and expectation that, this time around, the wonderful work teachers do in their classrooms will have the solid backing and moral support of administrators, peers, and parents.

Since your shift will be gradual, there is no question of suddenly relinquishing all of your tried and true ways of working. Instead, as you turn to more global ways of introducing children to reading and writing, you will become ever more intrigued and absorbed with observing which teaching methods produce the most meaningful learning, how children learn, how much they absorb, and how well they function when you have them explore literacy and numeracy within the context of work that is interesting and meaningful to them.

Children are natural learners

Observing children at work and watching them become ever-more-independent learners form the foundation for the new mandates in education. The new curriculum documents acknowledge that children are natural learners. A look at recent process-oriented research about language acquisition, brain functioning, and general human behavior supports the practical information gathered in classrooms and homes, as teachers observed hands-on work and parents watched children learn to crawl, toddle, and walk. Children learn by taking in global information and abstract from that what they need and are ready for; and learning functions best in concrete contexts that engage both sides of the brain and when learners have taken a personal interest in deciding what to learn.

LINGUISTIC RESEARCH IS VALID IN SCHOOLS AS WELL AS OUT

The language acquisition research of the sixties and seventies (Ferguson and Slobin 1973; Moerk 1977) describes just how well infants are able to abstract what they need to learn, to derive their own rules, and to update their knowledge constantly and effortlessly. Our own in-class research (Forester 1975) builds on that linguistic research, and in chapter 5 we describe how children continue to apply their own effective ways of learning in school as they did at home. Language-based research and direct observations of children working in different settings (Graves 1983; Harste et al 1984) provide solid confirmation of the need for context-based work to make learning meaningful. And Wells (1981), looking at the differences between home and school as contexts for learning, writes:

> The relationship between language and context is one of the aspects of the child's experience which tends to change rather dramatically when he goes to school. Whereas most talk – and most learning – in the home arises out of contexts of practical activity, often ones the child himself has initiated, a great deal of learning in school, and the talk associated with the tasks through which that learning is planned to take place, is largely teacher-initiated and involves contexts which are unfamiliar to the child and ones which, in many cases, are also

relatively abstract. The result is that, for many children, strategies that have proved effective for interpreting and learning from the very varied situations that occur in the home are less effective at school and in some cases are even counter-productive.

Enhancing science study by concrete material from the environment always stimulates students' interest. A giant wasp nest produced extra excitement when loud buzzing announced that the nest was not quite abandoned. When a groggy queen wasp crawled to the surface, the teacher placed her into a jar and children had the opportunity to study her under a microscope.

The changes proposed for teaching for the year 2000 address the need to give learners the same opportunity to initiate learning and to create settings that invite them to continue to learn in their own best ways. Adding further weight to the evidence accumulated by direct observations of children's learning is the latest brain research, which draws a distinction between learning within and without a context.

ACTIVE INVOLVEMENT SHAPES THE BRAIN

Children learn with their whole beings, not just the left sides of their brains. Brain research confirms what linguists and other observational researchers have described so eloquently.

Discussing the importance of children's active involvement in their learning, Jane Healy (1990) reports that physiological research has confirmed that children's physical activities in exploring their environ-

ment actually create new brain patterns and build new synaptic connections. Sitting passively in front of a television set or listening to a
lecture in school does not develop the solid connections that are necessary to stimulate learning that can be readily transferred to new situations and settings.

CREATING "INNER MAPS"

Brain researchers (Caine and Caine 1991) refer to the building of these
brain patterns as the creation of "inner maps." They point out that
through our interactions with the world around us, all of us draw on
our "map memory" to create and then update highly personal inner
maps of our experience. At home, children pick up vast amounts of
information and master a tremendous number of skills seemingly
without instruction and, to all appearances, with little effort on their
part. They learn about their homes, the people around them, and the
ways of getting what they want when they want it. As they begin to
walk, they find out about their backyards, their streets, and their
neighborhoods. They are using their senses and personal experiences
to build their inner maps and they are expanding, refining, and elaborating those maps every day.

We seldom give enough credit to the amount of learning a child
does before entering school, probably because it seems so effortless.
But if you imagine having to devise lessons to teach your children
about all the people, places, things, and how-tos they already know
before they come to school, the magnitude of the job comes into
focus. Children begin with their knowledge-base of their homes, but
once they are taken outside they quickly learn about houses in their
neighborhoods, stores, streets, parks, the Dairy Queen, the local
supermarket. In short, their maps of the world around them have
considerable detail and are updated and elaborated constantly with
very little specific teaching from their parents.

The seeming lack of effort is perhaps the most striking characteris-
tic of map memory. We adults are also building and updating our
inner maps continually. As we experience the world around us, our
inner maps for preparing foods, dealing with money, expanding our
vocabulary, going to movies, and participating in sports and hobbies
are constantly expanded and enriched by our daily encounters. Generally, we are neither consciously aware of that continuous learning

nor see it as a difficult task. Lozanov (1978) refers to the effortless learning from information in the environment as "peripheral learning," and the popular term "superlearning," which has been attached to his system of foreign-language learning, attests to its ease and productivity.

In superlearning, as in early language acquisition, learners construct their inner maps by using all their senses. Their instructors orchestrate lessons that have them interact with people in realistic settings for language learning to help them see, feel, hear, smell, and – when possible – taste what it is they are talking about in their new language. As a result, learners incorporate all that information into their inner maps for language and communication – a kind of knowledge base that is far more effective than the mere storage of vocabulary, rules of grammar, or sounds. In fact, this process is much like the initial language learning of children, when they learn to talk and to understand.

Emotions as well as sensory information enrich language learning, and learners are more deeply involved – more excited – about their learning. Describing the joys of introducing reading to his infant son, David Doake (1986) writes, "When the child, a parent, and a book came together something almost magical happened. The inner need to develop ways of gaining independent access to his books so that he could retrieve these moments of magic and pleasure for himself was already evident in Raja's behavior by the end of his first year." That kind of peripheral learning had Raja "hooked on books" by the time he was a year old. That same inner need to retrieve the pleasure of reading on their own is stimulated in children in classrooms that introduce them to the magic of reading aloud and sharing stories. As a result, they build inner maps for reading that include those warm feelings that draw them irresistibly to books and reading.

Once we acknowledge the ease and efficiency with which children use peripheral learning in the home to acquire vast amounts of learning, then creating concrete contexts for learning and maximizing peer interactions and peer modeling at school become both eminently sensible and wonderfully effective. Multi-age classrooms, in which teachers provide open frameworks

You're never too young to enjoy books.

for working on projects and themes, seem particularly well suited to help children build inner maps for the crucial concepts of literacy and numeracy about which we worry so much. Because reading, writing, and math work are constantly interwoven into the daily classroom routines and are operating at a number of levels, children observe and take in far more than "the basics."

The inner maps the children build about the utility and enjoyment of reading, for example, are rich indeed. As they listen to stories and nonfiction reading and observe their more mature peers interact with the printed material in class in many different ways, even children who do not yet read establish an awareness of the fun and many uses of reading. They know that books are sources of information and pleasure, that reading material can be produced by writing, and that reading is very much a part of everyday life. In time, their inner maps for reading will include knowledge of book language, story grammars, information about left-to-right and top-to-bottom progression of print, and the use of phrasing, rhyming, and drawing inferences to anticipate what appears on the page.

That inner "literacy map" is built and constantly updated without conscious effort on the part of the children, as emergent and more advanced readers practice reading far more extensively than they do in classrooms in which carefully structured lessons guide their reading. At the same time, their learning is far more lasting and integrated into their knowledge of the world than learning produced by the very best "drill for skill." Their literacy maps have been created in a concrete context of daily interactions with books and reading. They are enriched by wonderfully positive feelings, and they serve as a receptive matrix into which the learning of details will fit, as emergent readers are introduced to phonic skills, sight words, cloze skills, and ways of making sense of complex information.

"ROUTE MEMORY" REQUIRES DRILL FOR SKILL

In contrast to this global learning and the creation of map memory, there is also "route memory" for more specific detail and discrete skills. Caine and Caine point out that, unlike map memory, route memory requires instruction and concerted effort to be accepted by the brain and then to become permanent. Traditionally, much of school learning has fallen into the category of route memory, as teachers have introduced children to lists of letters and sight words or to tables of math facts and rules for working with them. Because these mental "routes" were all too often laid down without the benefit of the concrete, multisensory background that fosters the building of inner maps, route learning led to difficulties and tedious aspects for students and teachers alike.

To clarify the distinction between the two types of learning, it may be useful to stay with the example of children learning about their neighborhood. By building his map memory, a quite young child can readily learn the way to his best friend's home, to the corner store, or to the neighborhood park. Walking along the route and building an inner map of all the landmarks makes that learning quite effective. But if you were to try to give a small child verbal directions for getting to a destination, chances are that the learning would be difficult, if not impossible, at a certain stage. Imagine trying to direct a young child to "go south along Main Street, turn left at the third intersection, and follow the street for two more blocks to get to...." Would you then feel secure in sending the child out? Yet when you walk out together, and the child knows where you are headed, more than likely he would turn south, get ready to turn at the third intersection, and then head down two more blocks without you having to lead the way. The establishment of an inner map through concrete exposure and physical practice makes the learning easy, while the same job done through the abstract verbal directions suggested would be quite difficult, probably impossible, for a young child to absorb and apply.

Route memory – the learning of specific, out-of-context detail or skills – requires a concerted effort to become fixed. It depends on specific outside guidance and must be rehearsed consciously before it settles in. Even then, the information established in route memory is not as useful, flexible, or rich as information built up and stored in map memory. The example of "telling" a young child how to get to a specific location is quite similar to much of school learning that "tells" children how to work with letters and sounds, how to deal with numbers, and how to put letters on paper to create a *b*, *d*, or *p* and then to form those letters into words based on rules of phonics about long and short vowels.

Route memory and giving specific instruction certainly are useful and important to school learning. Teachers continue to introduce, explain, and reinforce the building of specific skills. But to be meaningful to young children who are used to building their inner maps

Figure 1

TWO KINDS OF LEARNING—NATURAL MEMORY VERSUS MEMORIZATION

Features of natural or map memory

All of us constantly and automatically monitor the sensory input we receive from our
environment. Without conscious awareness
we create inner maps of our physical interactions with the world around us. This inner
map is a record of our ongoing life events
and has a number of distinct features:

* Map memory is survival oriented and its
capacity virtually unlimited.

* Initial maps form very quickly. Sensory
information is taken in instantly and stays
in memory without conscious effort.

* Map memory is open-ended and flexible.
We constantly update our inner maps as
new information becomes available.

* Map formation is motivated by curiosity,
interest, and the desire to explore.

* Intricate maps are formed over time and
on the basis of many experiences. As new
information is perceived the updating feature of map memory enriches and elabo-
rates the existing map - often without
conscious awareness on the part of the
learner.

* Mental maps can be formed from such
things as stories, metaphors, imagery, and
music.

* Inner maps form interconnecting patterns
that aid the application and transfer of
knowledge.

Features of memorization or route memory

Memorization or route memory tends to be
abstract - like memorizing a list of items or
the exact route to a destination. It is more difficult to establish, and its features differ
markedly from the natural learning that is
fostered by day-to-day living and the concrete
settings in which it takes place. Route memory
has a number of distinct features:

* Information placed into route memory
needs to be practiced and rehearsed –
remembering the steps in math work or
following directions for the use of equipment are not instant.

* Route learning is mostly directed by others
and relies on external motivation –
rewards and punishment such as grades or
indications of approval or disapproval.

* Route memory, once acquired, tends to be
inflexible, difficult to transfer or apply, and
resistant to change. Unlearning a habit or
way of working can be difficult once it has
been carefully drilled and rehearsed.

* Items in route memory tend to be specific
details or facts that can stand alone or be
called up to be connected to the broader
field in map memory. Acquired skills, facts,
or lists of steps to follow can assist the
updating feature of natural memory.

Much of what is stored in route memory
may not be meaningful to the learner at
the outset. Routines may be blindly followed without a clear understanding of the
reasons behind them, and facts may be
recited without comprehension of their
significance.

(Caine and Caine 1991)

by working with concrete, experiential aspects of their environment, that kind of abstract learning needs to be set into the much broader context of reading, writing, and projects. Multi-age classrooms are eminently suited to provide the context for this effortless, yet profound, learning.

Teaching math is perhaps the most cogent example of the importance of map learning. If you think back to your own math learning, from elementary school through university, were you able to understand, translate into concrete terms, and then apply the lessons you were learning? In looking back, we are faced with the fact that, though we may have passed the higher demands of arithmetic, algebra, and even statistics, our learning was beset by the need to memorize rules, formulas, and abstract concepts. Applying that kind of rote learning was difficult indeed. To this day, our own math work is often labored and inflexible. By divorcing math learning from its everyday context and concrete applications, many learners become convinced that they are not "mathematically minded."

Many teachers who in their own learning have had to follow prescribed routes to only-one-right answers have great difficulty making math come alive for their students and finding everyday examples that set the learning into a concrete context. Like their students they may continue to feel that they are not mathematically minded. But many of the new resources and curriculum guides offer suggestions to help teachers build a repertoire of activities and a collection of concrete materials so that students can create rich inner maps of what math is all about. These suggestions include games, patterns, estimating, educated guesses, and the urge to try different ways. As with language arts, students learn best and with the least effort when their learning is connected to real-life experiences – hands-on, manipulative work; dealing with money; playing cards or dice; and measuring distances or volumes for practical purposes. Real-life contexts and settings and the teacher's daily references to practical math invest the necessary learning of abstract math skills with down-to-earth reality and solid inner connections.

As the teacher, you create the learning environment that makes it possible for map learning to flourish, because children use math in everyday applications, read for enjoyment and understanding, write for meaning, and see writing used for many purposes every day. But you also observe the children closely to discover where specific gaps appear and offer on-the-spot lessons to fill them: math facts and ways of working with numbers; comparing *to*, *too*, and *two*; looking at the many uses and pronunciations of *ea*; recognizing the function of the silent *e*; working with *ed* and *ing* endings; and discovering the use of apostrophes and exclamation and question marks.

Those kinds of lessons use route learning to best advantage. Though you direct the lesson and children rehearse the more abstract skills or rules, they learn to integrate what they have learned because your lessons are set into the matrix of more natural learning. The inherent ability to see parts and wholes simultaneously can come into full play because children are focused on using math in practical ways and on reading and writing to communicate rather than to memorize specific lessons. Their desire to communicate and to explore new areas of their own choice infuses learning with interest, understanding, and fun. The motivation to learn flows freely and naturally from within.

Meeting children's needs

We have given the concept of map learning prominence in this chapter because it seems to encompass so much of what we have observed in children's learning during the years of our teacher–researcher partnership. Caine and Caine have drawn together the latest in brain research in their work, and it has served to consolidate both our theory and practice of fostering children's natural ways of learning. But there are many more researchers and practitioners who are adding their voices to the growing chorus affirming that, to learn naturally and meaningfully, children need the type of learning environment and conditions that are implicit in map learning.

CHILDREN NEED A RICH ENVIRONMENT TO BE ACTIVE LEARNERS

Babies explore their worlds with all their senses. They initiate that learning themselves by exploring all corners of the house, grasping for everything in and out of reach, and experimenting with what *they* find *in their very own ways*. Eleanor Duckworth (1987) calls that experimenting "the having of wonderful ideas" and refers to it as "the essence of intellectual development." Unlike traditional schools that regulated strictly how, when, and where children used prescribed materials, the rich context of the home and the encouragement – or tolerance – of the parents leave young children free to have wonderful ideas about *how* to interact with the many interesting things they find. *They* raise such questions as: How does this work? What would this look/feel like upside down? Can I pour this into that pot? Then they investigate with tremendous concentration and remarkable persistence.

Tolerance for messy activities helps foster "the having of wonderful ideas" in class as much as at home.

Working with school-age children in environments that encourage them to have wonderful ideas about how to explore materials in their own ways produces the same concentration and persistence. Describing several instances of children bringing their own wonderful ideas to their explorations, Duckworth makes a "powerful pedagogical point that ... the right question at the right time can move children to peaks in their thinking that result in significant steps forward and real intellectual excitement; and ... although it is almost impossible for an adult to know exactly the right time to ask a specific question of a specific child... children can ask the right question for themselves if the setting is right." Bruner (1957) spoke of much the same intellectual excitement when he described the power of "messing about in science" as a way of drawing children into using their own ways of inquiry. (See figure 2.)

Duckworth goes on to say that wonderful ideas don't happen in a vacuum. They build on other ideas and flourish in a climate that values and encourages them. As a participant in a primary science curriculum project, she traveled to Africa with her team to evaluate a project that had used everyday substances like wood ashes, baking soda, and lemon juice as experimental materials. Children had been encouraged to raise their own questions or to experiment with the materials in their own ways. When these students were given the opportunity to work with unfamiliar science materials, they demonstrated that – as their teachers reported – they "had improved greatly

Figure 2

METHODS OF RESEARCH AND INQUIRY USED BY BOTH SCIENTISTS DOING RESEARCH AND CHILDREN EXPLORING THEIR WORLD

Both will

- decide what *they* want to investigate, what is important to *them*;

- observe, listen, physically examine, test, use all their senses to gain knowledge;

- use prior knowledge and previous experience to aid information gathering;

- follow the lead of their peers;

- draw on the experience of others to aid research, ask questions;

- note recurring patterns, similarities, differences, predictable patterns;

- develop hypotheses about the materials or activities they are testing;

- experiment to test hypotheses;

- draw inferences on the basis of experiments and observations;

- make retests to confirm or deny findings;

- anticipate what will happen next;

- generate rules and theories based on observed patterns;

- update or correct previous findings on the basis of new evidence;

- refine knowledge and test its fit with prior information;

- consider the entire situation or context to interpret findings;

- work actively to acquire new knowledge;

- use imagination and intuition to further their research;

- stay with a problem of their choice;

- take risks exploring and advancing new findings;

- show curiosity and enthusiasm for exploring unknown territory;

- work hard to solve problems and overcome obstacles.

at having ideas about what to do, at raising questions, and at answering their own questions.... Typically, the children in these classes would take a first look at what was offered, try a few things, and then settle down to work with involvement and concentration.... Their work became so interesting that we were always disappointed to have to stop them after forty minutes."

In contrast, students who had not had experience with working independently on the science project had a smaller range of ideas; some of the classes ran out of things to do after thirty minutes; and there were few instances of complex work in which a child spent a lot of time and effort to work out an interesting problem. The exciting finding, as summed up by Duckworth, is that "the development of intelligence is a matter of having wonderful ideas and feeling confident enough to try them out, and that school can have an effect on the continuing development of wonderful ideas."

She points out that Jean Piaget in his work on sensorimotor intelligence maintained that "the roots of logic are in action" and that he "followed this logic of actions through to adolescence, finding at every step of the way that children were able to carry out activities that demand a good deal of intelligence without necessarily using language that reveals this." Fostering independence of learning, which forms an important part of learner-directed classrooms, sets the climate for the having of wonderful ideas and provides growing room for the roots of logic.

Howard Gardner (1983) added six additional intelligences to Piaget's sensorimotor intelligence. His work on defining not one but seven human intelligences – linguistic, musical, logical-mathematical, spatial, bodily kinesthetic, interpersonal, and intrapersonal – relies heavily on the environmental input that shapes action and, with it, intelligence. Exploring the concept of apprenticeship as a way of learning, Gardner (1991) points out that that kind of learning is "heavily *contextualized*." He observes that many advanced, industrialized countries are reverting to the use of apprenticeships. For example, in Germany "over half of all adolescents participate in some kind of an apprenticeship, in which scholastic competencies are tied as closely as possible to the needs and demands of a workplace." With that combination, school and workplace collaborate closely to fit abstract academic learning into the concrete matrix of work. Considering Germany's level of technology and excellence of products, the system appears to work well for the young learners. Teachers know from long experience that students at all levels will make special efforts to do jobs well when they perceive that they are working on projects that have practical connections to the world beyond school. Such jobs create involvement and levels of thinking no textbook exercises could produce.

CHILDREN NEED MODELS THAT THEY CAN FOLLOW

Along with a meaningful context, apprenticeship learning includes competent models. Children are used to learning from models and respond to that style of teaching far better than to being told what to do. They do all their language learning by following models, and at school working with their peers lends depth to the modeling

A field trip to a salmon spawning ground reinforced classroom learning about the life cycle of Pacific salmon.

and practice the teacher provides. Describing the Spectrum classroom created to give children opportunities to use a range of intelligences, Gardner (1991) speaks of the benefits students derive from working in mixed–age groups:

Each student participates each day in an apprenticeship–like "pod," where he works with peers of different ages and a competent teacher to master a craft or discipline of interest. Because the pod includes a range of ages, students have the opportunity to enter into an activity at their own level of expertise and to develop at a comfortable pace. Working alongside a more knowledgeable person, they also have what may be a rare opportunity of seeing an expert engage in productive work. There are a dozen pods, in a variety of areas ranging from architecture to gardening, from cooking to "making money." Because the focus of the pod falls on the acquisition of a real–world skill in an apprenticeship kind of environment, the chances of securing genuine understandings are enhanced.

Our own work certainly confirmed that a shift from lecturing and "telling" to modeling learning behaviors produced learning at levels of understanding far beyond the dutiful repetition of teacher talk.

CHILDREN NEED TO WORK AT THEIR OWN PACE

While Gardner sees the close correlation between working at a comfortable pace and securing genuine understanding, teachers have been beset by time lines and requirements to move children along to fit adult-designed schedules. There is, moreover, what Piaget calls "the American question," that is, researchers who demand to know how children could be moved more rapidly through the various stages of intellectual development. Duckworth provides the metaphor of building a tower by quickly setting individual bricks one on top of the other. The job can be done speedily, but there are limits to the height that can be achieved, and the tower is definitely unstable. In contrast, if the builders take time to create a broad foundation or dig down to add depth to the structure, then towers of wonderful height and stability can be built – in actuality and in learning.

Teachers have always known about empty learning that was internalized by rote and that remained shaky. Now Jane Healy (1990) points out that brain research confirms that trying to hurry learning along actually runs counter to normal brain functioning. "The value of excessive stimulation to enhance development is unproven and risky. External pressure designed to produce learning or intelligence violates the fundamental rule: *A healthy brain stimulates itself by active interaction with what it finds challenging and interesting in its environment*" (Healy's italics).

The risky part of trying to hurry children along involves their internalization of rules that run counter to their own common sense. When Kamii and Derman (1971) examined the results of an experiment to teach kindergarteners notions that usually develop much later, they "found fascinating instances of conflicts between the rules the children were taught and their own intuitions – their common sense." Part of the work dealt with the concept of specific gravity as an explanation of floating or sinking. "The rules led to nonsense not normally encountered in children their age. One child hefted a large candle in one hand and a birthday cake candle in the other, but having seen that they both floated, maintained 'they weigh the same.' Another child said that a tiny piece of aluminum foil that sank weighed more than a large sheet that floated on the surface. Clearly these children were trying to apply the rules rather than coming to terms with the objects."

The experiment may have taught them rules, but the children failed to assimilate the knowledge as their own. Perching loosely on top of a rather shaky tower of learning, the bits of information they acquired did not help the children deal meaningfully with problems they needed to work out over time and in their own ways. Preparing children for the year 2000 asks for more solid, independent thinking than force-feeding rules that undermine the children's own common sense.

CHILDREN NEED TO GENERATE THEIR OWN RULES

Years of working closely with students, both children and adults, have shown us that it is counterproductive to try to hurry students along. As we watched students, they showed us clearly that providing them with rules, telling them the right answers, and giving them solutions to problems certainly built shaky learning towers. Students could repeat rules of spelling or grammar but failed to apply them. They repeated the correct answer to difficult math problems but looked unsure or blank. They accepted the adult solution but did not internalize its message for future reference. But when they explored what needed to be learned in their own ways, they were well able to generate rules and then refine them. Their map minds functioned effectively and easily as they worked on invented spelling, manipulated math materials, and worked on hands-on projects of all kinds. As Sternberg (1988) points out, "inductive reasoning [is] the kind of reasoning we most often use in our lives." And children are well able to abstract "general principles from specific information" from an early age.

Our own in-class research (Forester 1975) certainly confirmed that young children will generate important and productive rules even when taught in what we have since found to be counterproductive ways. While learning to read in a basal reader program, the children we observed developed two fundamental rules of reading:

1. To read you have to look for meaning.

2. To abstract meaning from the printed text, you work with patterns of language.

They did so, in spite of the fact that the focus of instruction centered on words and their sounds, with little explicit mention of meaning or making sense. *They* focused on *what it means to read*, while the structured lessons of the morning sessions focused on *component skills*. Virtually nothing was said about patterns of language, yet the children induced these two fundamental rules about the nature of reading. Both these rules flow naturally from children's language learning. To them, language consists of meaning and patterns. They do not examine language as an abstraction to be talked about on the basis of sounds or particles of speech.

Using their knowledge about language is one way children induce rules about reading, spelling, and writing. They make connections between what they know and what they are currently working with. As Jane Baskwill (1990) puts it, "Children are always making connections. They connect what happened yesterday with what's happening today; they apply what they know about one situation to many others; they predict what might happen in a new situation and then adjust their predictions and explanations in the light of new observations." Valuing their knowledge and encouraging the making of connections build knowledge and generate rules that are integrated with children's own experience and ways of learning.

CHILDREN NEED TO BUILD ON WHAT THEY ALREADY KNOW

Listening to children's concerns, inviting them to elaborate on their knowledge and personal experience, and valuing their special talents stimulate talk, foster reflection, and generate writing that becomes rich and expressive. Perhaps more important, children develop self-confidence and assurance in pursuing their own ways of investigating and representing new information. Connie White's (1990) poignant account of her year-long research into the learning and development of one of her students confirms many of our observations of students' ways of using their personal experience as a springboard for evolving new skills and branching out into unfamiliar work. In *Jevon Doesn't Sit at the Back Any More*, White writes, "I still believe that a shortage of literature dealing with rural life played a major part in keeping Jevon out of books. His entire being radiated 'farm,' and there hadn't been a lot for him to connect to in the Story Corner – or anywhere else in the classroom, for that matter!" When Jevon became the "recognized and respected expert on farm life" in the classroom, it gave him the courage to take risks and "confidently say to his friends: 'Help me!'"

His teacher goes on to describe how Jevon, who had shown her that remembering letters and their names was difficult for him, went on to devise his own way of learning the ABCs by using the familiar names of his classmates as his research base. Once he had gained confidence and "was able to use what he knew in pursuit of new knowledge, Jevon was set free in the classroom to learn in every corner." Acknowledging his life experience and personal knowledge not only opened the door to reading but gave him the courage and incentive to apply his own ways of learning in class.

The teacher as learner in the year 2000

There really is nothing new in connecting learning to what children already know, but in structured lessons that are intended to direct the work of thirty individual children in the same way, there is no room to help each one make connections that have personal relevance. To prepare children for living in the year 2000 we need to provide a learning environment that invites them to explore, to make connections between school learning and their own experience, and to help them – and us – integrate our map and route memories to their very best advantage. The having of wonderful ideas functions well in a climate that affirms the value of children's own knowledge and own ways of making connections.

The bonus for us is that when we work with children in ways that foster their personal growth, we as teachers reap all the same benefits we provide our students. We are the ones who set the pace, generate the rules, and build on our knowledge and observations. When we are observers and researchers in our own classrooms – watching for new ways of making connections – the having of wonderful ideas becomes part of the teacher's way of fostering learning. Connie White sums it up when she says, "To take the research out of my teaching would be to remove the learning. And learning is what I believe teaching to be about."

2.

The Teacher's Role

CELEBRATING THE TEACHER'S WAY

When you enter a class of eager, busy students working at a variety
of tasks and staying right on the job, you know that you are in the
presence of effective learners. As you observe all the independent
work children are doing and note that the teacher seems to intervene
very little in classroom activities, you might assume that these are
exceptional kids, that the teacher is lucky to have them, and that she
probably doesn't have to do much to keep them on track. In fact,
classes like that have very little to do with luck, and you are probably
in the presence of a wonderfully effective teacher.

At times we overheard visitors to Margaret's classroom comment
to one another, "But she isn't *doing* anything!" These visitors noted the
children's independent and purposeful learning and the fact that
Margaret could spend time talking to visitors, or even leave the room,
without any change in the activity level. Her students stayed busily
on task and readily referred to the visitors or each other if they felt
they needed some additional input to their work. When questioned
about how she managed to keep children on task without intervening, Margaret might even say, "Oh, I'm not doing anything in particu
lar to keep them on task." But the facts are otherwise.

In this book we want to celebrate all the things that teachers *are*
doing. In *The Learners' Way* we provided detailed descriptions and careful
analyses of what it is children do when they learn to read, write, and

think. Now it becomes important to celebrate what teachers do when they foster that kind of natural learning, to give credit where credit is due, and to help make manifest the crucial role that teachers play.

What teachers do to foster learning

In classrooms where children have the freedom to work at their own pace and on topics of interest to them, learning does not *just happen*. Instead, the teacher orchestrates what is being performed and how each member of that orchestra of learning performs, and makes certain that all members function in harmony. There may be many variations on the theme being played at any moment, but the activity in class is not random. The teacher sets the parameters for what will be done that day, conducts the overall activity, and makes contact with individual players to encourage them to participate, tone down a bit, or do a solo performance for the entire class. This book contains many concrete examples of just what has produced good results for teachers and students alike. Here we provide a list of vignettes as a reference to use when questions or doubts arise about what teachers *do* in classrooms where learning flows freely and children are eager to participate.

SETTING THE CLIMATE

Much of our teaching energy is spent on compensating for an unfavourable environment. It would be far more sensible to use our energies *first* on the environment itself (Holdaway 1980).

First, and perhaps foremost, the teacher establishes a learning climate in the classroom. Acknowledging the uniqueness of each child, she makes it her first priority to create a community of learners in which all the children will feel comfortable to talk, join in activities, and work independently at their own levels and in ways that fit their particular needs and interests. As Holdaway puts it, the teacher works to "put the pupil in a situation where he cannot help doing what is required, quite naturally, and without conscious effort."

To engender the independent, natural learning that characterizes an effective learning community, the teacher infuses the work in class with joy and enthusiasm. Reading, writing, artwork, hands-on math, science projects, social studies themes, field trips, and special work-shops are connected to the students' interests and real-life concerns. The teacher has gathered personal knowledge about her students' backgrounds, interests, and special talents from her discussions with the children and their parents, and she continues to update that knowledge daily by listening attentively to her students as they talk to each other and participate in classroom activities. Students know and feel their teacher's keen interest and gradually relinquish their shyness, belligerence, or reluctance to try new and different ways of interacting with those around them and with the learning materials.

To set the learning climate and develop a learning community, the teacher designs the activities to draw learners into the excitement and fun of discovery, and to generate real "can-do" attitudes. Having dis-covered that direct questions beginning with why, what, who, where, and when are sure-fire ways of curtailing open communication (think of the times when you, feeling put on the spot, closed right down), Margaret does a great deal of "wondering" as she talks with her stu-dents. "I wonder how we can do this?" "Did you ever wonder where your pussycat goes all night long?" "Do you suppose we could use some other materials to make this more colorful?" "Wow, what a big word! Scrumpchedelicious! I wonder what it means?" "I wonder if we can remember other words that begin with...." Those open invitations to engage imagination as well as logical thinking are nonthreatening, provide time and a clear invitation for reflection, and give no sugges-tion that the teacher has one "right" answer in mind. Since she is inviting them to muse and is herself opening her mind to all possibili-ties, divergent thinking has a chance to blossom, and there is a feeling of mutuality of learning right from the start. The climate is one of partnership and community.

Trial-and-error learning, being playful, and encouraging dialogue and sharing foster an attitude of being open to all possibilities. That way of working with children builds their self-esteem, confidence, and willingness to try any job at all that the teacher or other students might suggest. In fact, students become collaborators in planning top-ics to be studied – snakes, trains, ways of working in school a hun-dred years ago, growing a garden – and are eager to suggest novel ways of collecting or presenting their research. Collaboration and excitement run high, and the climate is one of productivity and eagerness to participate.

Then there is freedom from anxiety and threat. The teacher makes it a top priority to erase negative comments from her teaching vocabulary and focuses instead on steps forward, on good tries, on new ways of looking at work, and on problem solving and conflict resolution. The evaluation of progress is built into the learning activities and enhances learning instead of engendering test anxiety in children.

Courtesy and tact are very much part of setting a positive learning climate. As the teacher interacts with the children, she accords them the same consideration she would give adult co-workers. If a visitor comes into the classroom, the teacher introduces him (or her) to the children, gives a bit of information as to why the visitor is there, and then informs the children that while the visitor enjoys looking at their work, it isn't necessary to show it to him (or her) if they feel that they don't want to share what they are writing or doing at the time.

As they do at home, the children observe and emulate what the adults in class are doing, how they interact with them and with each other. If the adults are obviously interested in learning and if the tone of the classroom is friendly and cooperative, learning and cooperating become as natural as breathing. But that climate of delight is not happenstance. The teacher sets the climate the first day of school and maintains it throughout the year – by her friendly attitude, patience, relaxed manner, willingness to laugh with the children, careful listening, frequent wondering or musing, enthusiasm for learning, and above all her profound interest in the children and their development.

In *The Learners' Way* we devoted an entire chapter to setting the climate because the safety and encouragement that characterizes an effective learning climate are truly the foundation for all

Inviting children to bring in their family pictures for the class "family tree" builds a feeling of community.

learning. Unquestionably, it is the teacher who creates that physical and psychological climate for her students. In chapter 3 of this book, we discuss the many ways in which teachers create the spirit of independence that makes for lifelong learning and is a crucial part of the learning climate; in chapter 7 we offer suggestions on getting the classroom ready for incoming students at the beginning of the year; and in chapter 9 we discuss the importance of setting a context in which interactions can flow freely and productively.

PROVIDING LEARNING MATERIALS

Part of an effective learning climate, one that invites exploration and offers every opportunity to engage students in discovery learning and endless practice of skills, is the provision of learning materials. Based on her knowledge of the topics and skills children need to acquire during the months ahead, the teacher assembles a wide variety of materials, including

reading materials of all kinds, such as books, magazines, directions for making things, poems on large charts, and the children's own writing from this and the previous year

visual aids, such as charts, pictures, game boards, puppets and a puppet theater, individual name tags as well as a name book (with students' names printed in a looseleaf binder) to help the children acquire the names as sight words, colorful alphabet pictures, labels for things around the room, a family tree for the children in the class, the children's own artwork

center supplies, including the following:

* writing center materials (envelopes, stick-on stamps, crayons, colored pens or markers, paper of different colors and sizes, roll ends of newsprint, rubber stamps and pads, alphabet samples both printed and made of plastic)

* manipulative materials in the math center (Unifix cubes, tubs with pattern blocks to make beautiful designs, boxes of buttons, beads, miniature toys to count and group, scales and weights, games to teach math, measurement tools)

* reading center materials (books – as many and of as wide a variety as possible; a listening station with cassettes, earphones, and books

to follow along; games that teach spelling or letters and their sounds; charts with familiar poems or nursery rhymes; cloze games that invite filling in words)

✳ art center materials (colored paper, newsprint, pencils and colored markers, paint and paintbrushes, scraps of cardboard, cloth, plastic, and so on for creating imaginative things on "invention day"

✳ seasonal center supplies, which are collected in collaboration with the children

For children to learn naturally and profoundly, they need a rich variety of sensory stimulation to open their very beings to learning. Their map minds function best when body, mind, and spirit can explore and experiment in concrete, familiar settings – the classroom store, the playhouse, the water or sand table, the dress-up-and-drama center. That kind of rich physical and psychological environment doesn't just happen.

The teacher sets the tone as she creates the learning climate, and in the spirit of extending the feeling of belonging to a learning community, she invites everyone in the class to contribute to the rich mix of resources in centers around the classroom. She also encourages children – parents, visitors, and resource personnel, too – to add books, poems, and legends to the reading corner or to bring interesting recipes and supplies to the frequent cooking sessions that nourish body and mind. The climate of delight may be of the teacher's making, but it draws in and involves everyone.

Reading along with an emergent reader recreates the warm feeling of reading aloud at home and encourages fluency.

ORGANIZING THE LEARNING ACTIVITIES

The teacher is also an organizer. As she initiates projects and themes, she works with large and small groups of children and with individuals, draws on many of the resources available in the school and the community to augment the learning climate in the classroom, and coordinates activities both in class and out.

A GOOD ORGANIZER LEAVES LOTS OF ROOM FOR INDEPENDENCE
After a train trip to the Forest Museum, some of the children wanted to create a mural to depict that outing. Margaret discussed with the group what materials were needed to get started and then stood back to let them get underway in their own time and ways. She conferred with them as the job progressed to help them negotiate the items to be included and the colors and placement of the pictures on the mural. As the opportunity presented itself, she used the discussions to clarify and spell such words as *trestle* and *tie*, to enhance spelling and vocabulary within the concrete context of their work on the mural. ✳ By helping them initiate the artwork and then being available as a resource person, Margaret orchestrated the project but stood back to let the children do the work and solve most of the problems. Like the best of organizers, she stayed in the background to give the project engineers the feeling that the project was theirs.

At the beginning of the year she establishes routines – setting a sequence of activities for the day, modeling and talking about appropriate conduct, starting such daily features as story reading, news time, writing workshop, and center time. Throughout the year she draws together small groups of children to lead them through specific spelling or math practice that they – not the whole class – need at that moment. For example, as children work on the floor to create new groupings with Unifix cubes, she will observe, draw together a small group of those who are finding the job difficult, and give them the opportunity to work together and practice at their own pace without being overwhelmed by their more advanced peers, who need no such trial-and-error practice.

During center time, when children are busily pursuing their own interests, Margaret will sit down with individual children to play a math game, to do some one-to-one reading, or just to talk quietly about day-to-day events or an interesting book to help a child overcome hesitancy about speaking up in class.

When field trips and special occasions add extra interest to learning, the teacher collaborates with parents and staff to see that the events run smoothly, delegates roles and responsibilities, and leads the discussions both before and after the event to open and close the activity effectively.

Being very parent-friendly, the teacher may also organize the provision of regular parent help (or that of other volunteers). To minimize work and maximize parent input, Margaret kept an exercise book marked *Parent Help* in bright letters on its cover. Keeping the book handy at all times, she entered all the jobs she needed help with on a given date: photocopying song sheets, cutting out special shapes for decorative chains, reading with Lee or Noel, driving on the next field trip, bringing in milk cartons for a special math demonstration of volume and size. When parents came in and Margaret was busy, they would simply consult the Parent Help book and start a job of their choice until Margaret could give them a specific job for that day and perhaps discuss more long-range plans for some of the outings. Margaret also integrated the cooperative work of parents, children, and staff as they worked on joint projects or school-wide events such as plays or the giant potlatch given in honor of the principal who was moving to another school.

KNOWING HOW TO DELEGATE   At South Park School, the music teacher, Marne St. Claire, is the all-time organizational expert. When the school was putting on the musical *Joseph and His Technicolor Dreamcoat*, Marne involved everyone she could. She brought in former students to play in the string section and parents to lend their expertise in costume design and making props. She organized the stagehands and found people to choreograph and teach dances, to look after classes during rehearsals, and to help obtain special props. She did not hesitate to call on her friends to give a hand with the many small jobs that cropped up during rehearsals and performances. Most important of all, she involved every single student and teacher in the school in some way. She imbued all the students with the excitement of the important major production they were putting together. Discipline was at an all-time high as Marne demanded and got the children's top effort and attention. No one was left out; everyone felt part of the fun – and the success!

PROVIDING INFORMATION

Naturally, the teacher continues to be an information giver. The myth that *teaching is not acceptable* in classrooms where children learn through integrated activities, projects, and themes is just that – a myth. As always, the teacher supplies information on letters, spelling, punctuation, math facts, and any of the topics under discussion. But she does so in the context of meaningful activities – reading, composing, printing notices, counting, and so on. Keeping a close eye on the children's response to the activities in class, the teacher spots the specific needs of her students and presents lessons either to the whole class or to small groups on topics that need to be introduced or elaborated: structuring a piece of writing, the use of paragraphs and punctuation marks, specific spelling rules, or factual information on math or a social science theme the children are working on.

There are countless interactions with individual students during which the teacher provides the specific information a child needs at that moment – sitting at the computer with Robyn to go over the booting-up process one more time; joining the children at the water table to participate and, at the same time, demonstrate the function of syphoning; sitting on the floor to help a child who is puzzling over how to arrange Unifix cubes in threes, fives, or tens. But most important of all, the teacher shows how to learn by being a participant learner herself.

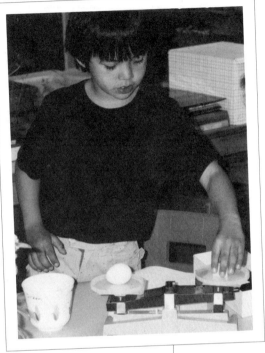

Weighing eggs before placing them in the incubator becomes a lesson in estimating and hypothesis testing.

MODELING LEARNING BEHAVIORS

The chief instrument of teaching is modeling. Throughout the day, the teacher demonstrates the skills and abilities the children need to learn. From the first day of class she models reading in all its forms – reading stories aloud; tracing the words of a song or nursery rhyme with her hands as she reads to and with the children; using recipes and making a point of indicating the parts she is reading aloud as they assemble and then use the ingredients. While everyone is reading at "book time," Margaret also becomes absorbed in her personal reading and will tell children who are becoming restless, "Please don't disturb me. I'm reading something really interesting, and I need to concentrate."

During news time she demonstrates printing, spelling, composing, and editing on the chalkboard as she elicits news items from the children and then prints the words while giving a running commentary: "I need a capital letter here because it's the beginning of the sentence. That's a soft *c* at the beginning of *ceiling*." To model a quiet personal

SH!

HERE COMES A SPELLING LESSON ✳ Like all significant learning, spelling needs to be based on experience and tied to concrete knowledge. Children will readily repeat spelling rules, but if you then examine their spelling, you will find that they are not applying the "knowledge" that "*e* tells *a* to say its name," or "that word needs a capital because it's the beginning of a sentence." ✳ Once the children begin to write and to invent their own spelling, they perceive the need to distinguish more exactly between sounds and letters that are hard to tell apart. Building on that experience and the fact that the children are actually looking for information that will help them with their writing and spelling, Margaret will call together a small group whose written work has revealed the need for some special work such as distinguishing between the *sh* and *ch* sounds. ✳ She begins the session by reading them the story *There's a Dragon in My Wagon*. As the children laugh and talk about the funny story, Margaret draws their attention to the girl in the story who says, "Sh! Sh!" She has the children practice saying "Sh!" to each other in different tones of voice and keeps the page open on the chalkboard rail. ✳ Next she asks if they can remember other stories that had that sound or can think of words that start or end with the *sh* sound. At this point she may read them *Sheep on a Ship* to give them examples of words she has in mind. Once they have had time to play with the *sh* sound and Margaret has put their words on the board, she moves on to "a sound that is *almost the same* as *sh* but feels different in the mouth as you make it – *ch ch ch*." As she exaggerates, shaping her mouth to sound *ch*, children join in and produce *ch*, then *choo*, and move from there to finding words that begin and end in *ch*. ✳ To reinforce the learning and involve their hands as well as their eyes and ears, Margaret will ask them to take cards and print words that have those two sounds. She then plays games with the children using those personalized spelling cards: saying a word and seeing who can hold up a matching card; mixing the cards and re-sorting them; giving clues about words and then having children say the correct words; having the children look through books to see if they can match their cards to words in the books. The children will find variations and play with their personalized spelling cards either singly or in groups. Knowing that lessons don't necessarily transfer to other contexts, Margaret will watch the children as they write during the next week or two and, if they still mix up the two sounds, she will remind them of their session. That gentle nudge generally helps them make the transfer. (Chapter 10 is devoted to an extensive discussion of spelling.)

way of composing, the teacher will sit down during writing workshop and write a short item, which she may later share with the children. Throughout the day she draws children's attention to the fact that she is communicating in writing: "I need to send a note to Marne to tell her about our buddy time"; "If we leave a message on the board, people will know we are in the park."

Living math is very much part of everyday modeling as the teacher calculates (with the children's help) answers to such questions as: How many children are present/absent? How many can go to the library at one time? How much taller have the bean plants grown over the weekend? How many quarters does it take to make a dollar? How can the treat be divided so everyone gets a fair share? As the teacher engages in roll call, counting money, measuring plants, and being curious about how to do a job, the children watch and then emulate those mundane activities without worrying about the rules of math or prescribed ways of doing the work. Knowledge of more formal paper-and-pencil math will arise from that concrete modeling and practice.

Modeling learning behaviors is a wonderful departure from the old ways of unfailingly modeling *knowing behaviors* and having all the answers. Working on a recipe requiring cream of tartar, the teacher might comment, "Oh, I'm not sure whether *tartar* is spelled with an *er* or an *ar*. Let's get the dictionary and look it up." As children or visitors bring in interesting items such as a meteorite, a live snake, or an arrangement of dried flowers, the teacher will often begin the exchange with the visitor by asking open-ended "I wonder" questions, being puzzled and curious, and by demonstrating how to pay close attention to the answers.

The teacher's way of listening to the children and taking a keen interest in them and their ways of working is unquestionably the most important modeling of listening and attending. As children talk,

THINKING ALOUD AND WRITING

Just before writing workshop Margaret may comment, "I'm thinking about what I will write today. Let's see, I want to write a make-believe story about a fairy princess. Hmm, I want to make sure my story will have a beginning, a middle, and an end. How will I start my story? Oh, I know, I'll tell about what kind of princess she is." After continuing along that vein for a while, she will ask the children what their ideas are for the day's writing, and invariably many of them will want to write fairy tales. As they sit down to write, Margaret also sits down to model writing, concentrating, sounding words out, rereading, looking up to think, and making final changes before concluding her writing for the day. Like young children at home, the children in class watch and imitate every mannerism – including the thinking aloud – of the teacher.

give information, or do artwork in class, the teacher gives each speaker in turn her undivided attention. She makes eye contact with the speakers, waits for them to finish, and encourages them to elaborate: "Can you tell me more about....?" "What kinds of things did you do to get your kitten settled in?" "How did you feel when....?" "What else do you suppose we could do to make this work?"

The teacher continually observes the children's language development, their willingness to speak up, and their ability to formulate coherent answers, and she is genuinely interested in the children's responses, because the information becomes the basis for special interest themes, individualized sessions, or the reading of a book or story to expand the children's knowledge or interest. Since it is genuine and purposeful, the quality of that focused listening conveys itself strongly. With that model of intent listening, children begin to reciprocate and listen to each other and the teacher with courtesy and attention.

Modeling learning also includes sharing information, being excited about new discoveries, thinking aloud, solving problems, being curious, asking open-ended questions that leave room for lots of different answers, looking things up, wondering and musing, being puzzled – doing everything a learner does, and, above all, being enthusiastic and interested. To be effective, that modeling has to be genuine, and herein lies much of the joy of teaching in holistic ways. Throughout the day, the teacher is exploring, thinking, wondering, and discovering new ways of teaching/learning. Children reveal new depths and unexpected sides of their beings, and the focus on steps forward more than on mistakes makes the work highly positive.

The old saying that children do as you do and not as you say is certainly borne out when the teacher models those all-important social skills: caring about others' feelings, getting along, speaking softly, demonstrating a sense of humor, taking turns, being independent and responsible, taking risks, venturing forth with opinions, accepting comments or corrections gracefully, collaborating with others, working harmoniously in a group, being friendly and welcoming to newcomers and visitors. When mothers bring their younger children into class, students follow their teacher's lead and vie with one another to be helpful and friendly. Similarly, when someone is hurt on the playground they can be heard to emulate their teacher's manner and words exactly, "Oh, Liam, are you all right? Can I help you? Don't be embarrassed; it's all right to cry. Here, let me help you up."

WORKING WITH PARENTS

A highly important aspect of the friendly cooperative spirit is being parent-friendly (see chapter 14). The effective teacher very much appreciates the role parents play in teaching their children. She sees parents as the most important collaborators in the children's learning and invites parents to participate in every possible way: visit the classroom, act as teacher's helper, correspond or phone at report time and whenever they want to communicate with the teacher, be an appreciative audience for the work children take home, provide information and help children when they need to gather outside information, take the children to the library, act as a driver or helper during field trips, and come in for student-led parent conferences or other information-sharing sessions that will help them appreciate their children's growth. When the teacher and the children's parents have frequent occasions to interact in a friendly, companionable way, that does wonders to help them appreciate the new ways of learning and turns them into the most ardent supporters of their children's independence and productivity in learning and socializing.

BEING ACCOUNTABLE

Keeping track of progress is another important role that continues to be very much part of the teacher's work. No matter how informal or open the learning climate may be, the teacher continues to maintain records and accounts of children's progress. From the first day of class, the teacher keeps field (or anecdotal) notes describing what skills children are bringing with them and what steps forward they are taking as they participate. Keeping an alphabetized notebook with a page for each child (or a sheet of paper with a space for each child) handy, the teacher enters comments daily about who is participating in group discussions and who simply mouths responses quietly without actually speaking up; who is coming forward to "help" with spelling during news time; who is sitting quietly with books enjoying or even reading them; who has a sense of numbers and is working with them; and who listens attentively during story time and who still needs a lot of coaxing to sit still and attend.

The children's conversations in class offer many opportunities to gain insights into their learning, their language development, their feelings about school, and their hopes or fears. Particularly around report-card time, the teacher may collect some verbatim accounts of what children say to let parents know what their children are saying in class. Here are some samples Margaret collected:

Shirley, as she changed ones into tens: "Hey, I just figured out how this works! I can do it!"

Gwynneth, who had been working on being less aggressive when playing with other children: "I will let Charlene go first."

Maria: "I like school, and I'm a pretty good reader. I can write almost anything!"

Oona: "I like making stuff"; "Me and David get along well now."

Gabrielle: "I'm really good at reading, and the kids in the class like listening to me."

Tony, on why he likes school: "Because it's fun and we get to have book time and choosing time."

Megan: "I got used to lots of people and I feel safe in Marg's class. She is my friend."

To augment the written notes and simplify the record keeping, the teacher may decide to use a checklist to monitor specific skills from time to time. After working on writing skills with children for some time, the teacher may want to make a spot-check of how the whole class is doing on a given day in a specific area:

* spelling (how many words correct out of...)
* using upper- and lowercase letters
* making spaces between words
* printing from left to right
* using periods and question marks

Using a grid with the children's names along one side and the checkpoints along another is an efficient way of gathering comprehensive information that can reveal not only the progress individual children are making but also information on who has grasped the concepts and who still needs a lot of practice. Constructing her own checklists in this way, the teacher customizes assessment for her own class and for a specific time. On another day she may do a similar list on math skills or on motor development in gym class. These quick checklists and the field notes become the basis for drawing individual children or small groups into special jobs that offer extra practice where it is needed – working with many more number games, finding extra copies of the little books that offer easy reading, sitting down together to play with letters and their sounds.

As soon as students begin to write and draw, the teacher provides individual folders in which ongoing records of each child's drawing, printing, spelling, and composing can be collected. Coupled with the written records the teacher keeps, this kind of ongoing monitoring, which is so much a part of holistic learning, allows for closer assessment than the sporadic spot tests and quizzes of old. The maintenance of field notes, folders with collections of children's work, checklists, and children's notebooks filled with their writing and notes on reading make it possible to do far more than assign a grade. Parents, supervisors, and the children themselves can look for detailed descriptions of steps forward, achievements, areas of need, suggestions for ways of proceeding next, and comments that include social and emotional aspects of the children's classroom interactions. Such accounts are neither threatening nor anxiety producing but serve as further aids to fostering yet more growth – and the teacher is very much in charge of gathering this information. Far from being vague or not very rigorous, the sheer weight of the variety of evidence gives this kind of evaluation at least as much or more reliability and validity as standard grades.

The important benefit of these global, ongoing ways of keeping track of progress is that they provide a well-rounded overview of how a child is growing and developing. Spot quizzes focus on limited numbers of skills or bits of knowledge, while the ongoing accumulation of children's work and notes about their functioning give the teacher much more of a sense of the manner in which a child is maturing. Instead of fretting about the fact that Lee is still not participating in oral spelling or reading aloud, there is the recognition that the child, though reticent orally, is beginning to write quite elaborate stories. Instead of worrying about Parminder's puzzling over math facts, there is the recognition that Parminder is still immature in many ways and simply needs to have lots more practice and playtime to allow that natural growth to make itself felt.

OBSERVING LEARNERS—"KID WATCHING"

While acknowledging the importance of keeping track of students' progress, watching learners – kid watching – is the teacher's most important tool for discovering the scope and sequence that individual children follow quite naturally. After years of university study and learning about "stages of development" in the abstract, the teacher becomes a researcher in the concrete setting of her classroom. She will often discover that children have a scope and sequence quite different from that prescribed by a curriculum document.

For example, the suggested teaching sequence for initiating children into reading used to begin with drills on long and short vowels. Careful observation of children at work reveals that consonants are first to emerge in children's sounding out and spelling. Vowels are far more difficult for them to hear and to produce accurately in their writing. That discovery influences the teacher's emphasis and timing when working on spelling and writing with the children.

If during news time all that the students offer are beginning and ending consonants as they help with spelling, the teacher simply puts those letters on the chalkboard and then comments about the remaining ones as she prints them, secure in the knowledge that median consonants and then vowels will make their appearance in the children's writing and spelling when they are ready for them. So in the meantime she simply acknowledges, "That's right, *Forest Museum* starts with an *f*. Now we also need...." And then, "*Museum* is a new word. Say it to yourself. Can you feel it in your mouth? How do you think it starts?"

When thinking about math, many people believe that children begin with adding and subtracting. A look at the intensity with which they puzzle over how to share toys or a treat, however, suggests that dividing things up is a very early *concrete* math job, one that children tackle happily. Similarly, being able to count to ten or more doesn't necessarily mean that a child has a sense of numeric values. Careful observation of Annika playing with beads or blocks may reveal that while she is happily counting away, the number of beads she is handling and the words she is saying don't match. After watching many children at that stage of development, the teacher develops a sense of the sequence in which children learn to connect the number words with the actual numeric value of what they are handling. If a child seems to linger inordinately long at the rote repetition stage, the teacher may decide to sit down with him to play some number games (counting fingers, finding the number of red beads, or doing some buying in the classroom store using pretend money to pay for their purchases).

Having learned about Piaget's concept of "conservation," teachers who observe with care will finally get some concrete examples as they note how children spell *today* or *going* orally during news time but continue to write, *TD we are goen*.... We call that oft-repeated phenomenon of showing mastery in one context but not in another "levels of knowing." But it is in fact a fine example of children not "conserving" knowledge or skills from one context to another. So concrete examples of children's behaviors begin to make real the theoretical knowledge teachers gained in university. Seeing these principles at work in their own classrooms reassures them that children are developing normally and that such seeming inconsistencies are something to expect rather than to worry about.

Scope and sequence charts used to prescribe the order in which skills and facts were to be presented, but increasingly there is the recognition that those charts were based on adult logic, not on the careful observation of children and their ways of learning. While there is research available to describe some of these natural sequences – we offer details and charts in *The Learners' Way* – it becomes important for the teacher to make her own careful observations to develop a sense of how the children in her class sequence their learning. She can then build on that very personal learning. Instead of simply following guidelines or sequences laid down long ago when direct observation of children was not part of educational research, the teacher uses her own judgment, informed by what she has carefully noted in class, to work with the children in her care. Workbooks (rigidly structured sequences of presenting facts and building skills) are replaced by day-to-day real-life events in class to determine what will serve children best to help them take the next steps in their individual journeys of learning.

Having children of varying ages in the same class broadens the scope for noting different ways of unfolding. As well, by working with children for more than a year, teachers experience the joy of seeing late bloomers blossom, precocious youngsters find their social fit, and everyone collaborate to work on projects and everyday jobs.

In chapter 5 you will find a more comprehensive discussion of kid watching.

DEIRDRE ✳ The more you watch children, the more you reinforce the wonderful knowledge that they will all make progress in their own ways. At times, when progress seems slow, your faith may be severely strained, but if you compare notes with other teachers and look back to your successes and those of the children, you know that you can let Deirdre carry on dreaming – for a while anyway. ✳ She was not yet five when she entered kindergarten, fidgety as only a small child can be. No matter what the activity in class, Deirdre placed herself in such a way that she could watch the other kids. It seemed that never once did she keep her eyes on Margaret or the chalkboard. Her actions showed all too clearly that lessons from an adult were not going to be her way of learning at this stage. What she needed was social contact and play with other children. ✳ So Margaret trusted her knowledge of children's needs and gave Deirdre lots of time and space to interact with the other children. Peer modeling, social contact, and the freedom to explore proved the key to Deirdre's learning. At the end of the year, seemingly without having paid the slightest attention to any of the work in class, Deirdre demonstrated that she had absorbed everything she needed to learn that year according to the curriculum guidelines – from the alphabet to numbers to the all-important social skills. ✳ Margaret's observations suggested that having mature peers and the freedom to watch them would be more effective for Deirdre than the cajoling, not to say nagging, she might have done in the days when she rigorously followed every detail of the curriculum. The results proved her right, and Deirdre gradually joined in classroom activities and began to pay attention to the teacher. In the meantime, Deirdre's map mind had absorbed effortlessly and enjoyably what drill-for-skill teaching could have turned into a very unhappy and frustrating time for all.

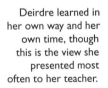

Deirdre learned in her own way and her own time, though this is the view she presented most often to her teacher.

MONITORING PROGRESS AGAINST THE CURRICULUM GUIDELINES

When assessing the progress of her students, the teacher also remains very much aware of the requirements of the curriculum and monitors how children are working to meet those requirements on an ongoing basis. (See chapter 12.) Giving students lots of opportunity to follow their own interests may seem overly flexible, but effective teachers never lose sight of what it is the children in their care are required to learn over the period of a year or two. The difference is that instead of using worksheets for spelling, grammar, and math or lecturing about specific content information in science or social studies, the teacher orchestrates the classroom environment to provide students with a variety of opportunities to learn what needs to be learned. News time and writing workshop double as composition and spelling lessons. Publishing finished stories can become a good occasion to practice careful penmanship. Reading workshop can be enriched by content reading to impart specific knowledge. And literature offers many opportunities to learn about history, geography, and social studies topics in general. Learning is not haphazard or random; it is orchestrated and monitored by the teacher throughout the year.

In fact, as we point out in chapter 12, curriculum guidelines have broadened considerably from the specifics of, say, the language arts curriculum with detailed lists of skills and facts to be acquired. Here in British Columbia, the Ministry of Education has developed five broad curriculum goals with guidelines that give teachers a great deal of scope to work independently in their classrooms to maximize children's learning and overall development. Under "Intellectual Development," for example, the Ministry guidelines suggest that teachers provide a variety of experiences to enable primary children "to sustain and extend natural curiosity; develop thinking through meaningful learning experiences; use language to facilitate thinking and learning; use language to communicate effectively; and develop and integrate the attitudes, skills, and knowledge of Fine Arts, the Humanities, and the Practical Arts and Sciences."

That kind of broadening of curriculum guidelines makes it essential that teachers observe children closely and keep the kinds of requirements listed above clearly in mind. There are no worksheets or tests that measure "curiosity" or "meaningful learning experiences." But as the teacher works toward extending the children's thinking and communication skills, she finds reassurance in referring now and again to those broad guidelines, especially when there are the occasional complaints from parents about "no worksheets, no homework, no spelling lists."

BUILDING ON CHILDREN'S LEARNING STYLES

Providing an integrated classroom in which many ways of taking in and expressing learning are encouraged is one way the teacher ensures that children with different learning styles have the opportunity to work in their preferred modes of learning much of the time. In addition, as she observes who relies heavily on kinesthetic work, who needs to talk in order to learn, and who seems to rely mostly on visual cues, the teacher provides games and center activities to encourage children to explore a broad range of learning modalities. At the same time, if Tony, a kinesthetic learner, continues to have difficulty remembering letters and numbers, she will provide practice materials that give him the opportunity to trace the letters and numbers in sand, cut out paper shapes, or manipulate plastic models of them; and build words and large numbers using movable cards or shapes of the letters and numbers.

For the auditory learner, the teacher will provide practice with audiotapes, songs, rhymes, raps, and games that require talking to make learning fun and memorable. For those who need strong visual

AND THEN THERE WAS... ❋ NICKY, who needed to play for a whole year before settling in. ❋ DARCY, who nearly drove Margaret crazy because he had a great need to talk – usually to her. ❋ LAUREN, who was a born leader and wanted to take over the class. ❋ LI TRANG, who needed to be with the teacher all the time. For the first three months Margaret didn't get a chance to eat lunch with the other teachers; she had her lunch with Li Trang. ❋ A WHOLE GROUP of children who needed to look at the pictures in books in order to "read" and who wouldn't move from that stance until *they* were ready to do so. ❋ A GROUP OF CHILDREN who needed to do exactly the same printing/writing job day after day, until they were ready to move on. ❋ KRISTIN, who read the same little book thirty-five times before she suddenly announced, "Today I want to read you something else," and then quickly moved on to more and more reading.

At times, going along with those needs or styles of working sorely stretched Margaret's determination to let children proceed their own way. But year after year, she found she could step back still farther to give children room to work in their own styles and at their own pace.

aids to their learning, she may use pictures, filmstrips, or the children's own writing and artwork.

But catering to learning styles and being aware of children's preferred modes or idiosyncratic ways of functioning does not end there. As she observes the children interact with each other and with the learning materials, the teacher notes who is slow to react, who likes to do things quickly, who is a social learner, and who prefers solitary work. Such observations are important to creating a positive, productive relationship between teacher and learner. Honoring each child's way of working and occasionally offering encouragement to try a new, somewhat different way create a climate of respect and mutual trust in the classroom. When the focus rested on acquiring facts and meeting specific deadlines, teachers had little time and experience to build that kind of rapport.

ENHANCING CHILDREN'S OWN SEQUENCE OF LEARNING

The teacher also knows about and responds to the children's ways of sequencing their learning. Instead of simply following sequences laid down by commercially produced programs or by guidelines designed by adults, she develops and then draws on her knowledge and experience of children's reading and writing development that evolves when they are free to learn naturally: from picture reading and memory reading to emergent reading; from scribbles and babbling in print to emergent writing and composing; from using only initial consonants at first, to more detailed invented spelling, and finally to standard spelling. Through her knowledge of such natural learning steps, the teacher feels secure in guiding children's progress from one level to the next level, using judicious input that gives students the right kind of information at the right moment. She helps them stretch their learning without demanding that they must do something for which they are not yet ready.

Working quietly with the children's own sequence of evolving skills builds a climate of trust in the classroom and assures students, parents, and anyone concerned about the children's progress that learning is unfolding as it should. Though the children are doing their own unfolding, the catalysts for this progress are the teacher's knowledge, quiet confidence, and ready affirmation of every step forward.

"Pat, that's really good work. You've got all the beginning consonants. There are a lot of the other consonants that are right, and you are using vowels in all the right places. You're really moving toward standard spelling!" When you observe Pat's happy smile and then the confident manner in which she is expanding her writing, it seems that "doing nothing" has very powerful and positive effects on children's learning.

APPLYING KNOWLEDGE OF CHILD DEVELOPMENT

Aside from knowing the children's sequence of acquiring skills, familiarity with child development helps the teacher feel free either to stand back to give a child room to mature or to move in to give encouragement or suggestions – not demands or orders - when that seems appropriate. A look at Piaget's stages of development confirms that young children need a lot of concrete work and find abstractions difficult. So the teacher knows that it is counterproductive to begin instructions with such abstract concepts as letters, sounds, words, numbers, or sentences and that concrete work like reading stories, writing letters or picture captions, and counting up game tokens are far more productive ways of initiating literacy and numeracy.

The atmosphere of confidence that derives from the teacher's firm trust that the children are following their own schedules of development conveys itself to the children and removes the feelings of anxiety, shame, and frustration that so often assail late bloomers. As a result, the children have the freedom to unfold based on their own timetables. The teacher, because she observes closely and knows children's natural sequence of development – motor skills, coordination, verbal skills – also knows when to provide a gentle nudge to bolster confidence or reinforce a child's desire to "do what the other kids are doing."

BUILDING ON SUCCESSES

Being aware of the important stimulant that a feeling of success can be, the teacher makes sure that all students experience success. For example, if a child is a fine illustrator but lacks composing skills, she stresses the importance of good drawings to convey a story; if a

GENTLE NUDGES THAT WORKED ❊ GERYLYN When Gerylyn entered kindergarten at South Park School, she was not ready to apply herself to the everyday work of school. So she spent her first two years daydreaming, playing, and watching other children. Then she entered Margaret's class as a second-grader, and her overall growth and the knowledge she had accumulated despite her daydreaming gave Margaret the signals that the time had come to ask for some concerted work on spelling and letter-sound correspondences, for time dedicated to table-work, for sitting still for reasonable lengths of time, for putting out at least a minimum of writing, and for increasing that minimum gradually. All along, Margaret would affirm, "You are more grown up now; I know you can do...." And with that one-to-one coaxing on Margaret's part, Gerylyn responded well to the gentle but firm nudges and moved right along. ❊ DANIEL had confined each of his daily writing assignments to two brief sentences, but showed every evidence that he could produce those two sentences very efficiently and promptly. So by the end of October, Margaret talked to him and established a new minimum for him. "I know you are a good writer and can think of lots to say. So next week, I'm going to expect you to write at least three sentences every day." ❊ When TONY found himself unable to work quietly on his own during writing workshop, Margaret told him, "Tony, you've been bothering the children at your table during work time. I'm sorry, but I'll have to move you to an empty table. Let me know when you are ready to come back." ❊ BALINT had been stuck in his writing, but responded with a complete change of topics when Margaret reminded him, "You've been writing about happy land, space land, sunny land, and bubble land for three months now. I know you talk about other things, so I'd like you to find another topic to write about."

While these "gentle nudges" worked, a suggestion can sometimes be untimely. When Margaret told Bryan that she felt he would be able to print larger to make his writing more legible, he immediately lapsed into reversals, printing from right to left, and generally displayed much poorer printing. He had been working in the way that was right for him, and the suggestion to do something new completely disrupted his own ways for a time.

child's math skills are more advanced than his language arts abilities, she celebrates the fine math work and provides extra support with language arts. Even the acknowledgment of successes achieved outside of school – in sports, in connection with hobbies, in artwork – can set children on the road to success in areas that they have found difficult.

As the teacher builds on the success syndrome, the child who has been slow to develop begins to evolve confidence and skills in many areas.

PROVIDING FEEDBACK THAT ACKNOWLEDGES AND EXTENDS SKILLS

And so the teacher provides feedback that encourages, reinforces, and extends what it is children are doing. For example, she says, "Yes, and..." rather than "Yes, *but*...." That positive input and focus on steps

LAUREN TIES HER SHOES ✳ Though it may not seem like a major milestone, the day after Lauren had mastered the difficult task of tieing her own shoe-laces, her reading shot forward and her confidence about being able to work with letters soared ahead.

ROB GETS HIS VERY OWN PUPPY ✳ Receiving a puppy of his very own gave Rob a feeling of importance. Being a member of a large family made owning something that he did not have to share particularly exciting. Rob had the responsibility of looking after the puppy, feeding it, and generally taking care of it. He felt grown up and important. At the same time, his writing took a strong leap forward. From being uncertain of using beginning consonants, all of a sudden Rob was writing about his puppy and expanding his ability to spell and create close approximations of standard spelling. Success, feeling important, and having a purpose for writing all combined to allow Rob to leap forward in learning.

PETER FINALLY GETS THE MESSAGE ✳ Peter wrote a lot and progressed well in his writing, but all his stories started, "Jimmy and me." During writing conferences Margaret would listen to his stories, acknowledge the message, and then suggest in a quiet voice that to be grammatically correct he should write "Jimmy and I." She also suggested other writing topics, but "Jimmy and me" continued to appear and continued to be a subject of discussion during conference time. Then suddenly, without any sign of what produced the change, Peter arrived for his writing conference with a big smile on his face. There it was, "Jimmy and I." He was totally awed and pleased with himself. After the conference – and lots of praise – he just glowed. That aura of success stayed with him for several days, and he moved right along in his writing – picking new topics – and transferred his success to his math work as well.

forward – the process – does more to foster learning and enthusiasm for productive work than any number of worksheets could achieve with praise about "an excellent job" or marks of red ink and the request to "do more careful work." What does help are comments like "I really liked the way you solved that problem" or "You really thought long and hard to get that answer" or "I really appreciate the effort you put into that work."

As children spell or write, Margaret will acknowledge their efforts to ensure that they continue to work and develop their skills: "You are right, that's what it sounds like. That's one kind of *to*. Here we need the number *two* and that takes a *w*. I wonder if any of you remember that third way of spelling *to*?" As a child volunteers *t-o-o* , Margaret prints the three words on the board as she has done many times before. Or she may comment, "I can tell you really sounded that out. That's an ∫ sound in *telephone*, and if we want standard spelling here, we

South Park Family School

Marg,

Two years at South Park. You've made it.

Your leadership in whole language, your flexibility in programming, your strength of conviction, your help and encouragement in our joint workshops, your service as social coordinator, your interest in research, your love of teaching and children serve as an inspiration to us all, especially me. Thanks

Trevor

Teachers, too, thrive on feedback that is specific, and Margaret's principal Trevor Calkins offered it in full measure, not just to her, but to all of his staff.

need a *ph. Ph* also makes an ∫ sound." If children are collaborating on recounting the steps in a project or a set of directions and one of them provides an example of a step that needs to be taken toward the end, Margaret acknowledges the contribution, puts it down low on the board or paper, and then asks for some of the other things that need to go on the list first.

Sometimes when children are working and have come to what they think is their limit, a word from the teacher will extend and enrich their ideas. Such questions as "Have you thought of putting a moat around your castle?" or "Have you thought of counting the rabbits in the border?" will renew activity without detracting from the child's own creative work. Looking at a diorama a student has created, the teacher might comment, "I really like the way you solved that construction problem. What a good way to work that out. I wonder if you could give the diorama even more of a 3-D look if you hung an airplane from the top of the box." Or a comment to Wang who is playing with large number cards, "Wouldn't it be neat if you put all these numbers in order from smallest to largest?" When working with the children in writing conferences, the teacher always focuses on the message first, acknowledges what the student is conveying, and then probes and discusses how the writing could be extended or polished.

INDIVIDUALIZING INSTRUCTION

Because the feedback is specific to the job at hand and to individual children's work, the teacher individualizes instruction to address the needs of children as they arise. Instead of concentrating most of her effort on broadly based lessons, the teacher frequently works with children individually in writing conferences, projects, and in the day-to-day classwork.

Talking to a child who is exploring the water table and its possibilities, a teacher will generate a shift from simply playing to observations of hydraulics by wondering aloud, "Maybe if we lowered that tube, the water would come through." The teacher helps children become aware of their own unique learning styles by asking such questions as "Do you need time to think about work before starting or are you always ready to get going right away?" or "Do you need to have a quiet time to work on your writing or can you write any time?"

Setting individual minimum requirements for writing assures that those who have the capacity to do more are challenged and those who need more time to talk and to draw are given time and personal assurance that what they do is fine. Simon, who could only sit still for a minute or two during writing workshop, was allowed to get up and be more active. He would do his "writing," which at first consisted of only the letters in his name rearranged in different patterns. Then he would jump up and Margaret would say a few words to him about his printing and the effort he put into it before letting him go on to one of the centers. Robert, who was sitting nearby, decided he would try to get by with just a little bit of work too. He brought Margaret his sheet of writing with just a few letters on it and started to head off to play at the transportation center, which with its trains and all kinds of signals and bridges was a totally absorbing place. In her own quiet way, Margaret brought him back to his seat and explained to him that she expected more from him because he was older, could write more, and had more experience in telling stories. Robert accepted that explanation and went back to work.

Reading offers many opportunities for the teacher to bring in books and articles to challenge advanced readers and to build on their personal interests. They often want to sit quietly, engrossed in reading such books as *Charlotte's Web* or *Little House on the Prairie*. As they do, Margaret singles out one or two of her emergent readers for a brief session of reading to and with them. She makes sure that such sessions are enjoyable and filled with laughter and good feelings as she shares favorite books and poems with the children. She does not structure the session as though it were a reading lesson or a test, nor does she demand that they participate orally. Her question "Do you want to read along or by yourself?" is an oft-given gentle nudge, but it is always a genuine invitation, and children receive it as such. They know that, if they say yes, they can be assured of as much or as little help as they need or want, and that if they say no, Margaret will accept their decisions and at the same time leave the invitation open by adding, "If you change your minds, just let me know." Books she may choose for such sessions are open invitations for the children to read on their own and to look at the pictures again and again. (Nelson's Breakthrough to Literacy series offers such popular titles as *I Fell Down*, *I Lost My Tooth*, and *Cup of Tea*. These are small books of six or seven pages with text that is easy – and at times repetitive and predictable – and that offer children a chance to chime in or to recognize familiar words. Ginn's Book Garden is a similar series with *The Chocolate Cake* being the favorite title. Peguis also has an excellent series of little books for beginning readers called Tiger Cub Books.) Having had the teacher's undivided attention while going over these books, children often seek them out afterwards and go over and over their spe-

cial favorite until their inner reading patterns become firmly established and they feel comfortable moving on to different, more
demanding reading.

During center or choosing time Margaret observes unobtrusively. If
Laureen is experimenting with the weights and a balance beam and is
on the verge of having the right combination to balance the weights,
Margaret may join her to talk about deliberately adding or subtracting
to come out with an even balance. Capturing such teachable moments
and enjoying them with a child is the best part of individualized
instruction. But you have to guard against *expecting* the child to accept
or put into practice what you are suggesting. Sometimes they will;
more often than not you will only see the results of your intervention
days or even weeks later. So patience and more unobtrusive observing are the answer. If children have learned to work independently,
opportunities for such personal interactions abound.

FOSTERING INDEPENDENCE AND RESPONSIBILITY

From the time toddlers begin to move around the home, they want to
explore and try everything for themselves. Their whole beings exude
I want to do it myself when it comes to feeding themselves, taking everything out of the cupboard, or piling blocks up and then knocking
them down. Children come to school with the same urges. If the
teacher has created the kind of friendly, safe environment that invites
them to take out the books, work with the materials in the centers,
and create their own artwork, she is simply building on every child's
natural urge for independence. With that, she sets the climate for
putting the children in charge of their own learning, which is, of
course, the chief aim of the holistic, integrated approach to teaching/
learning. It is also a core concept in lifelong learning, a survival tool
that students will require in the future and one that they should start
developing as small children. So as the teacher gives plenty of choices,
asks children to help her with simple classroom jobs, and seeks their
input for planning the work ahead, she is affirming that they are capa-
ble, responsible learners who can be trusted to work on their own.

From the beginning of the school year and throughout the term,
the teacher encourages students to take on jobs and to do things for
themselves – handing out supplies, choosing reading materials, picking the right centers to hold their interest, settling their disputes, find-

SETTING CRITERIA FOR SHARED READING   Shared reading is an enjoyable way to end reading workshop and gives children a chance to talk with
one or two special buddies about what they enjoyed in their book or to share
a passage and read it together. One day when the shared–reading session became too
noisy, somewhat unfocused, and disturbing to those students who wanted to continue
to read quietly on their own, Margaret called the children together to discuss the
problem.

MARGARET: Shared reading time doesn't seem to be working as we agreed at the beginning of the year. I notice that sometimes you don't even have a book there, and the
noise is becoming very disturbing to me when I want to read. Have any of you
noticed that?

STUDENT 1: Yea, I couldn't concentrate. I wanted them to stop.

STUDENT 2: Me too. But they wouldn't stop making a lot of noise. Why don't we just
stop shared reading?

MARGARET: How about those who like shared reading? How many of you would like to
continue having shared reading?

[Counts the show of hands]

All right. Let's look at what we can do to keep shared reading, make it really a time
of sharing your reading, and make sure that none of us disturbs the other readers.

STUDENT 3: We could make some rules.

STUDENT 4: Yea, you could just whisper as you talk.

MARGARET: That sounds good. What can you think of to make sure that you are actually
reading together and not just talking?

STUDENT 5: We could make sure we have a book and sit close together so we can both
see it.

From there the suggestions evolved and the rules for shared reading included:
  Have a book for sharing (either one each or one shared).
  Read together (choral reading or taking turns).
  Sit side by side so you can see the book and talk quietly.

Margaret recorded the rules on the chalkboard and left them there for a few days.
Shared reading settled down to a much more productive time.

ing solutions to problems of work or getting along, settling down to reading or writing, choosing their own topics for writing or projects, filing their own writing, keeping track of library books, cleaning up after art, putting away materials used in projects, helping younger peers, showing visitors around. The purposeful, productive atmosphere that visitors will remark on is created by the teacher's willingness to let go and to turn things over to the children. It is the direct result of the teacher's manifest confidence in the children's ability to "do the job." That spirit of independence also pays dividends in freeing the teacher's time to work with individuals or small groups. See chapter 3 for more details about and concrete examples of fostering that spirit of independence that is such an important aspect of preparing children for lifelong learning.

COLLABORATING TO ESTABLISH RULES— MAINTAINING DISCIPLINE

Part of the feeling of independence and responsibility engendered in the students stems from the collaboration between the teacher and students to evolve and enforce rules. (See pages 90–94 in chapter 4 and pages 160, 161 in chapter 7.) Whether dealing with rules of conduct or rules for completing a job, the teacher and students have genuine discussions to arrive at guidelines that are fair and reasonable. Students know that their opinions and suggestions are valued and received positively. As a result, they take discussions about rules seriously and then help to monitor their behavior and enforce adherence to the rules. Discipline in class becomes a shared responsibility. The teacher sets the tone, and the students take their cues from her. In fact, they often become the ones who call their peers to order.

(far right)
A visit to the local newspaper to deliver a check and a poster-sized covering letter prepared by the whole class provided a closing highlight for the class fundraising project.

CONNECTING LEARNING TO THE WORLD OUTSIDE

Just as the classroom rules are reality-based, so teaching in general strives to make learning meaningful and to connect it to the world beyond the classroom. To create that important link between school learning and the everyday world, the teacher sets reading and writing tasks that serve useful purposes and are much more than teaching/ learning exercises. Children's reading is not limited to fiction. As they

AN APPLE SALE FOR A GOOD CAUSE PROVIDES INVALUABLE LEARNING

AN APPLE SALE FOR A GOOD CAUSE PROVIDES INVALUABLE **LEARNING** ✳ Math skills, problem solving, and social skills all intertwined when Margaret involved her students in selling apples as a fund–raising project for needy families. The project began with a field trip to an orchard where the children bought a supply of apples (and in the process learned about all the steps involved in picking, cleaning, sorting, and storing apples). ✳ Back in the classroom, the children sorted the apples into small, medium, and large sizes doing a lot of comparing, talking, and estimating. Then they counted how many apples they had in each category, how many all together, and, later, how many were left after a day's selling. They made posters advertising their sale, prepared lists of all the things to be done, arranged for and practiced giving change, and took turns being apple sellers and change givers. ✳ Sales were made from a booth set up outside the classroom during recess and lunch. They used toy cash registers, which gave a satisfying ring as the drawers were opened and shut. Children sold the apples for twenty–five cents each for the large and medium–sized ones, and twenty cents for the small ones. Aside from making change, the children learned about dealing with customers. As some of the older children tried to get medium apples for the price of small, negotiated about quantity discounts, and talked about getting the right change, the children themselves worked out most of the challenges. In one instance, they took after one of the boys who dropped four pennies on the table and made off with an apple. Outraged, they confronted him and made him pay the sixteen cents he owed. ✳ Margaret often had to restrain those parents who had come in to help from stepping in and taking over the negotiations or more difficult transactions. As it was, they generally confined their help to directing students into lineups, if too many showed up at a time, and to keeping a general eye on the sale. ✳ Each day the children counted the money, and as the sum mounted up, the whole class walked to the bank around the corner to make a deposit. Margaret had taken the children to a nearby bank to establish the account, learn how to make out deposit slips and deposit the money. Bank officials were kind and cooperative whenever the whole class arrived to transact business. ✳ Once all the apples were sold, the students went to the local newspaper to hand over their check and have their photo taken for the next edition.

> Dec. 15
>
> Dear Times/Colonist,
>
> We went to the orchard and got apples to sell. We sold them at school to make money for the poor kids. We made $72.25. Please give our cheque to the 1000 Fund.
>
> Your friends,
> Grade K/1
> at Fairburn School

do research, they search through textbooks, reference works, and resource manuals. They consult recipes and directions, cull news from the local newspaper, and learn about looking things up in dictionaries and encyclopedias. Along with stories and reports, their writing includes making lists for shopping and field trips, posting notices around the room, writing letters, creating scripts for plays, and keeping track of group decisions in joint projects. Field trips and special projects are geared to the community around the school and draw on the special resources available in the area.

HOW OLD IS OLD? Visiting seniors at a home proved productive in many ways. As children visited a senior's home situated close to the school, they particularly enjoyed talking to the oldest resident, a gentleman 101 years of age. He greeted the children, shook hands with each one of them, and then shared some of his memories of eighty and even ninety years ago. As children talked about their visit once they were back in the classroom, Margaret noticed that they could not picture what a hundred years really meant. They talked in terms of "very old," but then they thought their teacher – then in her fifties – was "very old." So Margaret had them put Unifix cubes together in sets of ten and asked them to arranged ten sets of ten in different ways. Next she invited them to create a Unifix cube representation of their own ages. As they put together sticks of five, six, and seven cubes, she once again asked them to arrange them in different patterns and then to see how many sticks they needed to make up 101. A lot of adding, rearranging, and grouping by tens was the result. As a final comparison, children told Margaret that they would like to see her age represented by Unifix cubes. So the teacher, too, had her turn. She had created the framework for this purposeful, reality-based work, and her observations and input helped to expand her own work and that of the children.

COLLABORATING WITH HELPERS

To connect work in school to the world outside and to add richness to the in-class interactions, the teacher collaborates with as many "helpers" as possible. Within the school, the teacher actively seeks out partners for teaching special units or sharing resources. Fellow teachers, the librarian, the school counselor, the learning assistance teacher, the principal, the school secretary – even the custodian – are valuable aides to broadening the teaching base. Encouraging peer teaching is yet another way of expanding the learning opportunities for students and teacher alike and is particularly effective in multi-age classes and with buddy programs.

Helpers from outside the school include parents, special resource people, visitors, professionals, craftspersons, the local police and fire-fighters, student teachers – anyone willing to come into class to demonstrate or talk about their particular interest or expertise. Planning, organizing, rearranging prior plans, contacting everyone concerned, and coordinating activities to fit the school schedule are just a small part of the teacher's input to providing this enrichment. It definitely does not "just happen."

In chapter 14 there are examples of parent support, and in chapter 15 we describe the support and reinforcement Margaret gave and received in her networking with other teachers. Throughout the book, we give examples of projects that had special support from visitors, parents, or school staff.

CONTINUING TO LEARN

One of the most rewarding aspects of all the many things the teacher *does* – and there are many more – is that she continues to learn every day – watching the students, comparing notes with colleagues, abstracting information from interactions in class, learning alongside the students during special projects, taking advantage of in-service training, and reflecting on interactions in class to gain deeper understanding. The tedium of going over the same old lessons year after year simply does not exist because each year a new group of students presents new challenges and new needs. Teaching becomes continual professional development as teachers enter the excitement and challenge of finding even more and better ways of working with their students.

Reaffirming the professional status of teachers

We have entitled our book *The Teacher's Way* to reemphasize the importance of the teacher's role in classrooms that, on the surface, seem to function all by themselves. These are classrooms where students are learning with independence and joy. They are also classrooms where discipline problems disappear as the year progresses, because the children participate in setting and enforcing the rules and all work busily on projects that have meaning for them. In such classrooms the teachers are reaffirming their professional status. Instead of simply following directions and guidelines handed down from authorities who have never seen their classrooms, the teachers rely heavily on their detailed personal knowledge of the children in their care to devise programs that fit the children and their day-to-day needs. Far from being mere dispensers of lessons, these teachers are researchers and curriculum developers, and as such they themselves continue to learn and grow day by day.

Good teachers have always functioned in this way, but our contacts with hundreds of teachers during workshops and presentations have shown us that many of them felt they needed to conceal the fact that they were working in what they considered unorthodox ways. Now that we have ample theoretical backing and many forward-looking curriculum documents that encourage these thoughtful ways of fostering learning, teachers no longer need to hide their professional work. They can take charge of their classrooms and, within the broad curriculum guidelines for their specific grade area or discipline, they can decide what will best encourage children to become learners and thinkers right from kindergarten and grade one.

Throughout the book, we offer some comparisons of old and new ways of teaching to provide a framework for visualizing how you and the children – not a prepackaged, carefully prescribed program – make the decisions about learning in class. But we don't intend to focus on regrets about past mistakes. Instead, we want to celebrate teachers' ways of working productively – ways that build on the latest research on child-centered, brain-compatible ways of teaching/learning. Above all, we want to affirm that teachers who care about children and watch them closely have always known how to direct learning in positive, productive ways.

3.

Creating a Context for Independence

Once we acknowledge that whether working with a single-grade or multi-age class we are working with children of widely diverse levels of maturity, experience, and background (see chapter 6), we are faced with the need to create learning experiences that will challenge and involve all the children. There are many activities – projects, reading and writing, learning-center activities – in which all children participate and work at their own levels. But there is still the need to work with individuals and small groups if we are to challenge the more advanced learners, provide interest for reluctant readers, and offer extra help to emergent learners who need both encouragement and elaboration of the work given to the class as a whole.

The key to success in what at first may seem like an utterly impossible juggling act is to create a classroom environment that fosters independence, invites children to take charge of their own work, and lays the groundwork for the kind of lifelong learning, independent thinking, and decision making that they will need throughout their school years and then in the workforce. To build these skills from the ground up, we need far more than structured lessons that impart isolated skills and facts. But if the teacher *trusts* the children to know how to learn, she will know how to create endless opportunities to help them practice being independent and responsible at the same time as they are building skills in "the basics" – reading, writing, math, listening, and speaking.

Children certainly rise to the challenge of being trusted. Their learning and thinking skills flourish, and the independence with which they approach their work in class enables the teacher to individualize her teaching. As she establishes routines and clarifies expectations, her students know what to do and how to proceed to the next job while their teacher works with individuals and small groups, or even leaves the classroom - often without so much as a ripple to show that she is no longer present.

Children happily work on their own, especially if they have had a say in choosing topics and activities. To set them on that path of being self-directed workers, it is crucial that the teacher nurture their independence and responsibility in a wonderfully positive way from the very start of the year. If you have ever tried to lecture your own children or your students on the need to become "more responsible," you may have encountered blank looks or a direct question, "What d'you mean by 'responsible'?" We certainly have and found ourselves at a loss for words. In fact, talking has little or no impact, whereas creating a concrete environment that empowers children to be independent and responsible has a profound effect.

Setting a climate for independence and responsibility

Setting a climate for independence is a crucial part of that *change in attitude or philosophy* that undergirds holistic ways of teaching. You, the teacher, are the most important aspect of the learning environment, and if you cultivate a mind-set that affirms that the children in your care are eager and able to do jobs for themselves and that they are ready for "the having of wonderful ideas" given the chance to explore materials and ideas in their own way, then you have taken the first and most important step toward creating a context for independence and responsibility.

Children are astute observers of adults. Not only do they watch the behaviors of adults so closely that they can emulate them down to the finest detail, but they also know how to look deeply below the surface to detect the underlying feelings and thoughts that guide the actions of the adults around them. In *The Tone of Teaching* (1986), Max

Van Manen observes that parents and teachers frequently convey two messages, one spoken and one unspoken: "It would be fun to go skating" and "but underneath I really don't want to take you." So for children who "read" their parents' thoughts with amazing accuracy, life is "full of contradictions and ambivalences." If we want children to become independent learners, then our thoughts and actions must be congruent and free of the kind of ambivalence children detect so readily.

We may talk about independence and responsibility, but for far too long our methods of teaching and interacting with children have conveyed the message that we regard children as passive receivers of knowledge and the teacher (being an adult) as all-knowing, and that the only way they are going to learn is to follow step-by-step directions. In lessons that focused on imparting a fixed set of skills, there was little room for choice, independent action, or the development of creative problem solving. Children either had the right answer or they didn't, and the wondering that invites the application of right-brain spontaneity during reading, writing, math, and project work rarely came into play. When you change the way of interacting with children to two-way communication that helps *you* see and hear how much the children bring to their learning and helps *them* see that you acknowledge their ability to do things for themselves, then a different spirit pervades the classroom, and you and the children become co-creators of learning.

Writing about "the virtues of not knowing," Eleanor Duckworth (1987) remarks that in a classroom where quick right answers are prized most, *"the figuring out doesn't count"* (Duckworth's italics). She goes on to say, "What you do about what you don't know is, in the final analysis, what determines what you will ultimately know. It is, moreover, quite possible to help children develop these virtues.... Accepting surprise, puzzlement, excitement, patience, caution, honest attempts, and wrong outcomes as legitimate and important elements of learning, easily leads to their further development." She is talking about the can-do attitude that opens the door to moving from not knowing to knowing by way of learners' explorations that you can encourage from the moment they begin school.

Independence, responsibility, and cooperation grow in direct proportion to the opportunities you provide for exercising these qualities. The expectations and trust with which you imbue the classroom climate show themselves in all the small things to which we rarely pay attention. Cultivating an attitude of calm and acceptance is foremost among them. If we want children to be confident and secure in their ways of working, we have to radiate that confidence in them from within as well as display it in our actions. Max Van Manen (1986) eloquently describes how children experience our presence:

> A young and insecure teacher who desperately tries to feign an air of self-confidence soon gives away his or her real state of being. Children will quickly sense it in an awkward gesture, a false pose, a look in the eye.... We may be physically present to children while something essential is absent in our presence.

"YOU CAN DO IT YOURSELF!"

Starting with the first day of school, use every opportunity to give the unambiguous message, "You can do it yourself!" When you greet the children in a calm, friendly way as they enter the room, you let them know that you value their ability to do things themselves. Without fretting about the extra time it might take, you tell Clea, "I know you can take your coat off by yourself," or you encourage Kim, "That's right, you know where to hang up your jacket." If shoelaces need to be tied or zippers undone, you give the children time to work at these tasks by themselves and thereby affirm that they are able to handle these jobs, if not alone, then with the help of a peer and eventually by themselves.

That small beginning sets the climate of independence right from the start. Children perceive that you trust – and expect – them to do things for themselves, and they act accordingly. The confidence you show in their ability to take care of themselves does wonders for their willingness to listen, take the next step, and venture forth into untried territory. They feel safe to take on new jobs and do them to the best of their ability, confident in their knowledge that, without patronizing them, you will affirm, "You are doing just fine."

From those small beginnings that set the tone and clearly convey that you expect them to work independently, you expand to more demanding tasks:

✳ Leave it up to the children to find their seats for the day based on the name cards you have placed on their tables. (Children love to create and decorate their own name cards.)

* Hold the children responsible for keeping track of their belongings in their desks or in special supply baskets.

* Make children responsible for gathering and distributing supplies and equipment: handing out writing paper, choosing books to be used at reading time, gathering research material from the special tables set up around the room.

* Ask for help counting hot dog tickets for special occasions or other such math requirements.

* Enlist the help of more advanced students to take roll call and make the assignment sheet as easy or difficult as the child needs (for example, "how many half-day kids," "how many whole-day kids," "how many five-year-olds," and whatever else you can think of).

* Assign a child to be responsible for setting up the listening equipment for the first story of the day, for booting-up the computer, for setting up the paint easel.

* Hold the children responsible for taking home books (to be enjoyed and shared) every day and signing them out.

* Pick a child who is keen on science and make him responsible for planning and setting up a science experiment.

* Choose a child to take responsibility for talking to one of the children who is late every day.

* Make children responsible for cleaning up after artwork and cooking as well as putting away learning materials. (With a bit of modeling and some gentle nudges at first, children assume responsibility for keeping the classroom tidy.)

No doubt you will develop your own, far more extensive list, or you may already have done so. As you turn over more and more jobs to the children, your more mature students will demonstrate how to take charge, and the more timid or unsure children will begin to model themselves after their peers. There are even times when children begin to help out the teacher. In Margaret's class, Caitlin could always be counted on to remind her teacher, who tended to forget frequently, that the class attendance list was supposed to be taken to the office every day. Another time, one of the children noticed that Margaret was supposed to be on duty on the school ground during recess and sent her out posthaste.

Visitors to Margaret's classroom have commented that the children act with more independence and assurance than any children they have observed elsewhere. In creating that climate of independence and assurance, Margaret never loses an opportunity to turn things over to the children. She empowers them to be viable partners in running the classroom – doing such tasks as taking attendance, tallying money for field trips, counting up the books in the book order, taking messages to the librarian or principal, helping each other, setting rules and then enforcing them. Children perceive that the jobs turned over to them are important and relevant to the functioning of the class. Like a child who is allowed to help with real jobs at home or in a parent's business, they rise to that challenge. Without lectures or explanations about what it means to be responsible, children build inner maps of responsible ways of interacting. Based on that concrete learning and the inner picture they have of it, their responsibility and independence flourish.

If you consciously look for opportunities to turn as many jobs as possible over to students, they will become your partners in managing your class. Instead of spending precious time doing the many small jobs required in your school day and having to keep close control over discipline at the same time, you will find that your time and energy are freed up to attend to the management of learning and teaching. By imbuing the children with that spirit of responsibility and independence, you set the scene for effective learning that is not disrupted by discipline problems. As you gradually relinquish more and more jobs to the children, you will have to let go of your need to be ultra-efficient and to work within specific time frames or carefully structured guidelines. Undoubtedly many of the jobs the children assume within the classroom will take far more time than if you or an adult helper did them, but the dividends in learning and setting a climate of independence, responsibility, and cooperation far outweigh any "lost time."

As long as you are sure in your own mind that "letting go" of jobs does not mean letting go of discipline and order in the classroom, you will find more and more opportunities to help the children grow in responsibility and independence. In fact, they, not you, will quite often be the ones to keep order. Watching a group of first-graders participate in news time, a classroom visitor was startled to observe a tiny girl turn to her neighbor who was fidgeting and inform him, "That's inappropriate behavior." It was, and he stopped.

ESTABLISHING ROUTINES ALLOWS FOR INDEPENDENCE

Establishing routines and familiar daily patterns in class give children the opportunity to move on their own from one job to the next. Whether you begin the day with a talking session or with reading a story, children will know that after the ritual of greeting, making contact at the door, and a brief roll call, the first session of the day will be a group meeting and that they will move from there to the next job all by themselves.

By picking activities that children enjoy and want to pursue both following the morning meeting and right after recess, you assure that they proceed to the activities eagerly and settle down to work voluntarily and independently. If, for example, the children know that after recess it is reading time or drawing time or center time, they will come in, gather up what they need, and set to work whether you are there or not. In Margaret's class, students hurry in to be sure to get the very best selection of books they can for book time; in Karen Abel's grade-two-three class, "the daily draw" brings children to the classroom eager to take out their art supplies, and they set to work without the need for instruction or admonition to get on with the job. In fact, if Karen finds it necessary to eliminate the drawing session, students complain loudly.

Immediately after recess, Karen's students take out their art materials to begin their creative work. Without coaxing or special instructions, they eagerly begin to work on their current projects. At the teacher's suggestion and based on her modeling, they will experiment with line drawings, watercolors, continuous line drawings, or clay sculptures.

When it comes to general classroom seating, even kindergarten children quickly learn to recognize their name cards, and if you use the large cards as place markers for seating the children at their tables or desks, they soon find their assigned seats for the day – and get a lot of reading practice in the bargain as they move around on their own and look at all the name cards. Since you change the seating regularly, they also learn about getting along and sharing with different children without clinging to their one best friend or getting attached to one specific table or seat. They move freely and independently in the classroom as finding their seat becomes a fun mystery tour.

IF YOU GIVE THEM TIME, THEY'LL COME THROUGH　Pamela was working on her project for the upcoming health fair. She had chosen to create a diorama and was having difficulty producing some of the special effects she wanted to include. Her mother, who was a helper in the classroom at the time, was eager to help Pamela and was quite upset when Margaret asked her to let Pamela solve her own problems. Margaret knew that the child could do the work, but also knew that she was very much used to having her mother solve her problems. To give Pamela the chance to show her own creativity and independence, Margaret persevered in keeping mother from playing her customary rescue role. With a lot of encouragement about being able to do the work on her own, Pamela found that she *could* solve her own problems, and she fairly glowed with satisfaction and pride. She had done the job herself!

ALLOWING CHILDREN ENOUGH TIME

Then there is taking the time to let the children do jobs, accepting the minor mishaps and messes – spills, false starts, paints that run together, cardboard that tears when it is folded – as opportunities to learn from mistakes and to let the children help with the cleaning up if any is needed. Taking time also includes noting and encouraging even the smallest steps forward, celebrating successes, laughing together about unexpected outcomes, and cultivating a matter-of-fact voice in the face of all challenges and initial frustrations. Independence would not have a chance to flourish in an environment where sticking to a fixed timetable was more important than giving children opportunities to work and explore in their own way.

But it isn't always easy to let go of rushing in to "set things right." When Andrew had painted himself quite literally into a corner, had paint on his hands and shoes, and was sitting there debating how to solve his problem, Margaret's principal came in and in the best teacher tradition stepped right over the mess, lifted Andrew up, and hustled him to the sink, saying "Here take your shoes off. Hold your hands under the faucet. Get that paint off your shirt." Then he turned to Margaret with a broad grin of satisfaction to find her glaring at him: "I was just waiting to see how Andrew would solve his problem!" So much for being helpful! It takes time, conscious effort, and a gradual letting go of control to create that climate of independence.

DEVELOPING INDEPENDENCE IN READING

As long as basal readers with grade or level designations dominated reading instruction, children perceived a strong message – *This is* not *for you!* – when they looked at readers labeled for specific levels. They internalized the attitude that "reading" meant working at a prescribed pace and level, and that exploring literature or any material outside of today's lesson was inappropriate. With STOP signs like that, it was hard to develop a spirit of independence and adventure. But when children are encouraged to read anything and everything in class and out, they develop independence in reading without the need to discuss it or provide lessons in "staying on track."

If your classroom is covered from wall to wall with a wide variety of books, magazines, and all manner of games and charts that are not marked for specific reading levels but invite everyone to read them, then children will happily delve in and explore the literature available to them. They will, that is, if you encourage all forays into reading and reading-like behaviors.

Having the freedom to move about in class, children settle into their favorite place to enjoy reading.

Children who are not yet reading love to "play reading." They will ask to share at sharing time and hold the book just like an accomplished reader, make up a story, turn pages intoning "Annnd...," and then continue their "reading" on the next page. Memory reading of short poems and nursery rhymes is part of that early reading-like behavior, as is picture reading (looking at the pictures to find the right words). Often children will insist on taking home a book that is far beyond their ability to read. But they enjoy looking at the pictures, and as they look at the print they give all indications of envisioning themselves as readers.

During the early years of our partnership, Margaret would occasionally comment that she had always been able to teach children to read, but that with her new ways of working, children not only learn to read, but *love* to read and do so enthusiastically both in school and out. Teachers from the upper grades certainly confirmed that observation when they commented they could always tell who had been one of Margaret's students, because these children always had books in their desks, tucked under their arms, or peaking out of their backpacks. Moreover, they could be seen reading at recess, during lunch breaks, and even on the bus. Perhaps the most telling comment came from an enrichment teacher who remarked that whenever she suggested any reading task to Margaret's children, they were always ready to give anything a try, while children in other classes would frequently tell her, "I can't do this," or "I don't know how to read this," or "We haven't done this one yet." These children were unwilling to try anything that was not in their regular curriculum or had not been introduced by their teacher. Clearly their independence had not had a chance to blossom as yet, and they were missing out on a lot of the fun and excitement of reading.

"EVERYTHING IS JUST FINE" One parent, a professor of mathematics at the local university, enjoys telling the story of his young son coming home from Margaret's kindergarten with a huge book and announcing that he could read it. His father knew that the child could not truly read, but Michael insisted that he could. So the father visited Margaret to find out what was going on. When he tells the story, he gives a very good imitation of Margaret telling him, "Don't worry about Michael. Everything is going just fine!" At the end of the kindergarten year, Michael still could not read, and in mock worry the professor relates that he was "ready to go to see someone at the school board about this strange state of affairs" because Margaret continued to tell him, "Everything is just fine." Of course, Michael did begin to read and continued to enjoy big books, but he did so in his own good time confirming that indeed, "Everything is just fine!"

Encouraging free choices during book time and choosing time starts children on their own journeys of exploration. Books without words invite the free flow of imagination. Texts that are too difficult to read but are well illustrated may generate the same kind of imaginative work or simply a careful study of the pictures. Allowing children to reread the same book again and again makes for comfort and the establishment of language patterns that will then guide more adventuresome reading.

Comfort, enjoyment, curiosity, and excitement are the keys to developing voracious readers who choose their own reading materials and revel in the challenges of advanced works as much as the joys of rereading such old favorites as *The Balloon Tree, Where the Wild Things Are,*

Caps for Sale, Sylvester and the Magic Pebble, A Horse Called Farmer, Something Good, I Know an Old Lady Who Swallowed a Fly, and *Brown Bear, Brown Bear.*

Standing back, encouraging choices, and trusting the learners are as valid here as in general classroom management. There is plenty of room for suggesting titles, for modeling your own enthusiasm and enjoyment of reading, for whetting reading appetites with brief readings from interesting books, for stocking the classroom with books on specific topics or themes, and for reading aloud all manner of books, stories, or articles. But as soon as you impose strictures about this book or that being "too hard," "too easy," or "not relevant to our topic" the spirit of independence is dampened, and students begin to look to you for approval in their choices. Conversely, if you demonstrate your excitement about stories or articles you are reading, talk freely to the independent readers in your class about the pleasures of reading whole books, and laugh with the emergent readers about the funny passages in their favorites, you encourage the children to try whatever reading materials are in the classroom. Soon their independence of reading will carry forward to their home reading as well. Barriers of age or levels of maturity simply disappear as children make independent choices and become avid readers.

ENCOURAGING SELF-RELIANCE IN WRITING AND SPELLING

The same spirit of independence holds true in writing and spelling. To encourage self-reliance both for generating ideas and for evolving their own spelling patterns, Margaret leaves the choice of writing topics wide open, and as the children draw and then write, she provides neither dictionaries nor moment-to-moment help with spelling as children evolve their emergent spelling and writing. Years of observing students have convinced us that just as children generate their own primitive rules of grammar – and then refine them – as they begin to talk, so they need to develop their own rules for spelling and writing that fit their level of writing development if they are to become independent spellers and writers. (See more about spelling in chapter 10.)

Naturally, during writing conferences and as follow-up to projects, the teacher will provide help and on-the-spot phonics/spelling lessons to individuals, small groups, or the whole class, but children have no expectation of having their every question answered as they write. The teacher would be run off her feet trying to keep everyone supplied with accurate spellings. More important, such pervasive intervention sets up an attitude of "waiting for the teacher" or "the right answer," and then that independent, creative spirit fails to flourish. But if you encourage the emergence of invented – or temporary - spelling, the children will work at their own levels and pace. They know about "making drafts" and "getting things down" before polishing a piece of writing for publication. Neither strictures of spelling nor considerations of grammar hamper the free flow of their writing as they commit their thoughts to paper. Like adult writers, they think and draft first, and edit and polish their writing later.

Margaret's aim during writing workshop is to help children become fluent and expressive. As she begins to hold writing conferences with individual children, she focuses first and foremost on the content of the message. Then she lets children know how close they have come to standard spelling in tackling the spelling of unfamiliar words. "I can see that you really sounded this out. You have most of the beginning letters, and *today* and *mom* are all standard. If you want to see the standard spelling of the other words, I'll put them in pencil up here and you can change your writing if you feel you want to." During the early months, most children are content with leaving their work

> ## Publishing
> When you have 3 or 4 stories finished, pick the best one and:
> 1. read it to 3 friends and make changes
> 2. read it to Mrs. P. and make changes
> 3. help Mrs. P. fix the spelling
> 4. type or best printing
> 5. illustrate
> 6. read your story to the class

Posting publishing criteria prominently encourages children to use them, rather than the teacher, as their way of keeping on track.

The end.

This is a house.

as it is, but as the year progresses and they are moving toward publishing their work, increasingly they ask for standard spelling during writing conferences. In the meantime, they maintain their independence and that sense that they have inner resources for generating their own writing and spelling.

Choosing topics for writing and then finding things to say need the same kind of open encouragement. If the morning talk has failed to generate some ideas for writing, picking the same topic as your buddy is acceptable, as is writing again and again about rainbows, or wrestling, or liking this and that. Children need to feel that they do have a choice, and writing the same thing many times over can have the same beneficial effect on writing as reading the same book over and over has on reading development. Inner patterns are built, and, on that comfortable foundation, more evolved patterns of writing will emerge. But when, on occasion, the teacher suggests that the class write about Thanksgiving, the latest field trip, or a science project, children still have the option of writing about a more personal topic. If Noel asks, "Do I have to write about ...?" the answer is, "No you don't have to write about that. You can choose a topic of your own. Here are some of the specific things I want you to get from your writing at this time, and if you can find another way to achieve that, you have free choice." Children who are more advanced in their writing respond well to that kind of challenge, and their independent writing adds new interest to you and the rest of the class as you share and discuss everyone's writing.

At writing conference, the teacher uses a Post-it Note (far left) to provide feedback so that the child's work is not marked. Without further feedback, the child incorporates the message about the missing *is* in her next writing work (near left). Children don't always respond that promptly, but the expanded feedback given without nagging or demands for immediate correction fosters independence in the children's moves toward more standard spelling.

In writing, as in general classroom management, establishing procedures or routines early on makes for independence on the part of the students. Without waiting for the teacher to guide their every move, students gather their writing materials, date-stamp their current work, and file a finished piece in their folder in the box provided for that purpose. They move naturally and easily into peer conferences in the designated spots around the classroom, and they place advanced work in the teacher's "conference basket" to indicate that they are ready for her help with more advanced editing.

Children all work at their own levels and are at varying stages in their writing – writing captions for their illustrations, planning something more elaborate, working on their first or second drafts, having conferences, or completing their final edited versions. They do not need ongoing guidance or admonitions to stay on task. They are busily working at their chosen topics and feel confident about the steps they need to take to move right along.

When the class brainstorms a criteria list for drawing, the children refer to it rather than the teacher to check their work. If a student does ask, "Have I got everything?" Karen answers, "I don't know. Have you checked your work against our criteria list?"

Criteria
Continuous Line Drawing

1. animal picture
2. up to 4 colours
3. white painted in – not just left white
4. continuous line
5. paint – water colors
6. name – front
7. date – pencil – back
8. do 2 or more
9. compare – evaluate –
   choose for display
   explain what you prefer

You can get your sketch book out to use to give you ideas.

MODELING HELPS TO EVOLVE INDEPENDENT REPORT WRITING

Developing independence in extracting information from reading materials to prepare reports takes time and practice. Karen Abel works with her students on story maps and webbing exercises to model how to gather information from their reading. The web she produces on the board shows them how to organize the information, and from there how they can draw or write about what they have learned. To move them toward independent research and writing, she begins by working with the whole class, then suggests that they can do the same work in small groups or in pairs, and eventually on their own.

To foster a climate of open inquiry and the spirit of curiosity that marks good research, she takes time to discuss the information provided, enters into special interests expressed by students, encourages them to make connections with their own experience and other reading they have done, and conveys clearly that they are all gathering and weighing information together. There is a strong feeling of partnership and mutuality of learning. Karen's abiding interest in observing what children do and how they arrive at their ways of working conveys her genuine interest in the discussions. In short, Karen has developed "ways to catch their interest, to let them raise and answer their own questions, to let them realize that their ideas are significant – so that they have the interest, the ability, and the self-confidence to go on by themselves" (Duckworth 1987).

In the session of whole-group work on webbing that we observed, Karen informed her students that they were going to produce a web and would use it as a basis for their writing, but she made no demands that the students limit the discussion strictly to the facts given in the story nor did she curtail the time spent on information sharing. There certainly was time for "the having of wonderful ideas." The exchange of ideas had a feeling of openness that conveyed to students that their independent thinking was valuable and deserved whatever time it took to develop it.

MODELING WEBBING

After reading a story about the angler fish from a book called *Fish Do the Strangest Things*, Karen invited her students to think about all the things they could say about the strange fish that might be included in a web and later in their reports. Before beginning to record the webbing on the chalkboard, Karen and her students exchanged information about the angler fish and discussed the strange discrepancy in size between the male and female fish. Since the story told them that the male fish attaches itself firmly to the female, the children found it intriguing to debate how the male would get its food. One student commented, "I don't think his mouth is on her. The story told us, 'She does the fishing for him.'" At that point, another student remembered that she had seen a description of the angler fish in another book, and Karen asked her to see if she could find it.

The new source of information proved to be more factual than the story just read, and the comparison between the two books lead to a discussion of the reliability of sources and the need to consider publication dates of reference books. Karen commended the students for making connections with other sources and their own experience, and as the webbing got underway, she recorded their suggestions on the chalkboard as and when they were offered.

KAREN: I want everybody thinking about what we can add to our web. I might call on people who don't have their hands up. What should we put in the middle?

STUDENT 1: Angler fish

KAREN: Right. What do you want to put down next?

STUDENT 2: The female is one meter (three feet) long.

STUDENT 3: The male is seven and a half centimeters (three inches) long.

STUDENT 4: The female has a fishing rod.

KAREN: Where do you want that? Moving out from the center or connected to something?

STUDENT 5: Moving out from the center.

KAREN: [*Puts the information down as requested*] Does that connect to anything we already have down?

STUDENT 6: Yes, it goes with the "Female is one meter (three feet) long."

KAREN: [*Draws in the connection*]

Karen continued to lead the webbing, acknowledging the children's input and decisions about where to place the information. Since she put no time limit on the discussion and gave free rein to digressions about sources of information, ways of determining what is fact and what is fiction, thoughts about scuba diving and about the function of camouflage, and ways of inferring further information about the angler fish or any other topic they

Modeling information gathering and webbing, the teacher sets the stage for more independent research later on. Her web, done on the chalkboard from the students' input, reflects their decisions about if and when to connect items and includes her temporary spelling camaflouge, which will be checked in the dictionary later on.

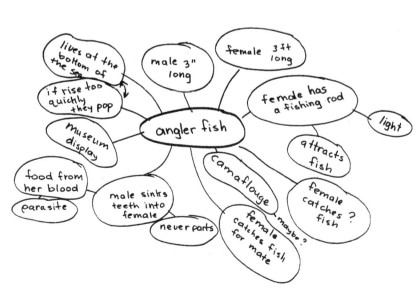

might encounter, the session lasted an hour and a half (much longer than Karen had intended).

Karen's willingness to entertain all student input kept ideas flowing and interest high. Insisting on a fixed time line and curtailing the kind of information that could be discussed would have curbed the rich input and high interest on the part of the students. As it was, they not only learned about the angler fish but acquired a great deal of practice in gathering and recording research information and weighing evidence.

In the same spirit of open time lines, Karen left the web on the board and students used it during the next few days as a guide for writing their reports. The criteria Karen laid down for the report included writing at least one sentence about each of the areas circled in color and accurate spelling in the finished copy of any word listed on the board. With that, she started the flow of independent writing and answered any questions: "Is that enough writing?" "I don't know. Have you checked to see if you have included something from each of the areas we circled?"

As a step toward greater independence, the children next used small books on various animals to create

The open discussion about research on the angler fish and students' comments about finding other books to separate fact from fiction inspired Mark to gather all the reference books he could find that provided additional information.

Mura Nov. 4, 1993

Ɛ Anglerfish3

The female Anglerfish has a fishing rod that has a light at the end. It attracts fish very well because the Anglerfish can camouflage. The male Anglerfish is only 3 inches long and the female is 3 feet long. The female is much longer.

There is a museum display of the Anglerfish. They live at the bottom of the sea. If they rise too quick they will pop becasse the water presher holds there body together. The male sinks his teeth into the female after that they never part. The male is like a parasite becasse he feeds from her blood.

Just as all students participate in gathering information, so all of them write at their own levels.

Alethela   Anglerfish   Nov‡

The male Siks his teeth into the female.
he pets his food from her blood. The Female
is 3 ft long The male is 3 inches. The female
has a fishing rod with a light that attracks
the fish. She Can Camaufloge She Looks
like a rock. the Anglerfish live at the
bottom of the Sea if they rise to quickl
they PoP.

The
Anglerfish   Nov.4,1993
by
Jean-Paul

The Female Anglerfish is a verey wierd fish.
It has a fishing rod with a light on it.
It camaflouges bie a rock than a Littel
fish comes along and it gets attracted
to it. And it gets eatin up by the big Fish.
There is another wierd thing about the
Angler Fish. The Female is three Feet Long
and the male is olny three inches Long.
The male is Like a parasite. Wean it Finds
a wife it sinks it's teeth into the Female
and they Never part. The Angler Fish Lives
at the bottom of the sea and the water
pressure holds it together so if they rise
to quickly they pop.

information webs of their own. Working in pairs they decided on
what to put where and then reported on their findings. From there,
the more mature students were going to move to individual work and
independent research.

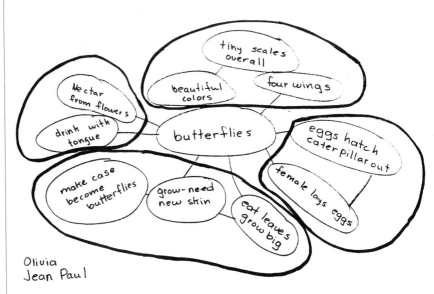

Olivia
Jean Paul

Collaborative work
produces a good research
job. The next web will be
an individual effort.

Setting a climate of independence leads to creative thinking and effective problem solving

The having of wonderful ideas needs a climate that values the unexpected and encourages children to explore, to take risks, and to celebrate their discoveries. The child-generated questioning, the wondering, and the physical explorations that lead to deep absorption flourish in a climate of open inquiry. Creative thinking and effective problem solving emerge quite naturally when you foster that climate of independence that tells children in no uncertain terms that they are trusted to work things out for themselves. They know that false starts and the occasional spill or messy hands are all part of solving problems. Here modeling of trial-and-error learning becomes a powerful tool, and children will take their cues from you as you involve yourself in science experiments, muse about the deeper meaning of words or metaphors, or show yourself to be willing to test your manipulative skills at some intricate game or task. If, as Margaret did, you find it is hard at first to give up your teacher-knows-all stance, you will soon discover the excitement of watching children follow your example of thinking out loud: "I wonder how we could get this to work." "If we go to a farm, do you suppose we will find...?" "Maybe we could try another way." "I wonder what would happen if...." "Maybe it would work if...."

Those kinds of comments leave the door wide open for speculating, for expecting more than one answer, and for taking two or three runs at the solutions to problems. They also invite students to follow your example and to generate their own questions or ways of approaching a task. When, as part of their work on a Mexican fiesta, Margaret's class struggled to produce God's eyes, students, teacher, visitors to the classroom, and even the custodian joined in the challenge of weaving the strands of wool around the crossed pieces of wood to produce the right effect. Comments like "Well, that didn't work; maybe we could try this way" or "Here's a different way of starting!" or "Wow, I got it! I got it!" show the dynamic of genuine problem solving that does far more for children and teacher than a carefully planned and executed demonstration. After all, producing

MARK SOLVES HIS PROBLEM WITH A LITTLE HELP ✳ When Mark had created a go-cart during invention time and insisted that the wheels should actually go around, everyone in the classroom offered ideas and concrete suggestions. When he found that despite all the advice available in the classroom, no one there could help him solve his problem, Margaret suggested he visit the principal to see if he had some more productive ideas. Half an hour later, Mark, accompanied by the principal, returned to the classroom showing off the go-cart that now had wheels that turned. The glow of satisfaction they both shared suggested that their cooperative problem solving had been very satisfying.

perfectly crafted God's eyes isn't nearly as important as learning the process of solving challenging problems through hands-on work, more than one trial, not giving up, trying a new approach, talking things over, comparing notes, looking at other people's work, being patient and persistent in the face of several failures. Neither lectures nor carefully planned step-by-step instructions teach that kind of problem solving. But the open, collaborative climate you create by trusting the learners teaches it effortlessly.

That effortless learning about the processes of problem solving and tackling jobs independently is aided immeasurably by the teacher showing herself to be a creative problem solver. Modeling a calm, re-laxed approach in the face of initial failure and starting all over again after some discussion of what might and might not work show children that the teacher also persists and works problems out gradually. That kind of modeling includes showing that problem solving does not have to be a solitary pursuit, that laughter and fun help you over tough ground, and that independence does not preclude seeking advice and expert help.

INDEPENDENCE LEAVES ROOM FOR *ALL* LEVELS OF WORK

Aside from freeing the teacher to give truly individualized attention to the children in her class, creating a spirit of independence makes ample room for students to develop their own unique talents. Since neither deadlines nor requests to "do it my way" hamper students' creativity, they feel free to work in their own best ways and to build on their own experience. That kind of productive spirit shows itself not only in the work the children do but in the overall classroom atmosphere. Children who are busily engaged on work that is meaningful to them are too busy to act out. When new students to Margaret's classroom create a disturbance, the children will frequently comment, "Settle down and stop that. We're busy!"

THE REWARDS OF INDEPENDENCE ACCRUE TO TEACHER AND STUDENTS ALIKE

Visitors to your classroom who comment on the purposeful work and self-assured independence of the children may get the impression that you were just lucky to get a whole group of responsible, industrious students. But there can be no question that it is your consistent stance of sharing responsibility for learning and classroom management that has created – and is maintaining – the productive independent work of your students. That climate of effortless management of the diverse needs of twenty-five or thirty students is the direct result of your attitude of trusting the children to do work on their own. The rewards for you and the students certainly merit the occasional frustrations or worries when things do not run as smoothly or efficiently as they would if you managed everything by yourself or with the aid of adult helpers. The relaxed, warm atmosphere created when children feel free to work in productive ways makes your day and theirs enjoyable and exciting. Children who can use their talents in their own ways become remarkably creative in both academic and artistic work, and you will no doubt find that that increase in creativity extends to your own work as well.

The most wonderful part for you is that once you have overcome your initial doubts or worries about sharing more and more responsibility with the children, the work becomes as effortless for you as it is for the children. When you adopt a calm, matter-of-fact way of meeting the challenges of the children's creative ways of learning and dealing with the minor and not-so-minor crises in the classroom – and always keep your sense of humor – the climate of safety that lets independence blossom just naturally evolves. If you share the minor problems of organizing field trips, getting drivers, keeping track of supplies and equipment, then the children will share their minor and major problems with you. A feeling of mutuality and genuine caring about the needs and feelings of others is the natural outcome of such sharing.

So the independence you create with your attitude and your willingness to empower the children creates a true learning community in your classroom. And when there is safety, the joy and excitement of learning can flourish. Both you and the children feel free to reveal and nourish your creativity and spontaneity. Together you create a climate of delight that makes plenty of room for the having of wonderful ideas.

4.

Who's in Charge Here Anyway?

We are far too concerned with discipline, with how to "make" students follow rules, and not enough concerned with providing satisfying education that would make our overconcern with discipline unnecessary (Glasser 1986).

One of the wonderful parts of acknowledging that the learners in your class are all functioning at their own unique levels is that this places you, the teacher, firmly in charge of what is happening in class. When it is official, thus accepted, that the children in the class are *not* all performing the same tasks in the same way, then there is no question of having your actions circumscribed by commercially designed programs complete with detailed guidebooks or somewhat rigidly framed scope and sequence charts. Because you know the children in your class and are tuned in to their specific needs, you are the best authority for designing and implementing individualized work to fit the unique experience and talents of each child. You are in charge of the day-to-day classroom work, and you are also in charge of shaping the social climate.

Being firmly in charge leads to an interesting paradox that is yet another wonderful aspect of officially acknowledging the diversity of learners and learning in your class. As neither you nor the children are any longer constrained by externally imposed guidelines that cannot possibly address the moment-to-moment needs of your students, you will discover that the need to control the children's activities diminishes day by day. Though you are definitely in charge, you will find that both learning and overall classroom conduct evolve ever more effectively and with less and less need for overt control. As students feel free to learn and work in their own best ways, they stay happily on task, and classroom management becomes a shared responsibility that focuses on "providing satisfying education more than on keeping discipline."

During author's circle when children read their published writing to the class, the author takes charge of the discussion.

Sharing power—enhancing power

Making others powerful makes the teacher feel powerful. And the power of both is a fact (Macrorie 1970).

As teachers we can think of few greater joys than the excitement of seeing our students unfold their powers to learn and to function effectively both in school and out. Participating in the unfolding of that kind of power is the essence of sharing power in the classroom. Later in this chapter, we describe more concretely how to transform energy in the classroom by gradually relinquishing external controls and exchanging them for internal discipline and the unfolding of students' potential. Here we want to take a look at just how it is possible to empower students while the teacher remains firmly in charge of overall classroom management.

WHAT IS POWER ANYWAY?

In her article "Defusing 'Empowering': The What and the Why" (1987), Leslie Ashcroft takes an in-depth look at the many facets of power and what it means to empower students. She points out that the most fundamental dictionary definitions of power are "to be able" and "to have the capability." Based on those definitions, *empowering* means freeing students to build on their strengths to enable them to learn, to use their abilities fully, and to participate responsibly in the day-to-day classroom management.

That view of empowering certainly does defuse the issue of relinquishing more and more power to students. It acknowledges that students are eager to take control of their own work and that they have inherent strengths which, if fostered, infuse their own work, and that of the teacher, with new energy. Instead of worrying that relaxing external control might lead to discipline problems, the teacher focuses her attention on enabling students to work freely and creatively. The energy in class becomes productive rather than disruptive.

Ashcroft draws parallels between *power* and *energy* by looking at the scientific world's vocabulary of power and energy and the fact that, in terms of physics, "Energy cannot be created or destroyed, but can be transformed." Applying that principle to working with students, we actually don't "give" them power or energy; we merely bring out what is already there. We foster the power to learn, to be physically active, to be curious and inquisitive, and we acknowledge the storehouse of energy that each and every child brings to school.

By acknowledging the reality of that energy, we defuse the latent charge that can build up if students feel that school inhibits their energy flow. And by recognizing that this energy can be released in either a positive or a negative form, we can find ways of transforming potentially destructive or counterproductive behavior into cooperation and mutual support, which not only affects individual students but transforms the entire classroom climate. To use Sylvia Ashton-Warner's metaphor, we are narrowing the destructive vent of the children's inner volcano of power and widening the creative vent instead.

MARGARET BRINGS OUT LES'S CREATIVE POWERS　✷　*Les was enrolled at South Park School when he was five. He had spent his kindergarten year in a very structured classroom in which isolated skills were taught in a rather rigid manner. At home, Les was raised primarily by his grandmother because his father was in jail and his mother was rather neurotic.*　✷　*On Les's first day of school he tried to kick my shins and swore at me, using very colorful language. The other children watched round-eyed and gathered around me protectively while I held Les off with my hand on his forehead to keep him from reaching my shins with his feet. He continued in this vein for days, and as I worked at staying calm and not showing my irritation, I reassured the other children, telling them, "Les is feeling uncomfortable now but will soon be all right."*　✷　*Our struggle went on throughout September — the same kind of behavior every morning, total frustration throughout the day. Les would irritate other children and laugh sneeringly at everything they did. I managed to keep my cool throughout. I kept telling him that he*

Identifying his teacher by tufts of hair, Les places her in jail and in front of a tank to give vent to his hostile feelings.

Margaret has certainly felt her classroom climate change as she has worked to transform negative energy into positive, creative work. And it is this aspect of empowering students that is so vital to the concept of control or being in charge. As long as we look at control and classroom management as a matter of "control over" the students and their behaviors and learning, we are in a constant tug of war with the energy inherent in every single student. Multiplied by twenty or more, that is a strong power, and controlling it can consume most of the teacher's time and energy. Once we adopt the philosophy that empowering means enabling and that learners can be trusted to use and develop their energies, then we find that classrooms become "communities of learners helping each other to transform latent capabilities to active powers for the enhancement of all" (Ashcroft 1987).

would feel better soon and that I would wait until that happened. At that early point he clearly could not handle the freedom the other children in my class enjoyed. He seemed to do everything he could to get attention, but I think my calmness got through to him and he began to relax a little. ＊ During writing workshop he would draw me in hostile situations - in jail, at the end of a cannon, being run over by a tank. By the end of September he began to write captions. If he had j and l for jail or t and k for tank, I would say, "That's wonderful, Les! Here you have the beginning and ending letters of the words." Perhaps it was time spent in class, perhaps the overall climate of encouragement, but gradually, day by day he began to be interested in our work, particularly in writing. ＊ As he became more and more interested in writing, he produced a lot of work. His writing continued to be concerned with hostile actions, but at least he was writing pages and pages. Bit by bit his behavior changed, and his

true personality began to emerge. Underneath all that hostility was a sensitive, neat little kid with sparkling eyes. His kicks turned to hugs, and by Christmas he would come in and hug me each morning. Still, when his mother came in to pick him up he would swear at her and run away. During the five hours I had him in school every day, he was a totally different kid. He had opened his creative channel and with that the destructive one closed down.

DISCIPLINE? KEEP IT POSITIVE

All too often discipline is seen as imposing order – often by punitive measures. Yet the first definition of "discipline" in Webster's Dictionary is "a state of order maintained by training and control." For Margaret, training children to help her maintain order has meant establishing a positive climate in her classroom, using ways of affirming her students' successes in both learning and social interaction, dwelling on the children's steps forward and overlooking their lapses into less than desirable behavior – unless those lapses interfere with the children's own learning or that of others in class.

Reflecting on the source of her own success and that of other teachers who maintain order in classrooms that are alive to learning

By November Les has shifted to writing. Though he is still writing about fighter planes, he no longer makes the teacher his target. The creative vent of his inner volcano is definitely narrowing the destructive one.

and fun, full of activity and laughter, Margaret feels that it springs from an inner attitude that is positive and at the same time very definite about the boundaries needed for order. Consideration of the needs and well-being of others is foremost in setting those boundaries. And so, in training children to become considerate, teachers model behaviors of caring, courtesy, and goodwill.

This modeling takes the form of listening attentively, showing with your eyes, your body language, and your smile that you are interested in the children and what they have to say. Thinking aloud about steps forward has a way of inviting many more such steps: "I really like the way you came in so quietly." "You are sitting right down to get to work." "You keep your eyes right on the book as I am reading." Children thrive on acknowledgments of steps forward and recognize a look, a nod, or a pat on the shoulder that tells them, "I see what a good effort [progress] you are making." Learning and order flourish in that climate.

Calling students to order when there are lapses works best when done in positive ways. As she sees children fidget or become inattentive, Margaret will say: "Isn't that right, Bobby?" "Tell me what you think of that, Judy." "What do you know about ... Mandy?" If the need arises to separate two children to make them attend, she will give a reason: "I need you to move over here, Jerry. I can't concentrate when you and Jimmy talk to each other." When she does not have the full attention of all the students, Karen Abel may comment, "I want you to think hard about what else we can put on the board, because I may call on some of you who don't have your hands up."

An important part of modeling caring, considerate behavior is to define clearly what your boundaries are, those of your students, and the specific requirements of your principal or supervisor. To establish those inner guidelines, you may need to ponder answers to questions like "How much noise is acceptable? When do I want children to sit still, and when can they move about? What are my most important goals for children's development? How important is it to me to have things done my way?" In time, you will want to discuss the need for rules with your students and have them help you brainstorm rules that will ensure that consideration for the needs of others is one of the important guidelines. But to help them see the benefits of such rules, you need to be very clear about your own inner boundaries and how they affect you, your students, and their learning.

Teachers who have observed Margaret have expressed their admiration for her ability to keep students' attention, to control the noise level in her class, or to draw children together with a quietly voiced, "I need you all really close by so you can see the great pictures in this book." At times these teachers commented that unfortunately Margaret's "tricks of the trade" would not work for them and their students. As long as they perceived her external behavior only, without recognizing that it stems from a deep caring and well-defined inner boundaries, they were right. "Tricks" or methods don't lead to discipline or order. A positive attitude that shines through in the teacher's modeling of focused, caring ways of interacting does.

The why and how of sharing power

Acknowledging that the children in your class are working not only on different levels and at different paces but also with many different learning styles frees you of the most energy-draining, frustrating responsibiliy – the need to see to it that all the work is done in *one* prescribed way and in *one* time frame. Teacher Anne Peterson speaks of the frustration and irritation she experienced when she felt constrained to teach math and specific reading skills in prescribed ways. The impossibility of bringing along all the children in her class at one pace and with one task had her tearing her hair out in frustration.

If you look back at times when you felt you had to make sure that children were following your instructions exactly, you may recall the frustration and irritation connected with keeping all those lively individuals in your class in close check. There you were trying to satisfy the demands of supervisors, parents, and the curriculum, and at the same time keep the work rolling. That responsibility may have invested you with the power to decide what should be done at any given moment, but at the same time it demanded that you find the method and energy to control twenty-five or more students and get them to work your way.

SHARING POWER TRANSFORMS ENERGY

South Park School grade–two–three teacher Karen Abel talks of the transformation of energy in her teaching once she opened herself to the fact that there are many ways of learning and solving problems. Mathematics was a particularly telling example for her as she worked with an experienced math teacher, Trevor Calkins, who invited Karen's students to try and find how many ways they could solve different problems. Instead of presenting the way, he demonstrated more than one and then worked with the children to see if they could discover even more. The many options possible in working with math came as a revelation to Karen, who now follows Trevor's example by asking children, "How did you work that out?" and then, "Did somebody have a different way of doing that?" Children continue to delight and amaze her by the variety of approaches they can think of to solve problems, ways that had never entered her mind because she learned according to the tradition of "doing it the way the teacher showed us."

The creative vent of the inner volcano certainly gets widened when teachers acknowledge children's ingenuity and ability to solve problems in unique ways. The pervasive attitude that affirms "you have many options and I, the teacher, value and celebrate how you work and think" sets a climate of empowerment that is highly productive. As children feel free to experiment and give their imaginations free rein, their awareness of the many ways of learning broadens day by day. For the teacher there is the joy of observing that creativity and at times being awed by the original approaches children bring to their learning.

CREATIVITY SHOWS ITSELF IN MANY WAYS

From time to time both Margaret and Karen challenge the children's reading and spelling ingenuity by placing several sets of blank dashes on the chalkboard " _ _ _   _ _ _   _ _ _ _   _ _ _ _ ?" and inviting them to read the message by filling in the blanks. As they puzzle over the possible words, the children will use the number of letters in each, the fact that the sentence is a question, and any other clues that might help, such as the fact that they have just discussed their ability to read well by now. The latter comment is sure to spark the hypothesis-testing and trial-and-error placement of words to discover the answer: "Can you read this?" Excitement and ingenuity sparkle as the children vie to find just the right words to fit that string of dashes.

When faced with math questions, they work in a variety of ways. Using multiple approaches was not permissible during Margaret's days of structuring math around set tasks. Now, after reading them *Over in the Meadow* – a counting book with a verse and one animal on the first page, two on the second, and so on to page ten – Margaret invites the children to take an inventory of all the animals in the book and to find out how many there are. As she puts it:

> It was totally awesome to see how many different ways they had of figuring out the answer. One child counted them all on her fingers, while another child made tally marks for each animal and then counted them. A third child wrote down the names of the animals to count them up, and still another made drawings of each of the animals. One did mental addition but continued to refer back to the book to keep track of where he was. As I watched, I saw so many different learning styles! And not one child said, "I don't know how to do that."

Linda Picciotto (1993), Margaret's teaching partner at South Park School, describes a similar experience arising from joining the two kindergarten–grade-one-two classes in a Hanukkah celebration (see also chapter 14):

> To complete the menorah ceremony for the eight days of Hanukkah required sophisticated mathematical thinking: two candles the first night, three the next, and so forth for eight days. I distributed toothpick "candles" they could use to help them do their calculations independently or with friends. The students who understood quickly were soon surrounded by classmates who were confused and wanted some help. After a certain amount of time we all met on the carpet to discuss the results.... While describing their thought processes, some of the students realized that they had forgotten to take one thing or another into consideration, so their numbers weren't right. I was fascinated by the number of approaches they'd used.

As long as power means having "control over" everything that happens in class, that kind of creative energy is blocked. Once you relax, accept that there are always more ways than one, and trust the children to find them, their creativity – and yours - will blossom. Margaret has certainly found that her own creativity has been stimulated immensely since she has shifted to observing the children's ways of learning and problem solving, and Karen's creative ways of teaching demonstrate that hers has too.

COLLABORATION GENERATES POWER

Inviting collaboration and joint planning leads to a complete shift in energy. Instead of feeling drained and frustrated from the power struggle inherent in imposing one-way rule, you receive a boost in energy. As you free the children to use their energy reservoirs to work in their own ways, they become your partners in seeing that the day progresses smoothly and productively. As Ephraim finds that his artwork is appreciated as a lead-in to writing, he abandons his tussling; as Louisa learns that she can take extra time to finish a job, she relaxes and continues in her own meticulous way; as Meredith observes how her best pal becomes engrossed in reading, she decides to give books more attention than games. No amount of talking or cajoling on your part could produce the same cooperative stance, but the knowledge

CHARTING MARIA'S TEMPER TANTRUMS ✴ Maria was a hostile, disturbed little girl. She was bright, and could function quite well in class until she felt pressured or pushed. Then her temper would erupt. She would shout and scream, slam things around, run out of the room, or invent new ways to show her displeasure in the most disruptive ways she could devise. Margaret suspected that child abuse of some sort may have been part of Maria's problem, but could not find anything definite. As she worried about the child, Margaret wanted to see if she could detect some pattern in the sparks for those terrible outbursts. ✴ To deal with the tantrums, Margaret stayed very quiet, telling Maria that she understood she was upset and giving her time to cool down by herself. Once Maria calmed down and turned sweet and compliant, Margaret would take out a clipboard on which she was keeping a record of the onset and manifestations of the tantrums. She recorded her dialogues with Maria, the kind of behavior she engaged in, the length of time it took her to calm down, and anything else she noticed. Once Maria noticed Margaret's record keeping, she looked over Margaret's shoulder to see what she was writing. Margaret told her what she was writing down and why she was doing it, and Maria began to make her input, reminding Margaret of what she had said, helping her spell, and describing how she had reacted to the tantrum. The charting process became interesting to Maria, and though Margaret never discovered a pattern, Maria's tantrums dwindled. Margaret's dispassionate analysis and quiet reaction helped Maria to narrow the destructive vent of her mind and to open the creative one more as she engaged in helping Margaret describe and analyze the tantrums.

that you are trusting them to proceed with work in their own ways and in their own time frames smoothes the energy flow for everyone. That trust and the willingness to make the children partners in learning transforms the classroom climate. As Jack Hassard (1977) puts it, "A high energy classroom is one which thrives on a cooperative use of power, promotes security, and enhances a student's self-concept."

Modeling calm deliberation when devising a variety of plans, finding many ways of approaching problems, generating multiple solutions, and having choices set the tone in Karen Abel's grade-two-three class. From the beginning of the year, Karen has open discussions with her children in which she coaches them in the art of reflecting on the possibilities inherent in the work before them:

"We have only one reference book per table of four students. What would be good ways of giving everyone at each table a fair opportunity to use the book?"

Collaboration enhances creative powers.

"Each morning there is a mad scramble for the beanbag chair in our discussion corner. How can we make sure everyone gets a turn without fighting about it?"

"We are going to create habitat murals for our dinosaurs. How will you go about planning your cooperative work?"

The children in her class are only six to eight years old but display remarkable acumen in generating solutions. Looking at the beanbag chair scramble, they started with a first-come-first-served situation that was clearly unfair. They debated different ways of deciding who would get a turn – drawing lots, assigning numbers, rolling dice, going down the class list, having the teacher pick whose turn it is. The final vote decided the issue in favor of using the class list and assigning the privilege on a rotating basis to each student in turn. Students also decided that whoever was in possession of the beloved chair on a given day should have the privilege of inviting one or two friends to share it.

That kind of joint problem solving invests the decision with a feeling of rightness; students abide by it willingly and actually become the ones who monitor adherence to rules they have helped set. More important, the time spent deliberating the matter has taught children the value of open discussion, the power of group problem solving, and the fact that there are always several solutions. That learning transfers to all their other work, and students in Karen's class are well aware of the benefits of formulating plans, following them, standing back to see how well they work, and then making adjustments to whatever can be improved.

Instead of telling the students how to proceed in their groups for creating dinosaur murals, Karen left it up to the children to reach decisions and then stood back to observe how they went about the job. Three groups formed; each decided on a different theme for its mural and then set out to reach a consensus on implementing the decision.

The mountain/lake group sat around in a circle, and each child in turn stated what she or he wanted. One student wrote down the ideas on a big sheet of paper, and the group made a mini-map to show the layout – mountains here, lake over there, and the river flowing this

Murals of dinosaur habitats attest to the students' ability to reach consensus and take charge of their projects.

way. The recorder used the initials of the students to write down who would do what and what part of the mural they would work on. They were very organized, reached consensus quickly, and produced their mural in record time.

The desert group worked quite differently. As the students sat in a circle, one child became the spokesperson and had everyone vote on each suggestion. "Who wants a red sky?" "Who wants... ?" But nothing was recorded. So the next day the group members could not remember what they had decided and just proceeded to do the painting as best they could. Once they realized that the mural was not what they really wanted, they covered over everything they had done and started again.

The rain-forest group decided to have everyone in the group do small sketches of different kinds of plants that could be incorporated in the mural. Then the students met as a group to choose the illustrations they wanted. But since they had not made an overall plan, they had to stop several times in the process of painting to find ways of resolving disputes over who was going to paint where. As a result, they learned a great deal about conflict resolution. Whenever two students wanted to work in the same area of the mural – as happened repeatedly – they and their teacher would sit down to discuss ways of

arriving at a decision. They looked at many different ways to resolve their differences. Karen led the way in modeling some of the problem solving and decision making, but she definitely stood back to empower the children to generate and then apply their own solutions.

At the end of the project, when the groups reported on the ways they had proceeded, they discussed the advantages and disadvantages of each, and everyone agreed that there is a strong need to write things down to make sure that decisions that are made are actually carried out. That kind of careful debriefing and the dispassionate examination of what worked well, what created problems, and what improvements could be made ensured that all the children learned from the different approaches they had taken. It also once again confirmed that there are always several ways of reaching a goal.

Figure 3

Derived from Dr. William Glasser's article on the work of Dr. W. Edwards Deming, which dramatically changed and improved the Japanese economy (*Phi Delta Kappan*, 1990).

USING A MANAGEMENT MODEL TO COMPARE TEACHING STYLES

The Boss Teacher	**The Lead Teacher**
Decides what will be taught and how it will be learned.	Sets the framework for learning but leaves room for options.
Keeps strict control of all aspects of the classroom.	Encourages students to make choices about their learning.
Decides on the rules and how to enforce them.	Discusses reasons for rules and asks for students' input to formulate and enforce them.
Keeps a strong focus on the curriculum to shape lessons. Is more concerned with the what of learning than the how.	Observes learners and their needs and interests to foster learning that fulfills students' needs as well as curriculum requirements.
Tends to use the lecture format to convey information.	Models the skills to be learned and uses experiential, hands–on work.
Relies heavily on Cazden's (1988) **IRE** model – teacher **I**nitiation, student **R**esponse, teacher **E**valuation.	Engages students in discussions about the relevance and quality of work undertaken in class. Makes information sharing reciprocal.
Tries to have all students work on the same job at the same pace.	Offers choices that fit the work to students' interests, abilities, maturity, and experience.
Generally has students work by themselves.	Often uses teamwork and cooperative learning.
Generally is the chief information giver and initiator of jobs, themes, or projects.	Encourages students to share information and to initiate projects.
Relies on outside motivation – grades, praise – to urge students to work hard.	Relies on students' inner motivation to excel. Trusts them to work to the best of their abilities.
Sees education as serious business that needs to be shaped by a knowledgable leader – the teacher.	Sees learning as exciting, fun, and arising from the students' own needs and curiosity, which has to be stimulated by interesting work.
Generally feels that students must be closely supervised to ensure that they will do the work.	Trusts students to work in their own ways and at their own pace.
Relies largely on tests, worksheets, and exams to evaluate students' progress.	Uses informal observation and ongoing anecdotal records to evaluate students' progress and to enrich information derived from exams.
Generally sees record keeping and evaluation as being the teacher's job.	Has students keep many of the records and uses students' self-evaluations to augment teacher observation.
Holds the power in the classroom.	Empowers students to work freely on academic tasks while observing social rules that have been established cooperatively.
Focuses on the end product of learning.	Focuses on the process of learning.
Manages the curriculum.	Manages people.

BECOMING A LEAD TEACHER

Empowering students means changing your role from that of being "the boss" who decides and controls what goes on in class to that of being "a leader" who points the way but is very open to delegating responsibility and fostering teamwork. A look at figure 3 may tell you that you already function far more like a "lead teacher" than a "boss teacher," but it also makes explicit what kinds of shifts are needed to free children's energies to become your partners in learning.

ESTABLISHING ROUTINES DIMINISHES THE NEED FOR CONTROLS

Sharing power with students is closely tied to fostering independence and, like it, needs to evolve gradually. At the beginning of the year you hold all the power and take time to establish routines and guidelines: coming in on time, greeting each other at the door, hanging up coats and putting down lunch boxes, moving quietly to the area for group talk and story time, taking turns when talking, choosing centers independently and cleaning up before moving on, not disturbing others who are trying to concentrate, being considerate and caring when interacting with others, coming in after recess and settling right down to silent reading. Children need and appreciate guidelines and frameworks that tell them what is acceptable and what is not. But within those guidelines they need to feel free to move and explore. By setting guidelines and routines you make it possible for the children to test and expand their powers gradually. Among these are the power/freedom for children to

✳ *make choices:* deciding what books to read, what center activities to select, what topics to study, where to sit, what games to play, what group to join, how much to write;

✳ *take time/make time:* staying with a job or shifting to the next one, working fast or working slowly, spreading a job over several days, sitting and reflecting;

✳ *solve problems in their own way:* working physically to create new solutions, debating, negotiating, trying new ways, turning problems upside down and inside out;

* *use their own learning styles:* approaching writing as an oral job, relying on mime and physical manipulation to work out problems, using hands–on work to discover patterns, using visual clues to remember spelling, testing "the feel" of letters to work with "sounding out";

* *move about:* being free to lie on the floor, under the table, or behind the coat rack while reading; moving freely from center to center; moving into the hall to work on a special project; using drama and physical movement to retell stories;

* *interact with other individuals and groups:* discussing, sharing information, forming teams;

* *engage in trial-and-error learning:* experimenting, testing ideas and methods, feeling safe to learn from mistakes, trying several approaches;

* *set and enforce rules:* participating in establishing and then enforcing rules to get along in class, making up rules for games, deciding on new ways to interact, discussing the rationale for rules, setting penalties for infractions;

* *choose partners:* deciding with whom to work, play, or sit; changing partners to fit the need, mood, or occasion; opting to be or not be part of a group;

* *participate or opt out:* choosing to watch instead of act, listen instead of talk, volunteer or hang back; choosing the extent of participation.

The list could easily be extended, and you no doubt have many areas in which your students are exercising their power and freedom. If you are working in a multi-age classroom, your older students will lead the way in demonstrating to the newcomers how and to what extent they can work independently at any given time. If you are in a traditional classroom, you will have to model, demonstrate, and explain how to use the freedom within the guidelines. Here are some of the ways to help students evolve their powers:

* Offer choices.

* Ask for opinions and value them.

* Look for suggestions and accept them.

* Model decision making and thinking aloud.

* Demonstrate collaboration – among teachers, staff, and parents.

✳ Make mistakes and work on solutions.

✳ Delegate responsibility at every opportunity, but be selective in delegating: consider children's ages and levels of maturity; encourage quiet children to do special jobs.

✳ Comment positively when students take initiative.

✳ Show that you value different approaches.

✳ Ask for as many answers or possibilities as possible.

✳ Use the same courtesy and tact as you would with adults.

✳ Turn more and more jobs over to the students.

✳ Refuse to settle disputes for the children.

✳ Stand back to give students time to solve problems.

✳ Enjoy the individuality of students' work and responses.

✳ Have fun entering into the children's games.

✳ Display enthusiasm for students' work and discoveries.

✳ Enter fully into the excitement of the moment.

✳ Talk about the choices you make in your own life.

✳ Relax and overlook as many lapses as possible.

✳ Build on the special talents of children to help them experience successes.

✳ Foster lots of physical activity and manipulative work.

✳ Model caring, considerate ways of interacting.

✳ Demonstrate how to interact with visitors or new students.

✳ Participate fully in reading workshop.

✳ Talk about your thoughts and feelings when reading.

✳ Show yourself to be a learner.

✳ Nourish, develop, and display your sense of humor.

This list can be extended further, and the longer it becomes, the more positive and potent will be the energy level in your classroom. As you show students how to initiate work on their own and how to take over more and more responsibility for their choices, and as you provide interesting lead-ins to jump-start new areas of work and choice, both you and your students will grow in creativity and spontaneity.

With a minimum of encouragement and modeling, students will set up mini-centers. Stewart, age 7, is showing his interest in King Tut's Tomb after his visit to the exhibit. Brodie, age 5, is setting up a center on snakes, because he became intrigued by a collection of reptiles a classroom visitor brought into school.

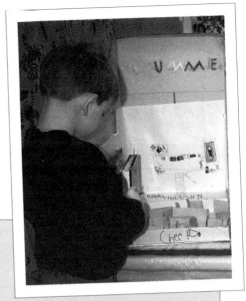

MAKING SPACE FOR MINI-CENTERS ✳ A word of encouragement – "Hey, that sounds like a really interesting idea to explore! Why don't you find some more books and see what you have at home" – is all children need to follow their special interests. Mini-centers sprang up when Brodie became fascinated with snakes after a visit from a reptile expert and when Stewart became enthralled with Egyptian mummies following his visit to the King Tut exhibit. Other students took their cue from these centers and set up their own on ballet, on black holes, and several on animals. Margaret followed suit and set one up on eagles after she had observed the nesting activities of bald eagles near a friend's home.

The more you turn over to the students, the greater will be your return in joy, excitement, productivity, and warm feelings. Because you are in charge and in the know, you are expanding the possibilities for learning not only academically but socially and physically. You know how much the children can handle and how much you are willing to relinquish at any given moment. Within your guidelines the children will learn how to develop the inner discipline and self-esteem that will channel their energies into productive paths.

Think of your classroom as a workshop for learning where you, the master learner, demonstrate ways of working and interacting with learning materials for the workers in your shop. The more experienced workers can work right alongside you and show initiative and understanding of the work, but the younger apprentices will need more time to become familiar with ways of working. They will observe both you and their peers and take their cues from the purposeful interactions. Like apprentices in a craft workshop, they will not expect to do the more difficult and demanding jobs until they have had time to become familiar with the work and have built some skills. But because they see the work as meaningful and exciting, they will strive to emulate what you and their older peers are doing. Like you, they know that they are building their strengths gradually and they are neither blocked in those efforts nor overextended. Their power evolves naturally and unhampered as you stand back to make room for their growth.

The gains you make from sharing power

Looking at sharing power in terms of freeing the children to work more productively changes the question "If I relinquish my power, what have I left?" to the realization that "If I stop trying to hold down the lid on all that energy, I am freed up to work at a far more productive level than ever before!" For, as you gradually step back farther and farther to give the children room to function freely, your time and energy are freed so that you can concentrate on fostering learning, on finding new ways to stimulate interest, and on

CHILDREN LOOK AFTER THEMSELVES
Children develop leadership qualities and personal responsibility as their teacher stands back to give them room. When Margaret had to leave her room briefly to answer a long-distance telephone call, she came back into the classroom to find that Orion had gathered the children around him on the carpet and was showing them a large illustrated book on fishing and the environment. He had not yet learned to read, but he displayed his experience and knowledge of the outdoors and had the children enthralled with his descriptions.

setting priorities for individuals and groups that will enhance their development still further. Instead of worrying about the minutiae of getting this or that job done exactly right, you are observing learners and are taking your cues from them to create an open climate for learning. You are still in charge, but you are functioning at a higher level of control because you and the children are working as a team.

5.

Child Watching Becomes a Guide to Teaching/ Learning

Many years ago as a young sole-charge teacher I faced a school of New Zealand Maori children in Wairau Pa, Marlborough— at that time a depressed rural community. They taught me some hard lessons which at first I undervalued. They taught me that literacy could be developed out of song and chant; that the preverbal expression of art could flower into language; and that fascination in stories led more directly to reading and writing than my competently prepared lessons in word recognition. They were kind and forgiving—as all *teachers* should be—setting me on a career of child-watching and child-admiration (Holdaway 1979).

When you shift your focus from teaching to learning, child watching ("kid watching" as it is known in North America) and child admiration become natural parts of your day to day working and planning. Many years ago, observing how children responded to Margaret's carefully prepared lessons set us on a path of acknowledging and admiring children's natural ways of applying their own effective language-learning strategies in class – in spite of the structured lessons that ran directly counter to their own ways of learning. And, like Holdaway, we discovered that reading familiar nursery rhymes and interesting stories full of rich vocabulary opened the path to literacy more surely and competently than the lessons and basal readers Margaret had been using. That was the easy part.

The hard part was letting go of the well-established beliefs and routines that had the sanctions of authority and tradition. Trusting our own observations and the lessons given us by the children was both difficult and unsettling when set against the authority of curricula and standardized tests that have held sway over education for such a long time. And even though Margaret had been searching for new and better ways to teach, making the shift meant rejecting what educational authorities had mandated for so long in favor of adopting what children were showing her to be the right way to proceed.

Shifting to the observation of children as a principle way of planning children's learning confirmed Lampert's (1981) remark: "For a teacher, looking honestly at what a child really understands can be a self-evaluative act; it can be seen as a measure of the teacher's own competence as a teacher." Margaret had to wrestle with many doubts and worries as she gradually built her confidence in the rightness of following the children's leads in shaping her lessons. She was indeed evaluating her former ways, and finding that they had not served her students nearly as well.

Connie White (1990) echoes that finding when, after a year of closely observing her student Jevon to get a glimpse of his way of seeing the world, she makes the rueful comment about her earlier, teacher-structured ways, "At the end of that first year, my teaching had failed six children." Once she moved past that self-evaluation and entered into a course of studies that made careful observation of students (particularly one student) the heart of her research, like Margaret and so many other teachers, she found that her teaching took on a new quality.

> I remember wondering: "What can just one child teach me that will be highly significant to my future teaching practice?" Today, my classroom is very different because of the understandings left to me by that one child. Jevon has made a tremendous impact on my teaching.... I've always had theories and beliefs about learning; every teacher does. But Jevon showed me that some of my theories were wrong.... As a teacher-researcher, I can continue to look to the learners to show me how I can best support their learning.

KID WATCHING GIVES YOU ANSWERS TO WHAT, WHEN, AND HOW

How will I know what to teach and when to teach it? How can I make sure that thirty children of widely different ages learn what they need to learn during the time they are in my class? How can I deal with learners who are of completely different levels of maturity and experience? The answer to all three questions is "watch the kids and take your cue from them." In this chapter we provide the how and why of kid watching. We will also reassure you that while you need to learn how to become an effective kid watcher, you already know a great deal about taking your cue from your observations of children.

START WHERE THE CHILD IS

You know that children entering school bring with them a wealth of experience with language and a wide repertoire of learning strategies that have served them well at home. So in order to build on those effective strategies, you need to trust and acknowledge them as learners. As Gordon Wells (1981) writes:

> Children, just like adults, constantly strive to make sense of their experience.... Recognition of this view of children as active seekers after meaning has important implications for those who teach them. For it calls for a much more thoroughgoing attempt to achieve continuity between home and school: capitalizing on the child's existing strategies for learning and contextualizing learning tasks in terms which make sense from the point of view of his coherent but limited understanding of the world. And this, in turn, means making a greater effort, through observation, listening and sensitive questioning, to discover what form that understanding takes. This, it is suggested, is what is meant by the slogan "Start where the child is."

At home the child's learning is set into the broad context of physical activity. Parents do not teach lessons that abstract the bits and pieces of language or factual knowledge their children need to learn. Instead, they create opportunities for their children to explore their environment and then stand back to let them initiate whatever learning they are ready for. Without tests or worksheets, parents observe how their children are growing and maturing, and they readily note the many steps forward their children make in their learning.

Linguists who have studied how children learn to talk at home have commented that parents seem to know intuitively how to expand the feedback they give their child to gradually extend and upgrade their baby's early language. As they observe how the child's language is taking shape – using nouns, then nouns and verbs together, then more elaborate phrasing – the parents subtly shift their ways of talking to baby to help him move to the next level of language development. Teachers who observe children closely and watch for those signs of growth do the same updating in their teaching as they fit their language, the materials they provide, and their ways of modeling learning to the children's stages of growth. And so, just as in the home, observing the learners at school becomes a way of noting progress and then of modifying the teaching input to help children move to the next levels of learning.

Experienced kid watchers will attest to the wonder and power of using close observation to read children's thought processes, but the suggestion that children will let you know what to teach when may sound more like magic than solid educational practice. It does take experience, knowledge about the processes at work in language learning, and careful reflection about children's reactions to teaching. It also requires a willingness to examine some of the strong beliefs you may have held about the rightness of teaching in a particular sequence and style.

When you shift to a mode of teaching where "the child-as-informant" (Harste et al 1984) guides much of your moment-to-moment decision making in class, it certainly helps if you have some good models to follow. So if you know of teachers who use close observation to guide their teaching, ask them for

Even children with short attention spans become rapt listeners when the school librarian reads an exciting story to them.

hints and for the opportunity to observe them in their class. In the meantime, in chapter 12 we provide a list of references we have found helpful. We offer specific suggestions on how to approach kid watching and how to see much more than the "errors to be corrected" and the surface behaviors of children.

What you already know about watching kids

The encouraging aspect about starting on this new way of planning your classroom work is that, whether you are aware of it or not, you already know a great deal about watching children and drawing conclusions about their ability to take on new jobs. Starting at home with your own children, or perhaps younger brothers and sisters, you probably took intense interest in the progress of babies as they learned to walk and talk and got ready to move out into the yard and then beyond. Though you may not have consciously enumerated the signs or behaviors that told you when baby was ready for the next move, you were quite sure when he was ready to sit up unaided, to stand, or to toddle. You knew when to turn jobs over to this small person – using a spoon, putting on clothes, tying shoes, getting his own coat. You were sure about the child's ability to watch and be aware of cars and other hazards before you allowed him to leave the yard. There was no magic about any of these observations or decisions. You watched the child and *knew*. Sometimes he even told you in no uncertain terms, "I want to do it myself!" Often these initial forays into independence were less than perfect, but the child needed and wanted that freedom to explore and learn.

Working with children in class is no different. At the beginning of the year you will do lots of group activities that draw everyone together: reading stories, gathering news for the chalkboard news bulletin, doing physical games, singing, providing lots of opportunities for artwork and hands-on projects – things that *all* the children can participate in, each at *his own level*. As you stand back to observe how children respond to the work, you will quickly spot those who are ready to do it themselves and those who still need a great deal of encouragement to venture forth and try something new. There is no magic in that – just your caring way of observing what the children are doing in response to your leadership within the rich learning environment you have created for them.

FREEDOM TO MOVE CREATES OPPORTUNITIES

You may have to remind yourself that independence, venturing forth, taking risks, doing things spontaneously and responsibly do not develop in a carefully controlled environment. At home, if you keep baby in the playpen, he will not have the opportunity to explore and to experience successes and dangers; therefore he will not learn or demonstrate independence and responsibility. In the same way, if you keep school children pinned to their desks and glued to prescribed worksheets or other table tasks, they will not have the opportunity to "show you" when they are ready for new steps forward or for more responsible interactions.

If you provide children with the opportunities to move about freely and take risks in trying out new jobs, they provide the opportunity for you to observe that students, like baby at home, *want* to do jobs themselves. Sometimes they simply demonstrate their readiness, for example, "now I am ready for writing on lines" by drawing their own lines on the blank paper you provide for writing workshop at the beginning of the year. But quite often, they will actually announce, "Today, I want to read without help" or "I want to go to the office by myself to take the principal a piece of birthday cake" or "Now I can start doing my writing in an exercise book with lines." If you encourage those moves toward independence, children will feel free to venture forth more and more often. Instead of waiting for specific step-by-step instructions, they will take the initiative to move from one job to the next on their own.

As we discussed in chapter 3, from the beginning of the school year children are ready to help with distributing supplies, willing to make choices about artwork or writing topics, able to clean up their own desks or work areas, delighted to work in creative ways in the various centers you have set up around the room, and eager to voice suggestions or comments during news time or when planning projects or field trips. The list is endless. And if you are willing to step back to observe and give time for the flow of ideas, you will be able to spot who is delving into jobs with confidence and competence, who continues to need play and social interaction, who is happily involved in writing or reading, who is making the most elaborate designs with math blocks or art supplies. Again, there is no magic in such observations, but your knowledge of child development will help you see what the child needs next, to give you clues about his interests or abilities, to decide what kind of program he needs, where to go next, what to encourage, and what to discourage.

YOUR KNOWLEDGE OF CHILD DEVELOPMENT GUIDES YOU

Perhaps the more structured teaching programs you have experienced placed greater emphasis on the scope and sequence of, say, language arts lessons than on the ways in which children learn. The programs probably made little or no reference to child psychology and the natural sequence of cognitive development from concrete manipulations to more abstract concept formation. But the fact is that you know a lot about child development, and that knowledge becomes your guide as you make in-class observations.

As you engage children in physical games – clapping, hopping, touching head, knees, and toes – you will note whose motor development is advanced and who is still wobbly when it comes to balance or coordination. You know that here you have a quite reliable indicator of levels of maturity. Though by no means infallible, motor development is a pretty good indicator of overall maturity, and so you will note that if Vito and Pat are still fairly uncoordinated, they will need extra time to develop all their other skills, and you will make sure to give them time to mature and extra opportunities to do manipulative work, handicrafts, artwork, and physical movement.

Looking back to your studies of child development, you will also remember the concept of "lack of conservation"   the child's inability to recognize that water poured from one container into another, taller one does not thereby become "more." In our initial research we were puzzled by the frequency with which children failed to recognize words or sounds that they had seen or heard only seconds before No doubt the examples we give below will recall your own experiences, and you may agree with our interpretation that they constitute lack of conservation.

Children working with cards showing endings like *and, ill, ook* and flipping initial consonants into place to produce words like *hand, land, sand* would continue to ask, "What does that one say?" referring to the ending. Even though they had already said it several times, the sound did not seem to be remembered. One child asked for the same ending three times in a row. In a similar exercise, children working with pictures as well as successive new consonants would say "hat, bat" and then look at the next picture of a mat and say "soap" because the picture looked like a bar of soap. The puzzling aspect of having children say and hear the same sound without using it as a guide to the next word in the sequence (or having the same ending in front of their eyes yet saying something quite unlike that ending) may be explained by the absence of the concept of conservation from the child's cognitive functions. Flipping a new consonant into place can be likened to putting the same ending into a new container. The child is not focusing on the intervening process but on the end result. The new word is a different entity from the one before. Besides, if the child is focusing on the meaning or concrete referent of the words, it is not inconsistent for him to say a word that sounds quite unlike the rest. If he is using mental images for each new word – possibly replacing the word just read with a more familiar one (say, *cat* with *pussy*) – he may not be very conscious of having just said *cat*.

Along the same lines, children reading short passages would ask for words that had just been discussed at length or that appeared on the board or in the line just above. The children would also hesitate on simple words like *want* or *make* and maintain they didn't know them. We could call those instances just a case of poor memory, but saying a word twice within a matter of seconds and then asking for it needs a better explanation. We feel it is another example of lack of conservation. Words are seen in a container of context – sentences, syntactic structures, or exercises. If the container changes, the word looks new and different. Children process the flow of language and use familiar structures of language to guide them. We found that they use patterns of language and context as cues to meaning. They are not word processors.

Observing those behaviors and speculating on what they tell us about children's ways of moving from being non-readers to emergent readers and then to fluent readers confirm the need to discover *their ways* of understanding the task. Building rhyming words and working with words in isolation do not appear to fit the children's way of making meaning. In the past, when children failed to respond correctly, we have resorted to the time-honored educational solution – doing more of it. As Mimi Brodsky Chenfield (1993) put it in a recent address, "In education, when something isn't working, we keep on doing it and doing it and doing it."

Here the power and magic of observation asserts itself. Kid watching shows us that children use meaning more than sound to guide their early reading and that they use "the container of context" to make sight words and written language patterns truly their own. Thus we can understand that modeling fluent reading and encouraging children to work with familiar stories and nursery rhymes will be far more likely to establish literacy learning than will further work with words or sounds in isolation. We can also understand that providing books with repetitive patterns (lots and lots of rhymes, jingles, and songs), reading aloud at every opportunity, and inviting children to read along so that reading becomes a multisensory experience will all help too. Practical applications of reading and working with familiar stories make the context for learning to read as concrete as the context for learning to talk is at home.

Your knowledge of child development tells you that abstract reasoning needs to evolve on the basis of concrete work. In fact, "Intelligence cannot develop without matter to think about. Making new connections depends on knowing enough about something in the first place to provide a basis for thinking of other things to do" (Duckworth 1987). In learning to read and write, children's knowledge of language is helped by their everyday experiences with communicating orally and visually through environmental print and familiar advertisements. So as you begin to observe children interacting with the learning materials in class, you value and enhance their ways of acquiring language skills – looking at pictures, drawing on memories of nursery rhymes or advertising jingles to help the move toward reading, and generally working in more global, concrete ways than those suggested in scope and sequence charts that start with rather abstract lessons about particles of language.

With teaching that takes into account the wide range of developmental levels assembled in a classroom, instead of worrying about each student's ability to follow step by step along the prescribed scope and sequence chart, you will watch all the children grow and mature naturally, secure in the knowledge that their ability to do fine-motor tasks will evolve along with their ability to distinguish numbers, letters, and sounds. In the meantime you can take pleasure in watching them enjoy story time, work with familiar poems or songs, make creative patterns with math materials, participate in projects and field trips, and work or play with materials in the learning centers around your room. As you initiate these activities and observe children at work, you will monitor their participation and note all the detailed skills embedded in those global activities. You know that all the concrete, global work they are doing is aiding both their overall development and their emerging functional literacy and numeracy.

OBSERVING THE BENEFITS OF INTERACTION

Being aware of the power of peer teaching and the stimulation it affords both inexperienced and more mature students, you can recognize the beneficial effects of the interactions between mature and emergent learners. This is particularly true in a multi-age classroom. Here you will find that the possibilities are endless and by no means unidirectional. The older students in your class provide leadership and caring for their younger peers. At the same time, the emergent learners inspire their more mature peers with their creativity, spontaneity, and lack of inhibition when it comes to playful solutions to day-to-day problems or tasks. Working on art projects together, the younger students often use materials more creatively: incorporating cloth in their collages or adding three-dimensional features to what starts out to be a two-dimensional painting. In brainstorming sessions to solve problems or plan an upcoming event, the younger students almost invariably volunteer the more unusual ideas. They are not yet worried about "saying the right thing" and therefore often lead the way in imaginative idea gathering.

Young students who set up special centers on transportation, dinosaurs, or Noah's Ark draw their older peers into a realm of imagination and playfulness. More mature students open new vistas to their

Children respond eagerly to the teacher's challenge to work with as many math concepts as possible while producing an invention from materials available in the classroom. They join the teacher in counting up the many different ways they include math concepts in their work: patterning, creating symmetry, counting, doing geometric work.

younger peers as they create dioramas from the "junk" materials in the art center, build bridges or construct arches with blocks, or experiment with the wonders of siphoning or the power of air pressure at the water table. As the younger members follow the lead of "the big guys," your tolerance for temporary chaos and messy floors may be sorely stretched at times. But as you note how much such peer interaction stretches everyone's learning, you also glory in the wonderfully positive atmosphere that makes learning both exciting and fun.

NOTING HOW FUN ENHANCES LEARNING

Of course, you have always known about the magic of fun in learning, and as you watch both advanced and emergent learners participate in story time and hands-on work, you will observe the intensity with which children focus on what they are doing when they are enjoying themselves. Kindergarteners will sit still for forty-five minutes while totally absorbed in creating birthday cards. All the children will hang on your every word as you read exciting stories full of suspense and expressing a whole range of emotions. And so you note that children are learning the highly important skills of attending, staying on task, and being creative. Those skills may not have been in your curriculum guide in the past, but they are the keys to further growth, and you are the magician who develops them.

RECOGNIZING INDIVIDUAL PATTERNS OF LEARNING

From those initial observations in which you simply noted activities and levels of participation, you will move to noticing patterns of learning – Noel needs to sit and muse for a while before beginning to write; most of the children are ready to give accurate beginning consonants when helping to spell during news time; Josi is drawing lines under the drawings and is ready to move to lined paper for writing. You will discover individual patterns and sequences of learning that don't necessarily coincide with your scope and sequence chart, but that indicate learning progress – hearing ending consonants when spelling orally during news time; using vowels for the first time during writing and spelling; making spaces to segment words during writing; shifting to more demanding stories when selecting books for personal reading. And you will learn to look for and acknowledge children's natural sequence of learning steps as you continue to watch them read, write, spell, and do math. In learning to write, students may move from scribble writing, to babbling in print with strings of letters, to emergent writing that shows the beginning consonants of the major words, to segmenting print into recognizable words, to the emergence of vowels, to refinement of the use of vowels, and to internalization of a host of familiar words that move children toward standard spelling and more elaborate compositions.

As you become increasingly aware that all students move through a sequence of steps from rough approximations toward greater accuracy, you will be reassured that your students are moving in the right direction. That knowledge will also become your guide for preparing materials to foster further growth – getting out new and more advanced books, finding specific games or offering suggestions for extending projects by making dioramas, creating visuals to illustrate reports, or preparing a demonstration for peers. A knowledge of the stages of development will also help you know when to offer suggestions for students' next moves ahead; to plan mini-lessons on spelling, penmanship, or math; or to provide in-depth reading on a new topic.

To document children's progress in writing, Anne Peterson produced collages of children's work for parents. The October and December samples demonstrate that progress often moves in spurts and includes strides forward as well as continuance of previous work.

Michael's Writing   Age 6   September to June

September 1980

October 1980

December 1980

March 1981

May 1981

OBSERVATIONS BECOME YOUR GUIDES FOR STIMULATING LEARNING

As you note how children react to the learning materials and activities in class, you will watch for signs of learning or indications that learners require extra help to move them toward meeting curriculum requirements. Inderdeep may need special encouragement to read with his classmates during unison reading, so you make sure one of his sentences is included in the news time bulletin, which he then reads and rereads throughout the day. For Peter, who still can't remember some of the letters, you tape a special chart of the alphabet right on his desk to help him practice seeing, saying, and writing the letters. Anita needs lots of manipulative work to develop fine-motor skills for printing, so you may suggest finger games, cutting jobs, and work with clay.

Folders of children's written work will help you note how the ability to print, spell, and compose all evolve together. You will not be in doubt about Carlos's learning and growth when you compare his pretend writing in September with his early letters and babbling in print in November and then sentences, and later pages, of writing during the new year. Throughout the year you have celebrated each step forward with Carlos during writing conferences, and all along you pointed to new steps he might take next: "You've got the beginning letters for almost all the words! And here you have a finger space in just the right place. Maybe tomorrow you can put finger spaces between all the words." Or "I really like the way you started your story. Now I wonder if you can tell me what else you did on your picnic. Can you continue your story tomorrow?"

You know the skills and facts that children need to learn and you can see their evolution in such an ongoing record. But you also know that children have their own ways of learning and, instead of keeping your eyes on the curriculum and making it the moment-to-moment arbiter of what happens in class, use it as a checklist. Rejoice as you check off the skills already learned and make a note of those that are still emerging. You will find examples of such checklists on pages 250–253 in chapter 12.

In the meantime, watch the students more than the curriculum. If you give them the freedom to engage in interesting work that arises out of their contact with the world beyond school, the curriculum will actually be enriched and expanded. Because the children are discussing genuine problems, such as a house on a trailer that was stuck in the street next to their school, they are all keenly interested and will participate in the search for possible ways to move that house without cutting down "their trees." Linda Picciotto (1993) describes how she capitalized on the real-life drama next door to the school:

We had a good look at the house and the moving equipment, and we discussed the problem: "How do you suppose they got those big logs under the house?" "What is that big crane for?" "Will our beautiful chestnut trees really have to lose some branches?" We decided that they shouldn't have to be cut down completely. The students proposed solutions: "Cut the house in half." "Take the roof off." "Put it back where it came from."

The house stayed there all day. We took sketch boards outside so the children could record the event in their drawings. That evening I videotaped a local television news clip about the house so we could watch it together the following day. During the night the unfortunate trees lost some limbs and the house moved on.

The next day we watched the news program and discussed the event again. Excitement was still high. I connected the computer to the large television screen so the students could watch as I typed a story we called "The Day the House Was Stuck on Michigan Street." We decided together which facts to include, and then we made the story more interesting by adding descriptive words and some details to "paint a better picture" for our readers.

While the children initiated the excitement and interest, the teacher facilitated the discussions, made room in the daily work schedule to allow the children time to examine the activities outside their school, encouraged them to record the events in their artwork and through writing, and provided special input by taping the news item. The amount of writing, drawing, problem solving, and idea generating certainly fulfilled many of the standard curriculum requirements. Observing the children's keen interest and changing that day's classroom routine to build on that interest was a very productive strategy.

Watching the curriculum versus watching the kids

Like other confirmed kid watchers you will discover that watching children is more rewarding, informative, and useful than keeping your eyes on the curriculum. Kids may be more complex and elusive than the curriculum, and it may be easier to keep your eyes on the curriculum's scope and sequence chart (if one is included), but watching it doesn't offer *you* much scope. It is clearly defined, relatively unchanging, and not very exciting – year after year, the same skills in the same sequence. When you feel obliged to impart the skills and information in the sequence in which they are presented and in the time span indicated, you are under considerable pressure to "cover the curriculum."

Now that she focuses all her attention on the children and uses the curriculum as an inner scoreboard on which to mark their progress, Margaret finds that students determine their own scope and sequence of learning and thereby broaden their scope of learning considerably, which, in turn, provides fascinating discovery learning for her. (Refer to chapter 12 for further discussion about the curriculum.)

The why *and* how *of* watching *learners*

Observation should never be perceived as police or detective work. Observing in the classroom, or wherever there are children, simply implies wide-open, interested eyes and ears. Through our eyes and ears we observe the day-to-day growth and refinements in learning that take place. Sometimes we observe major breakthroughs or mini-revolutions in a child's learning. At other times we see plateaus—times when the child is settling into a repertoire of new understandings (Braun 1993).

UNDERSTANDING AND APPRECIATING HOW CHILDREN LEARN

Understanding and appreciating how children learn is the prime reason for making observations in class. Everything else evolves from there. As we have pointed out repeatedly, to make learning meaningful we need to build on children's own ways of working and on their own experiences. We also need to respect their individual pace and style of learning. And so, observation that helps you understand the learners' ways becomes a tool for the following:

* fine-tuning instruction

* flagging fledgling strategies to fan the learning spark

* detecting counterproductive strategies early

* scouting for learner potential

* collecting data for effective reporting

* determining functional links between learning and instruction

* attributing success to learner strategies

(Braun 1993)

With these kinds of tools, the assessment of progress becomes a way of enhancing learning rather than interrupting it – as testing so often does. Observation becomes a positive way of keeping track of children's learning. Accepting its power and depth is also an acknowledgment that teachers are in the best position to plan and then update their students' learning.

Then there is the connection between language and learning and the need to examine our "current assumptions about language learning and instruction" (Harste et al 1984). Our own research started at that point, and as observational research expanded (Graves 1985; Wells 1981), we found our early tentative findings confirmed again and again. One of the most important aspects of the careful research conducted both in universities and by classroom teachers is the mounting evidence that curricula and lesson plans structured by adults do not necessarily coincide with children's ways of structuring their learning or the way language works in everyday communication.

You have the opportunity to rediscover how children use language as you observe them working with materials in class and interacting with each other. To move beyond the old ways of watching – looking for right/wrong answers – you need to work at developing wide-open, interested eyes and ears. As you do, you will deepen your understanding of how children approach learning and how you can work most effectively with your students to meet their very personal needs in enjoyable and productive ways.

BEGIN BY LEARNING TO DESCRIBE

Looking back at years of shifting from highly structured ways of teaching to the flexible, student-centered approach of watching learn-

ers, Margaret found that much of her early-day observing was directed at spotting "errors" of performance: "Is Michael forming those letters according to the rules?" "Does Betty start her sentences with a
capital letter?" "Is Parminder using the Dean's blocks as I suggested?"
"Is Josi spelling accurately?" The aim of such watching for Margaret
was to intervene and "correct" the children's work.

In retrospect Margaret feels that frequently she was actually
impeding the children's development. For example, she would not
allow them to move to written work until they could spell and print
accurately; she strictly controlled their reading to ensure that they first
worked with all the words; and she would not let them proceed to
the next page until they had memorized all the words. That way they
spent two agonizing days on the primer stories that might be no more
than two or three pages long. Margaret also made sure that the students worked on basic number facts before they tackled any problem
solving. So while she was watching closely what the children were
doing, and her motive was to help the children become more accurate
in their work, that kind of observing was a way of controlling what
they were doing just as much as the scope and sequence charts used
to control - or attempted to control – the work of the teacher and the
evolution of the children's learning.

To serve learning and the learners, observation needs to be a matter
of noting carefully what it is children actually *do* without letting judg-
ments of right/wrong or correct/incorrect get in the way. Seeing clearly *how* a child is dealing with a learning task and describing – mentally
or in writing – exactly what the child is doing opens the door to
noting just what he tackles or grasps first, next, and last. That kind of
nonjudgmental observation also reveals specific learning styles and preferred modes of approaching work: Ken responds best to oral instructions; Margot needs to try things out herself, to touch and manipulate;
Chou talks to himself when he is working out what to do next; Lisa
learns by watching (oral instructions go right over her head); Robyn
works best in a team where everyone is talking things over to find
specific ways to start work.

That kind of description takes practice and careful effort to restrain
the urge to intercede – to make sure all goes well and that work is
done correctly. "Teacherlust," as teacher-principal Trevor Calkins calls
it, is difficult to hold down. To help you develop your skills of observation and description, you may want to focus on two or three children
at a time and simply make a few written notes about their actions:

✳ Morgan clasps her pencil in her left hand for precise printing.

✳ Balint is working with pattern blocks, but does not count accurately.

✳ Tony draws first, then talks to himself about the picture, and then begins to write.

✳ Li Trang follows the reading of the news on the board with his eyes but does not yet say anything.

✳ Noel is beginning to choose more difficult books to read.

✳ Occasionally Gene silently mouths the words, but does not yet volunteer to come to the board to read.

✳ Anne continues to print from right to left.

✳ Pat at times holds her book upside down but still reads quite easily.

✳ Jan substitutes *mom* for *mother* and *teeny* for *little* when reading aloud.

INTERPRETING WHAT YOU SEE

By practicing such straightforward descriptions and then reflecting on their significance, you will find that plausible interpretations suggest themselves and give you insights into the children's ways of dealing with their learning. Substitutions such as Jan's (above) readily suggest that she is reading for meaning more than for sound. Though the words are not exactly as printed in the text, the meaning is preserved and maybe even enhanced. (Fluent adult readers frequently make such substitutions when reading aloud.) If you talk to Pat's mom and learn that Pat has always loved to watch the book while sitting across from her during story time, you will realize that Pat actually learned to read upside down and is just recreating a pleasant home experience by turning the book around.

As children become accustomed to telling you about their work, you will find that they can aid your observations with their own comments: "I am doing it this way because...." or "I like using...." Such explanations can shed much light on seemingly inappropriate behavior. When Marvin was asked to explain why some of his writing proceeded from right to left and some the other way, he replied, "It's fun. I get tired of doing it just one way." No dyslexia here; just a child who likes variety. And so, listening becomes a highly important part of observing students' ways of working.

Once you understand the reasons behind children's ways of dealing with learning tasks, you often find that no intervention is needed.
If a child is reading for meaning, remember that that is what you are
after. Demanding word-perfect renditions would merely impede fluency and enjoyment. On the other hand, writing from right to left is
almost impossible to read; once you explain that to a child and mention that when writing for others left to right is the best way to proceed, you will find no objection to the change.

As you observe you will also note gaps in children's knowledge
and will take those as signals to work with individual children during
center time – playing letter or number games with children who need
it; asking parent helpers to spend extra time on one-to-one reading
with a child; becoming a customer in the class store to help a child
practice making change and recognizing the value of the different coins.
The possibilities are endless if you observe to understand how and in
what ways the children are responding to your modeling of learning,
the mini-lessons you teach, and the learning materials.

EXPANDING THE ART OF LISTENING

Careful, attentive listening deepens and augments the visual observations you make in class. A child's tone of voice, hesitation, choice of
words, and way of phrasing information tell you as much as the visual cues of body language, gestures, and facial expressions. During the
early days of our in-class research, taping conversations among children as they debated just "what the teacher wanted" provided insights
into the children's perception of what the teacher wanted them to do.
And quite often those perceptions were not at all what the teacher
intended. When she set a task of answering questions about a story,
the children interpreted that comprehension check as a request to
replicate the text verbatim – "You can't use *had*! Mrs. Reinhard didn't
say it that way." When the intended task was learning about the
sounds of rhyming words and beginning consonants, the children frequently demonstrated that they were seeing the task as a game of
take-one-letter-off-then-put-another-in-its-place and produced
nonsense syllables like *mook* or *gan* as readily as *look* and *pan* on their
worksheets. They did what the teacher had taught them, but the
meaning they attributed to the job was different from what the
teacher intended.

SEEING WHAT CHILDREN DO CHANGES TEACHING   Reflecting on the underlying meaning of the children's ways of responding to seemingly straightforward phonics lessons became the turning point for Margaret's teaching. Our observations suggested strongly that while her teaching was focusing on sounds and parts of language, the children were looking for meaning, patterns of language, and ways of connecting their reading to the world they knew.

WORDS SUGGEST CONCRETE KNOWLEDGE   On a number of separate occasions, the children searched for an *r* (for *rabbit*) when the teacher asked them to circle the first letter of *bunny*.   Asked to write the first letter of *sister* on the board, a boy supplied *j*. (His sister's name is *Julie*.)   "Do you know what 'cake' looks like?" (meaning the word *cake*) elicited, "Sure. It's round and has icing on it."

MEANING TAKES PRECEDENCE OVER SOUND   No matter what the cue – written, spoken, or pictorial – children attended to meaning more than to sound: The caption of a picture of a very small bird was read successively as *teeny* or *small* when the printed word was *little*.   When asked orally, "What rhymes with *good*, and animals live in it?" the children responded with *zoo* and *cave*. The rhyming word *wood* did not occur to them.   The picture of a *hen* was identified by the children as a *rooster* and then a *chicken*, though the word appeared on a word wheel (complete with pictures) showing the words *men, ten, pen*, and the children had already correctly read those words.

Perhaps you will recall instances like the ones we encountered so often when Margaret was focusing her teaching on the particles of language more than on language as a means of communication. Once we acknowledged that the children were doing their best to follow directions, we looked for ways to build on their natural learning. We also tried to make our underlying messages clearer and above all more congruent with the children's ways of learning. For example, we decided to work with stories and concrete writing tasks rather than with particles of speech; to use writing and spelling as the means to teach phonics, spelling patterns, and ways of recognizing sounds. And we think aloud for the children on many occasions:

"Let's see, that says half a cup of sugar; so I'll measure that exactly. Can you see the half-cup mark?"

"I'm not sure about the spelling, so I'll put this down the way I think it's spelled and make a question mark next to it. That way I'll remember to look it up later."

"I guess this is really a question. So instead of a period, we need a question mark at the end."

"I wonder what we can remember about that story."

One key to sensitive listening is to ask yourself, "What was it in my instructions that sent the children off in a direction I did not anticipate?" As you look for answers, you may discover strengths you did not anticipate in the children's work, or adult logic in your instructions that was easily misinterpreted. For example, on comparing the children's performance in reading with the scope and sequence of Margaret's phonics lessons, we found that children were reading with quite good fluency and comprehension long before she had worked through all the phonics lessons. By the beginning of January, many of the children were reading, but Margaret was just then moving toward introducing the rules for long vowels and consonant blends. Many of them were well ahead of the scope and sequence for phonics lessons and announced proudly, "I can read. I know all the sounds." They did, and without the lessons.

Similarly, adult logic in abstract lessons does not necessarily achieve the desired results even when the children appear to have learned the lesson. Talking about sentences to children does not mean they understand the concept, even though they may repeat quite readily that a sentence begins with a capital and ends with a period. We found that their own writing did not reflect the adult-supplied rule. And their oral reading demonstrated that they were transferring their own oral language phrasing and sense of sentences to "correct" the stilted language used in their basal readers. For example, if the text showed "Oh Janet look" (which is an unnatural sequence), children would regularly convert that passage to the more natural, "Oh look, Janet." They know about sentences on one level, but they are not yet ready to transfer that knowledge – based on adult-supplied rules – to another level.

So once again, remembering not to evaluate or judge is important. Listen with your heart as much as with your ears and know that children *want* to do the right thing. Maintain eye contact while you are listening to a child and demonstrate with your whole body that you are fully focused on what is being said. Quite often, if you reflect on unexpected or "incorrect" responses, you will find the underlying rationale for what the children are doing. Then you can either acknowledge *their* way or steer them in the right direction.

Practice active listening by checking on your understanding. Instead of asking "Why did you...," which often elicits a defensive reaction, use information checks like "Do you mean...?" or "Are you saying that...?" or "How did you work that out?" Given in a matter-of-fact, information-seeking voice, such questions invite the child to confirm or correct your understanding. If answers or comments still puzzle you, reflect on them and ask for clarification – "Can you tell me more about that?" "I'm not sure. Can you show me what you mean?" "That sounds interesting. Maybe you can show me what you are planning to do." Questions and comments like these encourage further elaboration without suggesting that the child has said "the wrong thing" (as a *why* question often does).

Sharpening your listening skills and deepening your caring about the children's individual needs will infuse your teaching with interest, excitement, and a sense of accomplishment. You and the children will truly collaborate to produce the best learning possible at a given moment. Think back to the times when someone gave you total undivided attention with the sole aim of understanding your needs, hopes, and aspirations. Remember the boost that knowledge gave to your feeling of being cared for, of being important to someone, and of being able to build on those positive feelings. The children in your class will respond just as positively to your listening and will show you clearly that they trust and value you.

IF THE TEACHER LISTENS ATTENTIVELY, SO DO THE STUDENTS

Another important by-product of your careful listening is that the children will model themselves after you. Not only will the older students in your class follow your example and ask their younger classmates to "tell me more about that," but all of them will learn about the importance of eye contact and total concentration when listening to someone. As a result they will listen more carefully to each other and will go beyond the surface aspects of a message to find out what thoughts and feelings lie just below those words. Both young and more mature students in your class will soon model themselves on comments they have heard you make:

"You sound sad [excited, worried]."

"You don't need to hesitate. I can tell you will give a great try."

"It's O.K. to do it that way."

"If you want to give a try, we'll help you."

Since the climate of learning you establish creates a feeling of work- ing in a learning community, you can expect most of the children to give these kinds of encouraging remarks from an early point in the school year. After all, they continu- ally hear their teacher make just such remarks.

Even when working with the whole class, Karen models eye contact and careful listening in all her work with her students.

SETTING THE SOCIAL CLIMATE BY LISTENING WITH CARE

In an effective learning community, listening with care becomes the vehicle not only for guiding learning but for setting the social climate. Naturally, the two go hand in hand. But during our early observa- tions, once we measured our listening behavior in class against what we would do in the company of adults, we came up against some sad lapses in courtesy – not waiting for a response, not making eye con- tact, interrupting the speaker in mid-sentence, being impatient with a child who was slow to respond.

TAPPING THE CHILDREN'S ABILITY TO "HEAR"

Now that listening with care and caring about listening are integral parts of setting the classroom climate, the children's own acute ability to listen can come into its own. As you observe children's attempts to make the connection between letters and their sounds, patterns of spelling and sounds of familiar words, or patterns of language and patterns of meaning, you will find that children *hear* sounds we no longer acknowledge because we have internalized all those patterns and take them for granted.

Along with the common contractions of speech such as *sprised, cause, famly,* and *goen* there will be spellings like *mios* (for "miles") or *I youzed a hammer.* If you check carefully – without prejudicing your listening by your knowledge of accurate spelling – you will acknowledge that *miles* does sound like *mios* and that *youze* is a far better representation of the actual sound than *use.* And so you learn to appreciate the miscues the children produce and to recognize them for what they are: these miscues are attempts at listening with care and are quite accurate reproductions of the speech sounds they actually hear.

With that kind of listening and an appreciation of the children's ways of tuning into the patterns of sounds around them, it becomes easier to stand back and withhold judgment about seemingly inappropriate answers. Once you learn to tune into the attentive "hearing" children do, you will be able to acknowledge it – "That sounds exactly as you spelled it" – and then to continue in a matter-of-fact voice, "To make that standard spelling you need...." Because you appreciate the children's careful translation of speech sounds into spelling, you will not find it difficult to fully acknowledge that they are in fact hearing accurately. Your tone of voice will reflect both the appreciation and then the straightforward information giving that converts the invented spelling to standard.

You will find many such instances where the children's translation of their perceptions into written or oral expression don't match those of adults but are nevertheless accurate as far as the sensory input is concerned. Here is where your research and observation become intriguing and rewarding. Here also is the value in forming a learning community within your classroom that provides you with far more personal information about children than you would gather in a structured classroom.

TAKING FEELINGS INTO ACCOUNT

The children's fears, hopes, and dreams are very much part of their daily interactions in class, and it becomes far easier to understand why Marco is staring into space during writing workshop if he has just told you that his father has left the family. If Ginny is full of plans for her trip to her grandparents, she is not likely to be a careful listener that day. Listening with care explains so much about learning, and yet in the past we have felt that learning should be objective and serious and that feelings had no place in schoolwork.

The magic of observing the whole child

Careful observers of children learn not to interrupt the child who is deep in thought during writing workshop.

Observing, describing, listening, and keeping notes on children's learning behaviors are just part of the magic of letting children tell you what they are ready to learn. Experienced kid watchers make a whole range of connections as they build their knowledge of the students in their care. Physical development, social interactions, and ways of dealing with personal property or school supplies all tell you something about a child's way of growing. Knowing about the home background and personal aspirations of children further round out the insights you are gaining about their ways of learning and growing and why they are responding as they do on given days.

Extending your observations to the playground, to lunchtime, and to children's interactions with parents and siblings will add further depth to your understanding of their range of behaviors. Different contexts will show you different aspects of children, and at times you may be amazed at how a "nonverbal" child becomes quite vocal while participating in games or talking to parents. Map learning, that effortless taking in of vast amounts of information, functions most effectively in rich and varied settings. To find out about it, you need to look and listen not only in the classroom but wherever the children are.

RECOGNIZING LEARNING BEHAVIOR

Looking at the whole range of behaviors to be watched brings back memories of students and of the visitors coming into Margaret's classroom to observe. Some visitors took our hints and focused all their attention on what the children were doing, but many remained mystified and needed help to connect the children's activities with meeting curriculum requirements. Having fun with books did not seem like "rigorous teaching/learning"; discussing the relative sizes of Halloween pumpkins did not appear to add up to a lesson in math.

The prize comment came from a university student who had been sent in "to take notes on the behavior of one child." She dutifully spent the day in class and kept her eyes on the child she had singled out for observation. But at the end of the day she commented to Margaret, "I'll have to come back tomorrow. I watched him all day, and there was *no behavior!*" At that moment Margaret was too nonplused to inquire just what, in the student's view, constituted "behavior." She had watched the child read, write, talk, move to centers, and participate in news time without finding anything to record. No doubt she had misinterpreted her instructions as meaning "record misbehavior," and since there was none, she found nothing to report. Yet noting the full range of children's interactions with each other, and with the lessons, enriches teaching/learning immensely and lets the magic of observing come into full play.

TALENTS AND INTERESTS BUILD LEARNING

Gathering information on interests and talents through observation and listening is one way of tapping children's learning potential. As you find out about Jon's interest in gardening and growing things, Meg's talent for drawing, Pierre's passion for things mechanical, Marcia's involvement with gymnastics, and Robyn's love of puppets, you have a full repertoire of openers to help these children and their peers build on their strengths as they learn. Books, projects, artwork, and writing will be enriched if you encourage students to delve into, share, and expand their interests and talents.

Once children realize that your interest in them is genuine, they need little prompting to talk about their special interests during morning greeting, at news time, when you interact with them during writing conferences, or when they respond to some reading in class. The comment, "Oh, that sounds really interesting; I would like to hear more about [see] your books [equipment, puppets]" will be all it takes to start the flow of sharing. Inviting a child to prepare and demonstrate a specific skill not only engages that child, but often inspires others to volunteer to participate or to do a demonstration of their own.

As students work on and share projects that build on their special interests or talents, they become leaders who help other students open their minds and hearts to new interests or to reveal their own. And so the cycle of learning expands for you as much as for your students. As Jon sets up flowerpots with seedlings from his garden, several children volunteer to bring in additional plants, and a gardening center may emerge. If Marcia brings in books and pictures on gymnastics to prepare a special report or to get ready for a demonstration in the gym, the martial arts enthusiasts in class may decide to share their interest with the class; Robyn's work with puppets is sure to attract other students to use one form of dramatic presentation or another to act out stories and join the fun of creating characters with actions and voices. The suggestion that the children use center time to work on these special projects assures that the regular classroom work continues and that there is a definite time block during which students can expand on their personal work.

CAPTURING TEACHABLE MOMENTS

As you focus on the students and their interests, you will be able to capture teachable moments when students eagerly seek to participate and are ready to follow your lead along lanes they themselves have opened. In Margaret's class, a day when many children stayed home ill provided a fine opportunity to practice writing, describing, evaluating, and drawing in the course of creating "Missing" posters for each of those absent students. Watching the chicks hatched in the classroom incubator jump in and out of the box provided an opportunity for on-the-spot math practice: "How many chicks have jumped out? How many are left in the box?" Creating signs to alert the whole school that Raymond the classroom hamster had once again escaped invited exercise of the very best penmanship to be sure everyone could read the signs. (The frequency of that practice moved some teachers to suggest that Margaret was letting the hamster out on purpose, particular-

A lively discussion was sparked when the teacher used the term "missing" during roll call. Building on that interest, the teacher abandoned her plans for the day, and students eagerly launched into drawing and writing to produce "Missing" posters like those they had seen earlier at the police station they had visited.

ly since he chewed up all the phonics exercise books in the language arts room on one of his forays.) Field trips, cooking, fund-raising events all offer wonderful possibilities to practice math and planning skills. In all these activities all that is needed is the willing-ness to listen, observe, and then act on the opportunities or suggestions that arise.

Trusting the learners is the key

The magic of close observa-tion lies in the discovery that children are far more competent than we at times give them credit for. As they perceive that you are deeply interested in them and their ways of working, they reveal their strengths and talents to you at every turn. When you trust them to take over jobs in the classroom, to decide how to handle a given task, or to work independently on a project, your observations will reassure you that they fully merit that trust. In chapter 4 we described how discipline is maintained by involving learners in setting the rules, and here again careful observations of how the children interact show what is needed when. Children want to do well and to get along; your observations will affirm that you can trust them to do both.

A Multi-Age Classroom is Not a "Split Class"

If you are the parent of two or more children, you can begin to comprehend what teachers are up against with a classroom of many more unique characters (Sarason 1993).

Accommodating the needs of thirty unique characters simply cannot be done in a single classroom under curriculum guidelines that assume that all of them will progress at the same rate in all the academic subjects to be learned. The shift to multi-age classrooms that is taking place in many locations across North America acknowledges that fact and offers teachers the opportunity to extend their interactions with children over two or even three years. That extra time to work with students and, more important, the absence of fixed time lines or rigid curriculum requirements allow teachers and their students to learn about and acknowledge the many variations in children's ways of learning and maturing.

As Sarason points out, traditionally "schools give overwhelming emphasis to the learning of content and academic skills, not the confronting and accommodation by students of differences among them." Multi-age classrooms are one way of making that accommodation When the students working together in a classroom span two to three grades, the guidelines for content and academic skills have to be more flexible than for single-grade classes.

Sadly, many teachers and administrators hesitate to move toward multi-age classes, and many parents object to their children being grouped with children of differing ages. Though manifestly unsatisfactory, the *status quo* seems safer than a new way of accommodating the needs of the children. Acknowledging the pressures of opinion that favor graded structures, Goodlad and Anderson (1987) raise an interesting question: "Could this be another of those educational practices continued, not because teachers and parents have studied it together, but because both believe the other expects it?"

GROUPING CHILDREN FOR MULTI-AGE LEARNING

Looking back over more than twenty years of working in and observing multi-age classes, we are certainly convinced of their many benefits for teachers and students alike. Thoughtful and ongoing communication with parents of students in these classes has drawn them into the network of staunch supporters of multi-age grouping too. In this chapter we offer some of our observations on multi-age classrooms – what they are like and what they are not like, how they work, and the specific benefits they offer.

In moving toward multi-age grouping, classes that span two and three age levels gradually replace single grades. Teachers work with combinations such as kindergarten to grade two, grades two and three, grades three to five, grades four to six, and grades six and seven, although any combination is possible. Generally about three-quarters of the students span what used to be two grades with a few older children included if they need more support before moving to the next level.

Once multi-age grouping is well established in a school, teachers and administrators collaborate to establish – then update as needed – the combinations of classes and students to fit the learning and social needs of students and teachers. At times, parents are included in discussions to decide which class would fit their child best – both academically and socially.

Herein lies the key difference between multi-age classrooms as they are now emerging and the combinations that used to be referred to as "split classes." Split classes were the result of administrative, not pedagogical, considerations: "We don't have enough students enrolled in grade.... to have a full class, so we'll combine it with grade...." In split classes, teachers were required to teach two separate curricula and to keep the two partial classes on separate tracks of learning. Not surprisingly, having to meet the requirements of two separate curricula in one class was far from popular with teachers.

In a multi-age classroom that is based on the academic and social needs of the students, the teacher follows broad curriculum guidelines for *all* students to give them the opportunity to evolve their learning in *their* own best ways and in *their* time frames. As all the children work on the same projects or tasks - reading, writing, working at centers – the teacher offers specific help to challenge her most advanced learners and to provide extra support to emergent readers and writers. Personal levels of development – *not* age or two separate curricula – determine what children do with the job at hand.

TEACHERS OF MULTI-AGE CLASSES ARE ENTHUSIASTS

Unhappy memories of split classes still haunt some teachers, and understandably they are reluctant to try multi-age teaching. The worry that having children of differing ages in one class will result in a heavier workload and discipline problems is often based on unhappy experience. But subsequent experience with the new ways of working in multi-age groupings usually proves that these fears are unfounded. After they become accustomed to the more holistic approach to teaching, teachers develop enthusiasm for the many flexible ways of interacting with students. Comments like the following are the order of the day when you compare notes with teachers of multi-age classes:

"I would never go back to single-grade teaching. This is the only way to go."

"Multi-age teaching makes being a teacher so much more exciting. It's never dull and boring."

"Multi-age teaching gives me so much more scope."

"I love to see the interactions between kids of different ages."

"It's a true learning community."

"There's wonderful cooperation. I love the feel of the multi-age classroom."

"It makes starting the year so much easier. You have a core group to set up routines and you don't have to talk yourself hoarse. I used to feel exhausted in September because I had to talk and talk and talk!"

"Having children a second year is wonderful. When I had only one year with them, I always felt I could never get as far as I wanted to, and sometimes having them even two years is not enough."

THERE'S REALLY NOTHING NEW HERE

The introduction of multi-age grouping in primary schools is a fine example of the familiar saying that "the more things change, the more they remain the same." As large consolidated schools replaced the small, multi-age schoolrooms of old, it may have seemed that classes were grouped neatly by age, but teachers have known all along that their primary classrooms did not house thirty children of equal age and maturity. At one point in the year, all the children may have had the same official age of, say, six or seven, but far from being equally ready to absorb the prescribed curriculum for six- or seven-year-olds, their teacher had thirty individual children who varied as much as ten to eleven months in chronological age and more than that in readiness to absorb specific lessons. Home experience, the absence or presence of siblings, and cultural factors served to widen that age/readiness gap even further. According to Goodlad and Anderson (1987), "In the average first grade there is a spread of four years in pupil readiness to learn as suggested by mental age data."

Consider the difference that even three or four months can make in the maturity of a young child. Recall the frustration you may have experienced in trying to get Steph, Midge, or Raoul to follow your carefully prepared lesson plans, while Noel and Indra sat around looking bored or acting out, and the rest of the class followed along with varying degrees of success.

Naturally, you made adjustments in your approach to the different children in your class. But because you were asked to operate under the assumption that all the children in your class were equally ready to work in the prescribed way, you had no choice but to give a child's poor performance (or no performance at all) a negative evaluation. This, in turn, had a negative influence on the classroom climate. While you were trying to help all your students achieve a high enough level of proficiency to be promoted to the next grade, both you and the children were very conscious of that time-performance pressure. So when you are asked to shift to multi-age grouping, you are finally receiving the acknowledgment that you have been dealing with many levels in one classroom all along.

WHAT MULTI-AGE GROUPING HAS TO OFFER

Multi-age grouping makes it official – and acceptable – that the children in your class are working at their own levels and pace and will *not* all learn the same things from the activities in class. They will have many different timetables for learning. So multi-age grouping removes the pressure of time frames and fixed curricula. It allows you and the children time and flexibility to vary classroom activities and to fit the learning to the individual needs of the children.

Those needs include much more than the acquisition of basic skills – important though they are. What has become amply clear is that to prepare children for the the year 2000 and beyond, it simply won't do to wait until high school to impart such skills as problem solving, creative thinking, effective social interacting, and working independently. Multi-age grouping acknowledges the importance of building these skills – along with all the traditional basics. The need to work together in flexible groupings of necessity emphasizes the *processes* of learning more than the acquisition of narrowly circumscribed content.

So, while multi-age grouping increases the age span of the children in your class, it gives you – and them – the opportunity to make choices about the kind of learning they will derive from their classroom work. If you have filled your classroom with books about fall or sea creatures or monsters (at the suggestion of a few enthusiasts), all the children will delve in, look at the pictures, make drawings, write or talk about their own experiences, or read deeply and at length. As they do, they often absorb the essence of stories or factual infor-

Older students extend the reading of their young buddies.

mation that is far above their presumed grade levels. You won't have to prescribe or control the level at which each child "should" read. Instead you can stand back and observe – often with awe – how well the children themselves understand how they need to work in order to progress.

Because you have no mandate to see that children move along in lock-step progression, there is room to cater to individual talents and needs such as

✱ providing books and learning materials of varying levels

✱ working individually with children who need a challenge, such as Geordie who was ready to move into borrowing and carrying in paper-and-pencil math

✱ playing phonics games with children who have difficulty with letters and their sounds

✱ encouraging Mark, who is slow to develop his reading, to talk about his knowledge of fishing and environmental concerns and then to use that knowledge as a basis for his artwork and subsequent writing

Creativity and imagination flourish when students of diverse ages work together. On their own initiative these girls produced a beautiful miniature garden after their teacher discussed making miniature gardens as an alternative to the real garden that could not be planned that year.

Without the anxiety and humiliation of having to be kept back a year, the late bloomers in your class can take two or even three years to develop their latent talents to read, think abstractly, work with math, or write and spell. At the same time, those who knew how to read before they began school will be free to soar ahead as you make advanced stories, books of all kinds, and non-fiction materials freely available to them and encourage them to seek additional materials in the library. If these same students lack experience in math or still have a fair degree of social dependence, they will not be "streamed" out of their depth solely because of their linguistic skills, but will stay to be nurtured and supported by you and their classmates.

THE OPEN CLIMATE OFFERS MANY OPPORTUNITIES TO LEARN ❊ As there were no fixed lessons or sets of worksheets to be completed at specified times, his teacher was free to encourage Alex, who was moving beyond his classmates' math work on units. The teacher showed him how to group first by tens and then by hundreds. Then she answered his questions about what came next. That was all he needed to spend the morning putting together Unifix cubes in sets of tens and hundreds to come up with a final total of 2000 cubes, which he then displayed and explained to his classmates. ❊ Watching chicks hop in and out of a box becomes a concrete way to practice that difficult concept of missing addends. "We have eight chicks. Right now, two are out of the box. How many are still in the box?" Some of the children will simply look in the box and count, but a number will be ready to try to solve the problem using their fingers or in their heads. From there, they take over and repeat the game of adding up the number of chicks in and out of the box, starting with the known total and working on the missing addend. At some point the teacher may draw the children together to compare notes on the many different ways in which they did the job and to marvel at their ingenuity.

The math wizards in your class who, like Geordie, shine in their aptitude and experience with real-world mathematics and the recognition of patterns, can freely expand their skills and serve as models for their peers, and maybe even for you, as they display their original ways of dealing with problems involving math or measurement. And as cooperation rather than competition is the key to a well-functioning multi-age classroom, you can encourage the artists and outdoor specialists among your students to enrich projects and work on themes using their special talents or knowledge. You will discover these through their participation in news time, their planning of projects, or the informal talk that takes place in the classroom.

With just a small prompt from you – "I wonder if you could create a mini-center about...." – your young scientist will be off to research and collect books and materials, while other children will join in or decide on a special center of their own. Age differences do not create barriers to this cooperation. In fact, you will often find that two children of widely differing age work particularly well together. Just as kids who live in the same block will band together to play, so students who work in the same classroom will band together to learn regardless of differences in age, and sometimes because of it.

BUILDING A LEARNING COMMUNITY

Aside from seniors' homes, schools are perhaps the only other institutions that segregate by age. Anywhere else – in the family, the world of work, everyday life – people of widely divergent ages live, work, and learn together. In the past, the little one-room schoolhouse brought children of many ages together. Though these schools now seem outdated and inefficient, those who taught and learned in such settings often recount fond memories of the interest, excitement, and variety that was inherent in working with a number of different levels. The teacher had much more scope to develop the full potential of students, because the work flowed and developed over time without the fixed deadlines involved when you have to "cover the curriculum by...." The younger students had glimpses of advanced work in literature, math, history, or geography as they kept their eyes and ears on "the big guys." Older students' imaginations were reawakened as they listened to the teacher read some of their own favorite stories to their younger classmates and watched "the little kids" do creative work with art and physical movement. Their confidence grew as they realized they could help their younger classmates.

The divergent ages and levels of ability of the students made the one-room school a learning community that offered students opportunities to absorb lessons long before they were "on the curriculum." Since everyone shared the same room, it also removed the fear of "failing a grade" and being held back a year when all your friends were moving on. Perhaps best of all, it fostered habits of learning independently, working cooperatively, and dealing with problems in practical ways. Peer teaching augmented the work of the teacher, and students developed leadership qualities and social skills as they advanced from being newcomers to being the big guys. Learning and maturing together created a learning community that involved and nurtured everyone.

As it reenters the educational scene, multi-age grouping is recapturing the advantages of those learning communities where students of many ages learned and worked together. But the new ways of grouping avoid some of the disadvantages of having too wide an age spread among students. And the teacher now has the rich variety of materials and general support she needs to work effectively with students of diverse needs.

LEARNING TOGETHER AND FROM EACH OTHER

Meeting the needs of students stands at the heart of multi-age grouping, and finding the right mix for classes is just the beginning. Setting
a climate for learning, in which all students can find their own levels
and pace of learning, is the first priority in establishing a multi-age
classroom in which students and teachers learn with and from each
other. The mutuality of learning that gives the teacher the opportunity
to become a learner and active participant in projects and information
gathering, is the key to the enthusiasm with which teachers accept
and enjoy multi-age grouping. Far from being

When needed, the
hallway doubles as a
quiet space where the
South Park teaching
assistant gives students
individual help.

weighed down by the drag
of having to drill children
on the mysteries of long
and short vowels, the
teacher constantly experiences the same variety of
new learning that holds the
students' interest. As well as
observing learners to find
out more about ways in
which they learn most effectively, the teacher enlarges her
own learning as she research-
es science projects or enters
into the search for knowledge
about astronomy, the sea, or
the potlatch ceremony.

NO, YOU WON'T BE TEACHING SEPARATE LESSONS FOR EACH GROUP!

Instead of struggling with fairly
rigid scope and sequence charts for three separate groups in one class
– as some teachers imagine multi-age teaching demands – the teacher
draws children together into activities in which all of them can participate. (See chapter 7.) The teacher is free to build on students' special

interests or needs through projects and themes, and students are free to give the natural selectivity of their brains free rein. As they research spiders, build a transportation center with trains, cars, and tractors, create dioramas on North American native lore, participate in reading workshop or writing workshop, the students themselves determine the scope and sequence of their learning and skill building. The youngest members of the class may content themselves with artwork and a few cryptic notes dictated to a peer or adult, while the more mature students read and write prodigiously, study the symbolism of the totem pole, and learn about syntax and spelling along the way.

TEACHING BECOMES A MATTER OF CREATING CONTEXTS FOR LEARNING

The broad, process-oriented curriculum guidelines (see chapter 12) that are emerging as we move toward the changes advocated for the year 2000 and beyond, are particularly suited to multi-age grouping. They offer the open framework in which teachers can once again function as autonomous professionals in their classrooms – making decisions about time lines, adjusting the curriculum to fit the interests and needs of the children, choosing topics and learning materials that build on the children's suggestions; determining the sequence of learning based on in-class observations rather than printed guidelines, and setting flexible goals to accommodate the varying and changing levels of development of students:

"You have been writing three sentences very well now. After the holidays, you'll be able to move to five or maybe more."

"Now that you know many different ways of checking whether your spelling is standard, go over your draft to see if you can make some changes before you come to writing conference."

"I know that story about the tooth fairy is your favorite. How would you like to read it to Lee and look at the pictures together?"

"I know you are a real expert in..... How would you like to set up a mini-center to share your knowledge? Let's think how we could do that."

A flexible grouping of students to fit specific needs or interests and a certain measure of choice in the work and how it is to be done set the tone as the teacher creates frameworks for learning – hands-on work to start a project or theme, lots of discussions with students to get their input, working with centers, using literature to spark interest in history, geography, or specific human concerns. In chapter 7 we provide concrete descriptions of many activities, but here we want to emphasize that in a multi-age classroom the overall context and concrete work become the backdrop for learning specific skills. Age is no barrier to any projects or themes as long as all the students are encouraged to participate in their own ways, at their own levels and pace, and without the expectation that everyone will learn the same lessons from the same activity.

Why do we believe in multi-age classes?

This book includes many suggestions for working with children in flexible, open ways that accommodate their individual differences. The need to create independence of learning, to empower students, and to work in a variety of whole-group, small-group, and individual modes all have validity in any classroom. Then why do we believe so strongly in multi-age classrooms? The answer to the question really comes down to a matter of honesty. Educators have pretended for far too long that children all do the same learning in the same way in the same time frame. They have also pretended that within a short span of about ten months teachers can get to know children well enough to help them learn in their own best ways. And for far too long, educators have tried to fit the children to the administrative needs of the school.

Building on recent research into child development, normal brain functions, multiple intelligences, and optimal management principles, educators at all levels have reexamined the antiquated and structured ways of teaching that still characterize much of education but do not fit the realities of children's natural learning or biological maturation. The converging evidence that points to the need for a dramatic shift in the way we organize our schools has led to more holistic, learner-centered ways of teaching and the inclusion of multi-age grouping in many schools. Teachers have come to accept and value the change, and the evidence for the efficacy of multi-age grouping is accumulating. In *The Non-Graded Elementary School*, Goodlad and Anderson (1987) offer research that confirms the effectiveness of multi-age grouping. They point to "the unrealistic floors and ceilings imposed by the graded structure," and they document the fact that the practice of holding children back a year if they fail to measure up to unrealistic criteria does nothing to increase their academic achievement.

So here are the answers to our question, "Why do we believe in multi-age grouping?" We believe in multi-age grouping because

* it fits children's ways of growing and learning far better than single grades do

* it broadens the scope of learning and removes the "floors and ceilings" of content-driven curricula

* it emphasizes the process of learning and builds lifelong learning habits

* it creates a feeling of continuity and community that is difficult to achieve in single grades but essential to meaningful learning

* it is more effective than single grades in building leadership qualities and cooperation

* it eliminates the pressure and anxiety of meeting deadlines and specific curriculum goals at fixed dates

* it makes teaching and learning more exciting, more fun, and more rewarding for teachers and students alike

7.

To Start the Year – Begin at the Beginning

My kindergarten-grade-one teacher believed that the climate in her classroom was the most important factor. Her classroom certainly did create "a climate of delight," perhaps due largely to the fact that it wasn't *her* classroom: it was all of ours. All twenty-six of us five- and six-year-olds belonged in and to that classroom, and it belonged to us. Or at least that's how I felt. That room was not only colorful and full of fun stuff to do, but it was warm. I felt very safe (Jenny Miller 1993).

When launching into teaching that acknowledges the multi-age nature of your class, like Alice, you need to begin at the beginning. Getting to know your students and introducing them (and their parents) to your classroom before school opens in September – we suggest a June meeting – is a friendly and relaxed way to start. Meeting informally sets a positive tone for teaching/learning and for home-school liaison. Children have the opportunity to experience the interest and excitement that can be generated in your classroom; parents find that school is a place that welcomes them; and you gather valuable information on your prospective students, about their families and general backgrounds.

New Parents' Tea

At South Park School teachers enjoy holding a "New Parents' Tea" sometime in June. They have established a parent-friendly climate throughout the year, and so they know they can call on one of the "old parents" from the current year's kindergarten children to organize a party for the newcomers. The organizer of the tea calls on other parents for help, and on the appointed day the team arrives at the school and sets up the room with cups, baked goodies, flowers, and anything else that will make the event warm and welcoming.

The "old parents" greet the newcomers, serve them tea or coffee and talk about their children's experience in the classroom, what to expect, and how the new parents can become involved in useful and enjoyable ways. While the parents socialize, next year's kindergarteners talk to the children who will become their classmates and explore all the interesting things that will be available to them in their future classroom.

After the informal mingling and chatting, the teacher gives a brief talk on how children learn. She makes it a point to acknowledge the fine job the parents have done in teaching their children to talk, to think, and to get along. She then tells them that the school's job is to build on the solid foundation they have laid. After that positive introduction, she invites questions, comments, expressions of concern, and then schedules individual meetings for early September so she can get to know her new students and their parents. The home setting is ideal for these meetings. It gives more insight into the child's life and is a

OLDTIMERS AND ROOKIES ※ In Karen Abel's grade–two–three class, talk about incoming students inspired her experienced group to refer to themselves as "oldtimers" and to dub the newcomers "rookies." The oldtimers made plans to make the rookies feel welcome when they came to visit the classroom in late June. To make room for the rookies and to give them a chance to meet on a one-to-one basis with their prospective classmates, the grade-three students who were scheduled to move to the next grade in September went for a very enjoyable visit to their former kindergarten–grade-one teacher (who was sending up the rookies). ※ Karen and the remaining oldtimers welcomed the incoming rookies, introduced them to the classroom and its people, and then settled down to a read–aloud story session followed by an art activity. Each rookie was paired with an oldtimer, and together they created a piece of artwork. These were used to decorate the classroom in September to create a welcoming atmosphere for the whole class – rookies and oldtimers alike.

AND HERE'S WHAT WE DID THIS SUMMER! ✦ At the time of the June visit to class, Margaret talked to parents and children about their plans for the summer: "What are you planning to do? Are you going any place special? Are you going to visit someone? Are you going to enjoy summer in the city?" Then she gave each child a large piece of chart paper to take home, saying, "Now here's an expensive piece of paper just for you. If you go camping or on a trip or do anything that's interesting or fun this summer, why don't you draw a picture, or if you have pictures of places where you go, paste them on. Maybe you'll read some books from the library and want to draw pictures about those. I'd really like to know what you have been doing all summer, so bring your drawings or photos when you come to school in September." ✦ Children and parents alike responded to that sincere interest. In September most of the children brought in wonderful collages representing their summer holidays – brochures of places they visited, tickets to special events, maps, drawings, shells and flowers. Margaret used these collages to decorate the room. Those children who had not brought in their charts hastened to get in on the fun and one by one brought in their own creations. ✦ Aside from having interesting and colorful displays that had personal meaning for the children, Margaret used those collages to help children talk about their experiences. With the help of all the visual materials, she could coax the children into giving quite coherent accounts without being shy or tongue-tied in front of their classmates. Pride in their display and happy memories smoothed their entry to school and their participation during sharing time.

more comfortable setting for parents and children. However, some teachers and parents prefer to hold these meetings in the classroom.

Such informal meetings reassure both children and parents that you, the teacher, are deeply interested in them and are looking forward to acknowledging their individual needs and concerns. With that assurance both children and parents lose much of the nervousness they may feel about school and getting along with the teacher. At these meetings you can also begin to forge a positive link between home and school by suggesting a summer activity that would be fun for parents and children alike. Through these informal meetings you begin to build the mutual trust that becomes the foundation of effective teaching/learning.

If you are able to visit the children in their homes, you will gain valuable insights into their learning experience, their social skills, and their special needs or hopes. Watching parents, children, and their siblings interact on their home ground will give you a far better understanding of the children than seeing them only at school. Here, as in all direct observations, your skills in describing without judgment will be invaluable as you make mental notes, such as the following: "Children and parents talk freely to each other; it looks as if Kathy likes to share games; pictures around the room suggest a strong interest in sports." In the meantime you demonstrate to parents and students alike that, in addition to being *the teacher*, you are someone who shares the same interests, concerns, and everyday needs as they do, that you are a person in your own right.

Starting the new school year

The beginning of the new year will reinforce for the children that feeling of communicating and working with someone who is both friendly and approachable. The first and most important job is to establish an atmosphere that draws children into a cohesive circle of learning, that sets a "climate of delight" right from the start, so that children will continue to build on the power of their natural desire to learn and will enjoy exploring and participating in all the classroom activities. The approach you take to initiating children into the routines of everyday work will depend on the nature of your class.

If your classroom is multi-age merely by virtue of the gap in maturity among your incoming students, you will begin the year by establishing routines, helping your students to feel comfortable and effective in their new setting, establishing guidelines, and developing an atmosphere of cooperation, sharing, and mutual respect. In this case, you will do a lot of the talking, explaining, and modeling. It is important to base any talk on events that have just taken place in class. For example, if you are establishing guidelines for "indoor voices" or putting things back in their places, talk about them when the noise level needs to be lowered or after learning-center time when children have left lots of materials in disarray. Rather than simply laying down the law, you will find it effective to ask the children how to deal with such problems. In that way they will take ownership of the solutions. (See also page 90 in chapter 4.)

On the other hand, if you are working in a class that spans two or three grades, then the benefits of multi-age grouping will come to your aid in starting the new year. Your "mature" students will be the ones who do much of the explaining, modeling, and guiding to help the newcomers settle into classroom routines and find their way around within the physical and behavioral boundaries. When they take on the status of wise elders, your returning students will settle down quickly and happily. They know that their role is important, and they rise to that challenge. At the same time, the newcomers often find it easier to follow the lead of the big guys than to listen to the teacher.

In Karen's room, to stop the mad dashing and shoving to get a seat on the sofa in their classroom meeting corner, students developed a system of rotating who is in possession of the sofa on any given day. During writing workshop, students who need quiet time to work inform restless newcomers about the rules about not interfering with other people's work. Taking their cue from their teacher, students generally use a matter-of-fact voice to pass along such information and seldom use an unpleasant tone of voice or resort to pushing. The caring atmosphere established the previous year is continued as the big guys help the newcomers.

To orchestrate a good peer-support system, you will need to set the scene carefully. For kindergarten-grade-one classes in Margaret's school, returning students begin school a few days to a week before the new students to give the teacher the opportunity to reestablish

LEARNING HOW TO GET ALONG IN CLASS Learning to get along takes time, patience, and a lot of practice. At the beginning of the year, second-graders can still be pretty egocentric and simply take the attitude "I want it, therefore it's mine!" whenever there is a question of sharing or taking turns. To create a climate of cooperation, Karen Abel has a lot of discussions with her grade-two-three children about sharing, taking turns, and the need to be courteous and respectful. She comments, "This has been one of the biggest teaching changes for me. I used to set all the rules and guidelines. But involving the children works so much better when we first talk about how we feel and what we need and then set the guidelines." Karen role-plays bad behaviors – "I want that!!" "That's a stupid answer!!" – and puts a lot of steam into her performance. Seeing an adult display that kind of behavior comes as quite a shock to her students, and the subsequent discussion and reflection "What do you see? What do you hear? What do you feel?" takes on new depth and a lot of involvement for everyone. On that foundation of awareness the children discuss possible solutions to conflicts and problems, to fighting and bickering. Here too Karen lets the children take the lead in putting forth suggestions. As they develop rules, they themselves monitor each other's adherence to these rules.

Given the freedom to move, students find a quiet space of their own to do their work.

contact with them – an ideal way to begin. In many schools this will not be possible, but the teacher can take advantage of the fact that the kindergarten students usually attend only for half days. Whatever the case, setting routines and guidelines becomes a matter of encouraging your returning students to recall how their days unfolded the previous year. They will quickly recall the joys of story time, of working independently at learning centers, and of creating their own stories and artwork. They will also remember the agreed-on rules and the end-of-year conversations about plans and hopes for the year ahead. As you demonstrate that you trust them to fall into the easy rhythm you had created jointly by the end of the previous year, your students will quickly settle back into their patterns of working independently, and they will welcome the invitation to help their less experienced peers get settled in.

MAKING GRASS-ROOTS CHANGES

Margaret and some of her fellow teachers were instrumental in having some of the rules about the ways in which children first enter school changed. By contacting Ministry of Education personnel, she was able to obtain tentative approval of continuous entry – having children begin school on their fifth birthday – for her classroom. The superintendent and her principal acknowledged that tentative approval, and Margaret was able to celebrate each child's entry with her students to make the newcomer feel important and welcomed on coming to class.

Though many school boards now permit the gradual phasing in of new students, there are still many districts where staggered entry and initial half-day sessions to lay the proper groundwork are only a dream. Once you are convinced of the benefits of phasing students in gradually to provide each student with an excellent start to school, you too may be able to sway your local authorities. Always remember that you, the teacher, have the best insight into children's needs and can therefore be an effective advocate for them. In fact, many of the important changes in education come from the grass roots – teachers and their knowledge of students' needs.

GETTING READY FOR THE NEWCOMERS

As you comment on their ability to know what to do, to be effective, and to take care of themselves and each other, you are in effect reminding your continuing students that they are now the big guys, the ones who know what to do and where things are. With that feeling of self-confidence they will be ready to help plan how best to welcome the incoming younger students. Reminiscing with them about their first day in school, they will share their memories of how it felt – "I cried"; "I didn't want to leave my mom"; "I didn't know when lunch was", "I was afraid to go out at recess." You can probe what it was like to be greeted by the older students. What felt good and what was a little scary? What was fun and made you laugh? In what ways did the older students help?

From there you can move into discussions about how to make the new students feel comfortable, how to help them find their way around,

WELCOME-TO-OUR-CLASS CARDS   After discussing who was coming into class and reminding them that they had met their prospective new classmates at the time of the June New Parents' Tea, Margaret put the names of the newcomers on the board and together they worked at matching those names to the children they had met – "Leah was the blond girl." "Noel was the one who was crying." "Pat was the shy one."   Next the students discussed how they could make all the children feel welcome. They decided to create personalized welcome-to-our-class cards. They set to work with enthusiasm and creativity, and each one had a special message for the new classmates – "Welcome to our class. It is fun" "I hope you are not afraid. I will help you." "I will show you where the washrooms are." "Don't worry. Marg is nice." (Children at South Park School address their teachers by first name.) When the kindergarteners arrived, the children presented each of them with a card, which they read to them. For newcomers and oldtimers alike, it was a very special day.

and how to make their entry into school fun and exciting. As you invite your students to give you specific ideas for helping the newcomers settle in, there will be no dearth of suggestions. Children remember fondly what was fun for them the previous year and they are never at a loss to suggest some new ideas. Many of them volunteer to become buddies to the newcomers, to show them around and help them feel welcome, to invite them to join them in building things with blocks, to help them with artwork, or to join in special games. All are ready to think of special activities to make the first days of school memorable for the incoming students – lots of story reading, providing a special snack or treat, going on a short walk or field trip, playing special games at recess, putting on a play for the newcomers, having a welcome message on the chalkboard, decorating the classroom.

The more you involve the children in these plans and preparations, the more successful those first days will be. Teacher-designed schedules and materials may be more orderly or attractive to adult eyes, but they don't hold the same warm feeling for children as a welcome that comes from other children.

Discussing plans for the newcomers can help your six-year-olds set goals for their year ahead. Whenever children are faced with defining something for someone else, they tend to confirm and enrich their own concepts of their visions for themselves. Thus, rather than responding, "I don't know," when asked what they want to learn and what interests them, they will consider the question very carefully and become quite creative when you ask them to come up with ideas for their new classmates' learning as well as their own. Write these ideas down and encourage students to add to the list.

Here is a sampling of suggestions Margaret's oldtimers made when they looked ahead to their new year:

HERE'S WHAT WE WANT TO LEARN ABOUT THIS YEAR

pets	raccoons	dinosaurs	sharks
hospitals	pirates	spiders	art
fire engines	trains	ballet	computers
chicks	fish	reading	birds
snakes	writing	printing	cooking
space	water	numbers	Mexico

ADMITTING SPECIAL NEEDS CHILDREN　Since mainstreaming is now a fact of life in schools, and children who are physically or mentally challenged are joining regular classrooms, teachers need to prepare the way both for them and for the rest of the class. To be fully informed, the teacher needs time to meet with the current care team: nurse, parents, psychologist, teaching assistant, social work-er, and any former teachers. Ideally, the teacher needs half a day or even a full day free to meet with the team to gather information on which to base plans for the child's learning program.　Here are Margaret's suggestions for creating a smooth entry into class for the special needs child and for the rest of her class:

If I have a special needs child to be enrolled, I usually ask the parents to bring the child a few days after classes have started. I feel that I need to take time to prepare the rest of the class for the special needs child's entry. The students need to know what to expect and how to interact with the newcomer in supportive, caring ways.

Mostly we talk a lot about what to expect, what the child might do, what his mannerisms might be, and what his physical symptoms might be: shaking, drooling, crying, shouting, or whatever. Children may describe special people they know and how they have reacted to them. If possible, and if they are available, I show slides or a video of the special needs child to make the discussions more meaning-ful and to give the children time to look, so they won't feel the need either to stare or to avert their eyes when the child first arrives.

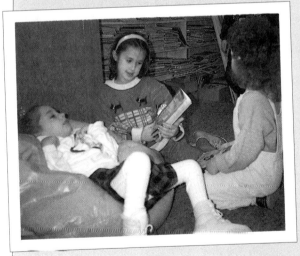

An important part of our discussions centers on ways of being supportive and caring without overdoing it. We also anticipate how our days or routines might have to be slightly modified to meet the needs of the newcomer. Those thoughts may lead to some creative problem solving on the part of the chil-dren. With that preparation, the entry of the special needs child is usually free of stress for all concerned and makes for a positive beginning.

Thoughtful preparations for the entry of a special needs child into the classrooms set an atmosphere of caring and understanding. Children love to read to Mavis even though she shows little or no response.

Just as you will refer back to the list of suggestions and plans for their own learning, so you will want to take time a month or so later to talk to your oldtimers about the success of their plans for helping the incoming students get settled – what worked well, how the newcomers reacted, and what more could have been done. Once a plan has been initiated and carried out, there should be closure. We often forget about that last vital step in working with students.

Generally you will find – and the debriefing will confirm – that the young newcomers are eager to follow the lead of the older students. Taking on the role of leaders and information givers creates a climate of caring and cooperation that draws the newcomers into a circle of friends. As you continue to affirm the older students' goals and more advanced work, the newcomers eagerly observe and imitate what the big guys are doing. As a result, your job of establishing routines of work and of introducing and enforcing guidelines for behavior and work habits becomes not only easier but effective. The climate of delight that had flourished by the end of the previous year will reemerge easily and naturally.

The first and foremost job— setting the climate

PROVIDING OUTLETS FOR CREATIVITY

Describing how she begins her year, Margaret tells of her priorities and first concerns:

> I like to start out in September by working on the tone of the classroom. I put concerns about the curriculum aside for the moment and just concentrate on getting the right kind of mix or balance. Early in the year, my primary concern is to have the children become independent learners – to think for themselves, to initiate activities, and to make smooth transitions from one activity to another. Since I generally have children who have spent a year in kindergarten with me and are now entering grade one, there is a core group of students who know the daily routines of our classroom and who have absorbed the ground rules for getting along. But sometimes I find that the newcomers are all pulling in different

CREATING A SENSE OF COMMUNITY ※ To establish that cohesive spirit in her class, Karen Abel makes it a point at the beginning of the year to take her grade–two–three students out to the playground during regular class time. This gives the children a chance to play together undisturbed by other groups, and in that informal setting oldtimers and rookies quickly form friendships. While she gives the children a lot of freedom of choice in the selection of work partners for projects or teamwork, Karen makes certain that all children get a chance to work with everyone during the course of the year. To ensure this happens, at times she will assign work partners to fill specific needs. She points out to the children that we all have something to give and that we should discover what it is like to work with many different partners.

directions, and so the first thing I have to attend to is getting the class to work as a cohesive unit in which everyone cooperates.

Margaret goes on to describe the power of creative work:

A key to harnessing all the lively energy children bring with them into the classroom is to provide lots of hands–on creative work. As Sylvia Ashton–Warner (1971) puts it, "I see the mind of a five–year–old as a volcano with two vents: destructiveness and cre–ativity. And I see that to the extent that we widen the cre–ative channel, we atrophy the destructive one." Looking at her work has confirmed our own observations about the need to involve children physically

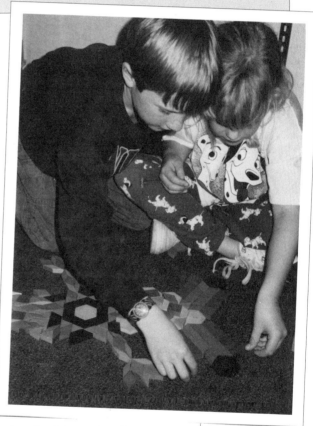

and creatively in the work they do in school. Lecturing them and making them sit still for extended periods of time just builds up steam in the destructive vents of their inner volcanoes. Instead of trying to control them with carefully structured rules, it is far more

Creative work with pattern blocks draws children into produc-tive collaboration.

productive to harness that power by channeling it into creative, expressive paths.

And so, to draw the children into working together harmoniously and creatively, I have an interesting language arts center ready for them when they start in September. To use that as a jumping–off point, I fill the center with games like Junior Scrabble, SPELLO, Phonic Fun, Word Lotto, Picture Lotto, alphabet cards, self–correcting phon-ics games, and Letter Bingo; writing supplies like paper cut in vari-ous shapes (e.g., trains, pumpkins, Christmas trees), pens and crayons of varying sizes and colors, rubber–stamp letters, and story starters; creative arts materials for making puppets or other items the children devise; and, of course, lots of books.

As the children interact freely with the materials in the center and with each other, I watch them closely to pick up on their inter-ests – creative work, sports, ballet, animals, the outdoors, building things. These observations give me the chance to provide the chil-dren with lots of positive feedback and to extend and enrich their work – make them aware of additional books and games, suggest they might put on a play that incorporates their dancing, help them convert the playhouse into a veterinary hospital, talk of my own childhood experiences, or invite visitors into the classroom to make presentations on snakes, special artwork, creative dance, and so on. The only guidelines I set at first have to do with sharing or taking turns, not fighting, and with putting back one set of materials before starting to work with another. Otherwise the children are free to interact with the resources in the center in any way they choose. They enter into the activities naturally and creatively and accept the guidelines because we talk about the reasons for having them in terms of everybody's needs.

USING STORIES TO DRAW CHILDREN TOGETHER AND WIDEN THEIR HORIZONS

Continuing on the theme of establishing a climate of delight, Margaret goes on to describe her use of reading aloud to introduce the joys of story time and personal reading:

> To draw the children together and into the world of reading, I read aloud to them often – sometimes three or more times in a day. Over

years of teaching I have accumulated a large stock of books and I know which ones are perennial favorites: *The Fat Cat, Matthew and the Midnight Tow Truck, Alexander and the Wind-up Mouse, Just Me and My Friend,* and *Curious George Rides a Bike.*

At times I use big books so that the children can see the pictures and follow the text, but if I have small books, I still hold the book in such a way that they can see the pictures. Naturally I put a lot of feeling into the reading, and children will laugh, cry, and talk with me as the readings evoke their own feelings and memories.

As well as the obvious benefits of introducing children to book language, to story grammars, and new vocabulary, I find that reading to children has a soothing effect and helps them take on other activities calmly. It also becomes the impetus for their own exploration of books, both at school and at home.

One year, when I had thirty–three children in my class – mostly boys – I read and read and read to them. It was the one time in the day when they became totally engrossed. They would sit very still listening raptly, oblivious to any distractions. That absorption also helped them participate more fully and appropriately in discussions and planning and certainly improved their willingness and ability to listen intently.

TALKING AND LISTENING LEAD TO
NEWS TIME AND WRITING

Emphasizing the crucial importance of listening to children as they talk about their interests and concerns, Margaret makes news time a daily feature that establishes a climate for attentive listening and relaxed sharing:

> Right from the first day of school in September, I start each day in class with a relaxed discussion that involves everyone. The children sit on the carpet in front of the chalkboard and discuss things that are important to them. If at the beginning of the year no one has any news to share, I tell them something that happened to me – stories of my dog doing funny tricks, a mouse startling me so much that I jumped on a chair, or my plans for a special event – anything that is likely to evoke a "me, too" response to start the talking and listening.

Margaret offering a demonstration lesson in a school in the Queen Charlotte Islands. When writing *their* news, children are drawn to participate, even when the teacher is a visitor to their class.

Asking pointed questions like "What did you do?" or "What news do you have today?" doesn't work nearly as well as modeling the kind of sharing you hope to evoke and "wondering" about their plans, their ideas, their ways of dealing with an incident you just related from your own experience. Once the children get into the swing of sharing their news, peer modeling takes over and I rarely have to prime them with my stories.

Talk leads into deciding what news to put on the board (see a more detailed description of this in chapter 9) and to spelling lessons embedded in the context of printing the news on the board. In the early part of the year, I keep news time brief and concentrate on involving the six- and seven-year-olds. I provide a modified version for kindergarteners when their older peers are busy writing or working on projects. But in all cases I listen carefully to everything the children have to say and convey to them that their news is of interest and importance to me. I accept their ideas, their thoughts, their attempts to spell, and their suggestions for editing. Once children have been heard, they are usually quite ready to listen to other suggestions and to have a particular idea included or excluded without feeling rejected.

These talking sessions give me wonderful opportunities to observe how children interact, to assess their verbal skills, and to learn about their special interests or concerns. As they talk I may also be reminded of a special book I have that relates to their news – losing a tooth, grandparents coming to visit, or getting a new dog. Reading that book aloud right then and there is attended with extra delight. Such acknowledgment of children's special thoughts or needs tells them that they are valued, and the intense listening I do not only models good listening for them, but also sets that climate of delight that tells them that their thoughts and feelings are important and that school is a very good place to be.

FIELD TRIPS AND MOVEMENT ADD PLEASURE AND CHANNEL ENERGY

Keeping twenty to thirty active children in their seats for extended periods of time certainly conjures up images of Sylvia Ashton-Warner's "inner volcano." Developing their muscles, motor control, coordination, and even the neural connections in their brains demands that children

MAKING READING PERSONAL ✳ Being lost can be a terrifying experience to a young child. After a child told a story of being lost, Margaret added to the sympathy and caring the child received from his peers by telling the children, "I think I have a story you will all be interested in. It is called *Out on the Ice in the Middle of the Bay.* Would you like to hear it?" (This story talks about the experience of a little girl lost on the ice in the middle of a bay.) ✳ Another day, a child was very upset at morning meeting because his mother had cleaned out his room over the weekend and had thrown out or given away a lot of his old toys. After much discussion by the group about similar happenings in their lives, the teacher read them a story that described just such a problem. *Setting Wonder Free* took on new meaning and depth for the children. ✳ Then there was the time when little Sarah and her mother had seen two Canada geese by the roadside. One of them was lying on the ground seriously hurt. The other goose was standing over her mate protecting him. The mother explained that geese mate for life and that the live goose would probably stay there for a long time hoping her mate would get up and fly again. Sarah was deeply affected by her experience and wanted to talk about it. To involve the other children in a story of loss and sadness, Margaret worked up her courage and read them *The Christmas Day Kitten,* and they cried together about the loss of a pet.

be physically active. Acknowledging that fact by including plenty of physical activities, both indoors and out, channels energy into productive vents. Outdoors, running and jumping, taking a walk to the park, playing games, and climbing on the jungle gym all serve to let off steam and to add joy to the day. Indoors, clapping games, singing with actions, dance, working in the gym, and even doing artwork provide the active, creative outlets children need and enjoy.

Margaret and Marne leading the children in the Mexican hat dance in preparation for their Mexican fiesta.

If you initiate and channel children's energy, they will quickly suggest other activities of their own – a singing game learned at camp, a skipping chant, a song with actions learned at home (sometimes rather risqué!), or a playground game they want to try inside. As with any activity, your careful observations of how the children respond will provide many insights into the children's levels of maturity, talents, and areas of difficulty. Without special tests, you will learn ways to help individual children grow – adding further challenges for the more mature students and providing special input for the less advanced – and pick up on individual needs or concerns that surface as children move about freely.

THE CLIMATE OF DELIGHT SHOWS ITSELF IN MANY WAYS

You will feel the atmosphere of calmness, cooperation, and joyful, purposeful learning once a climate of delight has become established in your classroom. You will know that the time you spent building that climate is now paying dividends in effective learning and harmonious interactions. The benefits springing from the right climate far outweigh any "wasted time" spent in establishing such a climate.

There are also specific signs and landmarks along the way to reassure you that you and the children are moving toward effective learning within that climate. Knowing those signs becomes particularly important when you start with a whole class of newcomers, because without a core group of experienced students to lead and model, it may take you two or more months to establish that learning climate. (One year Margaret found she needed four months.)

When watching for that climate to emerge, here is what you will notice:

* Children's attention spans lengthen.

* Routines become established and are followed.

* Children begin to initiate activities on their own.

* Children need few directions for much of the work.

* Children know what is expected and follow through.

* A feeling of calm and cooperation pervades the room.

* Friendships begin to form.

* Children are less egocentric and more team-oriented.

* Children feel free to make suggestions, negotiate, raise topics – "Could we stop now and have a story?" "If we finish this, can we...?" "Could we change...?"

* There is an absence of fear, tension, and nervousness.

* Children no longer cling to their parents.

* Children deepen their discussions to include personal and important topics like death or losing a parent.

* Children want to share and participate more.

* There are occasional breakthroughs: "I did it, I did it!"

* You need to talk less and less.

* Parents tell you that their child loves school.

* Children are turned on to literature.

* Children are willing to explore or try whatever comes along.

* You find out who is ready for more advanced work

* You offer enrichment and new challenges.

* Both you and the children share a feeling of ownership of the classroom.

* There is a general feeling of well-being and goodwill.

No doubt you will find many more signals to add to your list of indicators that tell you that you are on your way to establishing a warm, effective, and joyful climate for learning.

With all the information on how the brain works and how emotions affect learning, both positively and negatively, there can be little doubt that setting the climate is crucial to fostering learning. Yet it is one of those intangibles that tends to be omitted from curriculum guides. Fear, anxiety, belligerence, or anger shut down learning and disrupt the work of the classroom. That destructive vent may inject hot steam into any interaction. But harnessing that energy and converting it to creativity fosters feelings of joy, safety, and harmony. In that climate learning flourishes for all children. When they feel acknowledged, valued, and connected to the group, they work productively and effectively because you, the teacher, established a climate that exudes goodwill, patience, enthusiasm, laughter, and, above all, the willingness and ability to listen deeply to the children.

AT THE BEGINNING OF THE YEAR WHOLE-GROUP ACTIVITIES PREDOMINATE

Before your learning climate is well established and students have learned to move independently from one activity to another, you will need to rely on whole-group activities more than you will later in the year. Here again, if you have a core group of returning students, reestablishing routines and reaffirming their ability to act independently become much easier. However, to form a cohesive group and set the scene for a relaxed flow of productive work, here are some activities that will give everyone a chance to participate – regardless of their level of maturity or proficiency:

* morning meeting and discussion

* news time (mostly for the older students with a separate, modified version for kindergarteners, but also some joint sessions)

* story time, with the teacher reading aloud (including favorites of both the young and the more mature students)

* writing workshop (students all working at their own levels)

* choosing or center time (following writing workshop)

* reading workshop (with all children choosing books to suit their own levels and inclinations)

* math made concrete (using manipulatives and real-life applications augmented by some separate sessions to fit different levels)

* project time (with all children working to their best abilities and levels)

* science and social studies projects (extending the work of mature students and leaving less advanced children to work at their own levels, but with all students working on the same theme)

* field trips and special events

* viewing videos and putting on plays

* invention time (when all children create their own inventions)

In each one of these activities *all* children can participate at their own levels. There is no need to segregate children, to hold some of them back unnecessarily or to urge others along too quickly. If the guide-lines for participating are sufficiently broad – such as working quietly with books during reading time (even if a child cannot yet read and only looks at the pictures), producing a picture and some writing before moving to a learning center, staying within a theme but using different ways of working on it (drawings, stories, plays) – the children will find the right levels for themselves and will often surprise you with the advanced work they can do, despite the fact that "they may lack the basic skills." Remember that learning does not proceed in a neat linear progression. Instead, it moves forward on many fronts at the same time, with skills being learned and then refined in the matrix of multifaceted whole-job learning.

If you are working with a kindergarten-to-grade-two class, some of the work becomes easier because the kindergarten children are in school for only half a day. Working intensively with children from grades one and two sets them on the path of working independently on such jobs as writing workshop or reading workshop. They will happily carry on their work while you give the kindergarteners your undivided attention, and then everyone joins in choosing or center time. Setting those predictable rhythms helps greatly in moving into the more individualized instruction that will characterize the latter months of your teaching year.

Setting routines and guidelines

Children like and thrive on predictable sequences of events in their day. Without giving up the option to vary the shape of your teaching day for special events, field trips, or visitors, you will find that your students enjoy the security of knowing how their day will unfold. As you encourage them to take steps on their own, they will feel ever more comfortable moving from one job to the next without waiting for you to tell them what to do when. (See also chapter 11, "The Day in Class.")

Routines also include ways of dealing with materials and jobs. If you model how books, writing materials, and games should be handled, the children will watch and then emulate you. Cleaning up, putting things away, and getting ready to go out all fall into easily recognized patterns if you encourage the children to do as much of the work as possible on their own initiative. They rise to the trust you place in them and will collaborate readily in setting rules or guidelines as the occasion demands.

Your own modeling of tactful, friendly, consistent behavior will go a long way toward establishing guidelines right from the start. But talking to children about how they feel when the room becomes too noisy, when others hit or push them, or when they refuse to share becomes the starting point of mutually agreed-on guidelines that are updated and added to as the year progresses and new situations suggest the need for more. As the

BUILDING ON THE STUDENTS' EXPERIENCE Cooperation among teachers to make smooth transitions for students eases the way for everyone. For example, at the beginning of the year the grade–two–three teacher in South Park School continues some of the routines that the incoming children had become used to in grade one. While she works on establishing a cohesive atmosphere, morning news and choosing time – which were daily features in grade one – remain part of the day. Children relate well to these activities and to each other and settle in happily. As they move into the school year, choosing time is gradually replaced by project time, during which students have a lot of choice of activity but in more limited subject areas. Journal writing and other writing activities gradually replace news time as children need less and less priming to find activities about which to write. The students make these gradual changes easily, and the teacher has the opportunity to stretch their repertoire of experiences and move them beyond the habit of, for example, always choosing one favorite activity or remaining passive during news time.

SHOWING THE CHILD YOU CAN BE TRUSTED ✳ Mutual trust is probably the most important factor in establishing rules and having them followed. Children can sense that you trust them to do their best, but to help them build trust in you, you must find ways to appear trustworthy in their eyes. Thus, you must be fair, consistent, loving, understanding, open-minded, genuine, flexible, enthusiastic, positive, and firm.

teacher you certainly have the power to lay down the ground rules, but the more you base these rules on needs as they arise and involve the children in reasoning out why specific rules would be helpful to all of them, the more likely those rules are to be followed.

When their own creativity is challenged in devising workable rules for their classroom, the destructive vent of the children's inner volcanoes becomes narrower and narrower. The children are busy; they themselves have set the guidelines and they have enough freedom to move and express themselves within those guidelines. They feel no need to watch for opportunities to act out. Guidelines and routines keep the work moving along smoothly. (See also chapter 4, "Who's in Charge Here Anyway?")

The teacher's way of setting the scene

All along the way you, the teacher, are setting the scene – providing learning materials, modifying work to fit students' personal needs, offering suggestions, modeling social behaviors and learning. Above all, you are constantly affirming the children's ability to work independently. You are building their self-confidence and pride in being effective learners.

You are also teasing the content for themes out of their discussions and news items. As you listen to your students, you pick out the topics that could involve and interest, if not the entire group, then a large segment of it. In any given year interests may range from camping to Egyptian mummies, from dinosaurs and monsters to ballet. As you encourage children to delve into these areas, the content becomes the matrix in which reading, writing, thinking, talking, and listening evolve. Active, purposeful involvement draws children of all ages and levels together to do research and learning that moves far beyond the primary curriculum, yet "the basics" are learned in that context as well. Because you consider the interests and needs of your learners from the very beginning of September, you draw them into a community of learners that will thrive and grow throughout the year.

8.
Activities That Involve All Learners

Classrooms filled with books, writing materials, math equipment, art materials, a variety of learning centers that change frequently, a play center, and perhaps a dress-up treasure chest invite all children to be active learners right from the beginning of the year. As they enter school they are eager to explore their new environment and to join in activities the teacher has planned to introduce them to the cooperative world of the classroom. Though some of the younger or more timid children may need extra encouragement at first, there are no age barriers to the whole-group activities that start the year and become the springboards for more individual work as the year unfolds.

All the activities we describe in this chapter are drawn from multi-age classrooms in which teachers and students collaborate to learn so effectively that visitors often have great difficulty in sorting out who are the young students and who the older ones. (At times it is even hard to spot the teacher. Margaret's principal has come into class and asked, "Where is your teacher?" only to find her working on the floor with the children.) Enthusiasm for learning and sharing the excitement of stories and interesting information carry the whole class along as the teacher shifts from being an information giver to being a co-creative learner.

Reading is for everyone

READING ALOUD

Reading aloud and enjoying the fun of sharing stories, familiar legends, or poetry have no age limit. There is no need to choose books with limited vocabulary. You can make every read-aloud session a special event that touches all the children in your class. When you read with expression and verve and enter the story with your whole being, children are drawn into the magic of imagination, interesting pictures, and rich language. They revel in rolling big new words off their tongues as they listen intently and expand their vocabularies in quite delightful and amazing ways.

Listening is not a passive time, but an invitation to enter into the story with thoughts and feelings. You put the children firmly on the road to becoming thoughtful readers as you model thinking aloud, "I wonder if my dog could find her way home if she was so far away." "I wonder what else Amelia is going to get into." "I've never seen a house like that. Have you?" "I wonder what it felt like to be lost like that."

Once you model the many possibilities of interacting with the stories, even the youngest children in your class will gather around to compare notes on how that story relates to them, what they know about similar incidents, and what other possibilities there are. Very soon reading aloud will generate careful listening that extends well beyond the usual perfunctory surface attention to thoughtful talking and shared feelings – both happy and sad – as you select books that touch on the special concerns of the children. Stories kindle interest, curiosity, and eagerness to delve in and look at those colorful pictures or try out those beautiful long words. If you make reading aloud an important part of your day, particularly at the beginning of the school year, even the youngest children will want to explore books on their own. Learning to read for meaning and enjoyment becomes a natural part of the daily use of books, and there will be no reluctant readers.

UNISON READING

Using big books or large charts of familiar songs, rhymes, or directions makes it easy to invite children to start reading along with you.

As you model expressive, fluent reading, the children follow along with their eyes, voices, and thoughts. Here again, you have a fine chance to observe who is reading right along, who is chiming in on the predictable parts only, and who is simply tracking the print with their eyes and an occasional quiet whisper.

Aside from the fun of joining together in a chorus of reading, by modeling your leadership in reading aloud, you are able to induce your more mature readers to come forward to lead such sessions for their younger peers during center or choosing time. And so whole-group work spawns all manner of personal and small-group reading that flourishes in the atmosphere of independence you have established.

Reading is inviting for all children when they have many materials to choose from during reading workshop.

READING WORKSHOP

If you can augment your own stock of books by calling in at the local public library, the

SUPER QUIET **READING**   By grade two, children have had enough experience with books to sit quietly by themselves to enjoy them. In Karen Abel's grade-two-three class, children settle down to "Super Quiet Reading." Some concessions are made for the youngest members of the class, who are allowed to get up quietly to exchange their books if they find it too hard to sit still for more than fifteen minutes at a time. But some of the older students settle down to quite advanced reading, tackling Tolkien's *Lord of the Rings* or stories about the Knights of the Round Table that are not just scaled-down versions for children. When writing about or discussing their reading, they give every evidence of having good levels of comprehension.   During the early part of the year most of the children will participate in "shared reading": talking to two or three of their friends about what they have just read. But as the year progresses, they become more and more involved in their own reading and simply use that extra time to continue to read quietly. By then the younger members of the class have evolved their reading skills further and are quite content to sit quietly with a selection of books for twenty to thirty minutes. Super Quiet Reading time is definitely for everyone.

school library, and the school resource center, you will have all the resources you need to start reading workshop (or "book time," as Margaret calls it) for all ages right from the beginning of the year. Having modeled the fun of reading stories and the excitement of extracting intriguing bits of information from nonfiction works, you have set the tone, and the children will be ready to rummage through your supply of reading materials to settle down with a stack of books at their tables. Your emergent readers may content themselves with looking at pictures, some quiet talking, and pretend reading, while your more mature readers will seek out their favorite authors or subject areas and settle down to intense quiet reading. But all are using books, and you can count on longer and longer reading workshops each day as the children become more and more involved with books of their choice.

Reading workshop is a wonderful opportunity for you to observe which books children choose, how often they reread a favorite, how long their attention span is on any given day, and who is eagerly waiting to share a favorite passage. Readers' theater, artwork, story writing, research projects, special activities, and lots of talk evolve from the group reading session, and regardless of level of proficiency, all the children see themselves as readers. Reading time will become longer and longer, and you will note that many children will expand their choice of books and extend reading into choosing time or even into recess.

After much negotiating, some manipulating, and lots of discussion, boys are ready to present their version of readers' theater.

To keep reading workshop interesting, change your supply of books regularly. Encourage children and parents to bring in books or magazines, and be sure to include a good selection of nonfiction materials to fit the interests of your students, whatever these are – animals, hockey, space travel, dolls, rocks and minerals, trains. Once they have been introduced to the school library and you have established a procedure for borrowing and returning books, the children will keep the classroom reading materials expanding and evolving to meet their changing interests and needs. Here again, you will find that there are no age limits. Quite young children can be very responsible when you give them the opportunity to do important tasks, and often they are the ones who come up with creative ideas for special interest projects or themes.

Interest themes and projects draw students together

Whether you follow the spur-of-the-moment suggestions of children or initiate them yourself to fulfill specific curriculum requirements, themes and projects draw students together to collaborate and learn. They create that "concrete matrix" or background that Caine and Caine (1991) talk about in connection with the effortless quality of "map learning" that grows and expands as learners interact with the world around them.

HANDS-ON ACTIVITIES BUILD LEARNING FOR EVERYONE

Themes and projects generally demand hands-on interactive activities, such as creating dioramas, doing artwork, acting and miming, building things, running experiments, and producing illustrated reports. A key ingredient for success is your flexibility in responding to the children's suggestions, questions, or creative ways of working. Here are some ideas that might serve as catalysts for your own – and your students' – creativity.

Converting the playhouse into a space rocket was the outcome when Margaret read *Space Witch* to her kindergarten-to-grade-two class. Once she responded positively to the children's suggestion, "Let's make a space rocket out of the playhouse!", the children set about to gather materials, find illustrations to help them, and brainstorm jointly to see what else could be added. Researching, planning, building, collaborating, and problem solving were shared by all. Margaret stayed in the background, helped locate materials, offered constructive comments,

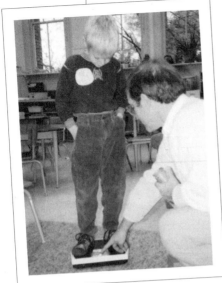

Weighing in the space travelers for their planet walk included calculating their relative weight on the various planets.

but mostly stood back to admire what had been accomplished.

An all-school astronomy unit drew in parents as well as the entire school, and here, too, hands-on, concrete work assured that all children were learning and participating fully. Papier-mâché models of planets, a planet walk that recreated the relative distances between planets, a delicious space lunch, and discussions surrounding the construction of a rocket ship were among the activities shared by the lower grades. Teachers provided materials, resource people from the community, and books and articles about space. And they joined the students in learning new and fascinating information about astronomy. In this instance, a science resource teacher came into the school to help the entire faculty make plans for their involvement in this all-school effort. Because factual learning was prodigious for teachers, students, and parents alike, enthusiasm for the unit was high right from the start, and the stargazing evening for the finale was an unqualified success.

Creating paper dinosaurs used the children's fascination with these prehistoric animals to foster research reading, careful drawing from observation, and comparative anatomy. The teacher provided a wide selection of books on dinosaurs and asked her students to create their very own dinosaurs. They first drew a number of heads, bodies, tails and limbs of the different dinosaurs they could find in the resource books available to them. Then they created composites of the body parts they had gleaned from their research and colored their paper creations in imaginative ways.

Their teacher Karen Abel had set the specific tasks of observing closely, compiling information, and thinking about the reasons for the different shapes and physical features of dinosaurs. In the fun context of creating imaginary prehistoric monsters, the children in her class learned research skills, information on comparative anatomy, lessons on herbivores and carnivores, and, above all, the skill of synthesizing information gleaned from books: first drawing out specific details, and then putting them back together in new and creative ways. The effortless map learning of which Caine and Caine speak certainly functioned at a high level. The context and activity – not a lecture on how to research and synthesize information – produced profound learning, and all children participated fully.

From there, the project expanded into team building, joint planning, problem solving, and cooperative artwork, as three teams gathered together to decide on and then create large background murals that depicted the habitats of their dinosaurs. As the three teams negotiated how to proceed and what to include, the teacher acted as a resource person who helped find additional information, suggested ways of reaching agreement during the planning and problem-solving sessions, and noted the different styles of teamwork and note taking that emerged.

To enhance the practical learning about teamwork, keeping track of decisions, and reaching a consensus, she then invited each team to describe how they had gone about doing the work. That debriefing became a highly effective closure that not only celebrated all the successes but also created an awareness of the importance of careful note taking and the need to respect each other's opinions and ways of working. Leadership qualities showed themselves, teamwork reached a new level, and all children were included in the work.

Creating a treasure map built a knowledge of cartography. At University Hill Elementary School in Vancouver we watched a group of about fifty children build contour maps. Two teachers - working together with their grade–three–four students - introduced the basics of map reading and construction by inviting their students to devise their very own treasure maps. They began by showing children examples of contour maps and then asked them to look at the many different features. With the help of the students, they created a list of the ways in which these maps provided information. Contours, symbols for north, color coding of elevation, legends to designate special features such as rivers, towns, and forests were included in the information. The teachers then provided paper, colors, glue, and scissors. She asked all the students, working in small groups, to create their own contour maps of secret treasure islands of their own designs using the information they had just abstracted from the contour maps provided.

Without lecturing about ways of reading and interpreting maps, the teachers created a concrete context for imparting all the necessary information to help the children build their own very effective inner maps of cartographic design and usage. The total absorption with which the children worked on their projects, pasting layer on layer of construction paper onto the base layouts for their secret treasure islands, left no doubt about the efficacy of the lesson for one and all. Since they were actually building maps to represent lakes, mountains, flatlands, and special surface features such as trees and houses, the learning was firmly anchored in hands-on work and engaged not only the right and left brains but emotions as well.

A look at the seasons as they change involves everyone. Sharing experiences of spring, summer, fall, and winter will elicit participation from most children. They will eagerly search out and share books that deal with the topics, and a unit on the seasons can get underway any time of the year. Scholastic Publishers includes a collection of books on the seasons in their "Reflexions" kit, but your own stock of books, augmented by those from the school librarian and others brought in by the students, will be the focal point for a discussion about favorite seasons. In fact, the invitation to find all the books that have anything to do with seasons can spark interesting discussions as children justify their choices.

Special holidays such as Easter, Christmas, Chinese New Year, or Rosh Hashanah add further impetus. When a mother came in to show the children the intricately decorated Ukrainian Easter eggs (*pysanke*) she had collected over the years, they asked their teacher to help them create their own *pysanke*. The parent produced design charts to help the students and came in to give a physical demonstration. The work became a fine example of students working at and benefiting from their own levels of ability. The youngest among them colored the eggs and added a few decorative details, while the most mature produced intricately planned *pysanke*, paid close attention to the symbolism of the colors and designs, and transferred their new-found knowledge to artwork they were producing in other projects. All learned about the special customs of another culture, enhanced their artistic skills, and participated in and enjoyed the project.

Reality captivates students and engages them in projects that connect to the world beyond school. As at

Even kindergarten children can participate in creating graphs when the topics are familiar and concrete.

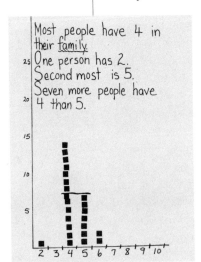

home, everyone collaborates on such work, benefiting greatly from peer modeling and mutual support. High on the list are such activities as cooking, making gifts or greeting cards for special occasions, and participating in fundraising or charity activities launched by the school. The latter certainly raise the math proficiency of all participants, and there is no question of declaring that students are too young or too old to take part in any of these activities.

Such projects as hatching chicks

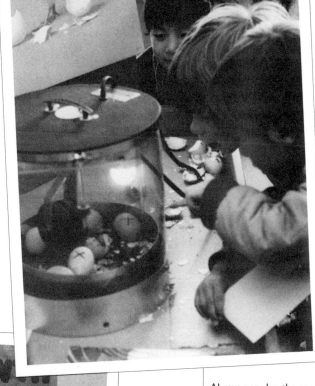

Always popular, the annual chick-hatching project stirs students' interest in learning about living organisms. Everyone participates enthusiastically— from students to the custodian to the principal. One year, even the assistant superintendent came into the classroom to help name the chicks.

in an incubator, raising salmon fingerlings in an aquarium and then releasing them into a local stream, looking after pets in the classroom, or raising plants for transplanting into home or school gardens are among the favorites. Children of all ages learn to chart growth, and keep track of conditions that foster or hamper development. Careful record keeping is practiced by one and all.

Devising ways of taking care of our environment and studying how each of us can contribute to conservation and the ecological balance is almost always of interest to students. They eagerly participate in the lunch-time compost collection of all food waste, the recycling of lunch bags, the use of cloth towels to cut down on the waste of paper, and many more such interventions of their own design. Serious discussions about air and water pollution and ways of cutting back on the deterioration in our environment elicit thoughtful suggestions and very intense listening.

No doubt you have your own list of favorite projects that connect to local activities and have found many ways of drawing visiting experts to the classroom to enhance your own knowledge as well as that of the children.

USING LITERATURE TO FOSTER LEARNING

Children's literature enlivens geography lessons and leads to close cooperation between teacher and librarian. As she was required to teach children in her grade-two-three class the fundamentals of Canadian geography, Anne Peterson sought the help of her school librarian to find as many books by Canadian authors and illustrators as possible. Information on the writers' homes and personal backgrounds enhanced the information packet, and everyone including the teacher not only learned about the home towns and provinces of the writers but also developed a feel for the many regions of their country.

On the surface it may have seemed as though there was far too much story reading and looking at pictures, but in reality all the children were internalizing very personal lessons about Canada and its geography as they read, listened, discussed, and then transferred some of their knowledge to maps and charts of Canada.

Creating miniature gardens based on stories from children's literature integrated biology, art, and language arts and gave even nonreaders a chance to express their appreciation of stories in concrete ways.

Kate from The Secret Ga... This is before Mary got into the garden to fix it up. The cat is sneaking up on a mouse. Mrs. Medlock is smelling the fragrance of the flowers.

Literary gardens foster reading and teach creative design. Faced with the need to abandon plans for planting a real garden on the school grounds, Karen Abel discussed possible alternatives with her grade-

THERE ARE MANY WAYS TO EXTEND AND ASSESS WRITING ✳ To extend her students' writing, Karen Abel asks her grade–two–three students to retell stories. She finds a straightforward retelling is an excellent gauge of her students' levels of writing development. The most advanced students provide a full account of the story and its high points. Less mature students may offer the beginning and end, leave out important parts, or focus on one aspect of the story only. Based on her assessment, Karen will spend extra time with her emergent writers to talk about how stories unfold with a beginning, middle, and end. In the meantime her mature writers are off on their own projects. ✳ After reading *A Horse Called Farmer* to her class, Karen invited her students to retell the story. To add interest, challenge, and fun to the work, she suggested they write the story as if told by the human farmer, by Farmer the horse, by the horse in the next stall to Farmer, or by a visitor to the island where Farmer lives. ✳ When her advanced writers sug-gested they do a research project on horses instead of retelling the story, Karen worked separately with them to model research strategies. Picking cows as an example of a research topic, Karen demonstrated different ways of finding and extracting information, taking notes using mind maps or a grid, and entering only two to three words on each topic to avoid copying whole sentences from the source books. Once her students had accumulated a body of information, she demon-strated how to put the bits and pieces into coherent sentences and then para-graphs. ✳ Here again, stu-dents worked at their own levels of development. Her most advanced writers readily produced para-graphs; those less skilled simply strung the infor-mation together into a continuous flow. But throughout the project all the students par-ticipated in writing about "Farmer the horse," all received the teacher's attention when they needed it, and all had satisfying writing practice that stretched their repertoires.

Spiders				
Kinds of Spiders	Body Parts	Size	Nets	What They Eat

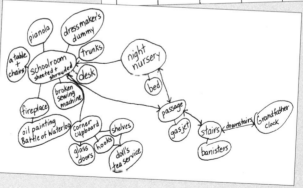

two-three students. Together they decided to create miniature gardens based on stories in literature. The stories selected by the children ranged from *The Secret Garden* to *Bambi* and *Jack and the Beanstalk*. As students set about creating figures and small creatures to people their gardens, parents assembled a selection of plants and brought in trays and potting soil. Needless to say, the custodian was an important participant, and the multi-age collaboration was stretched to its fullest with wonderful results.

Social studies and science are enriched by using literature and special stories as well as textbooks. Instead of relying principally on textbooks and lectures to convey information in content studies, reading to the children and inviting them to look at books and articles on the topic at hand enriches their learning and draws all children into discussions and information sharing. Here again, collaboration with your librarian will be wonderfully productive, and children will extend their reading in class and at home if an interesting collection of books is available to them. Parents will tell you about their own learning as their children bring books home, and many will volunteer information or send in additional materials that will enhance your learning too. Co-creative teaching/learning functions at its best, and children will demonstrate that their capacity to learn from books stretches far beyond the carefully controlled readers or textbooks of old.

(previous page) Students become proficient researchers when mind maps and grids serve as research tools to extract information from textbooks or details for drawings or retellings from literature.

Drawing a story map based on a list of criteria brainstormed by the students.

MAKING THE READING/WRITING CONNECTION

Reading and listening to stories build children's vocabulary and help them to internalize the patterns and conventions of book language. As a favorite is read and listened to again and again, its style begins to show itself in the children's writing. As they move beyond picture captions into story writing and reports, you will find that the writing style of their stories reflects more than just the once-upon-a-time opening, and that reports on animals or sports are couched in the language of the source materials you have provided.

Field trips are wonderful sources for learning

Field trips don't have to involve driving or going to the beach, the farm, or the forest. Instructive and exciting though they are, they can simply be the icing on a very rich cake. Here are examples of field-trip destinations that can provide unique and individual benefits for all students in classes from kindergarten to grade six:

* local stores
* fire station/police station
* hospital
* veterinary hospital
* home for the elderly
* public library
* local tourist attractions
* kitchen of a large hotel
* Chinese restaurant at Chinese New Year
* kitchen of a pizza restaurant
* local schools (high school, middle school)
* local radio and TV stations
* neighborhoods around the school
* legislature
* art galleries and museums

With the help of parents, students and teachers can also make special trips farther afield (often complete with picnics) to such places as the following:

* pumpkin farm
* local salmon stream to observe spawning salmon
* beach with tidal pools
* local parks
* nature sanctuary
* dairy

Such trips are neither unplanned nor are they wasteful of valuable learning time. Discussing with students what to expect, what to look for, how to collaborate or look after each other, and what rules of conduct to observe on the trip are vital to success. Obtaining children's input and having them help set the rules and decide what might arise from the trip enrich such discussions and allow students to make the information and rules their own.

Drawing things together in a discussion after the trip is equally important. Once everyone has settled back into the routine of the classroom, the students are ready to discuss what happened, what exciting discoveries were made, what questions or problems arose, what (if any) means of reporting on the trip might be fun and effective, and how future trips could be improved. If students know that you take their thoughts, questions, and suggestions seriously, they will advance comments and often quite ingenious ideas for interpreting or improving field trips. They are also open to suggestions from you. For example, capturing the enthusiasm engendered by their visit to a veterinary hospital, Margaret suggested that the children might like to change their playhouse into a veterinary hospital, and the kindergarten–grade-one class was on its way. They made suggestions and did all the work. All it took was capitalizing on their interest and enthusiasm when it was bubbling over.

Talking, reading, and writing about these field trips definitely extend the concrete learning. When making reports about some of these outings, the more mature students in a multi-age classroom will act as scribes for their younger peers and encourage them to contribute not only information but also illustrations and artifacts collected on the field trips. The caring, sharing, and collaboration in evidence while the students are outside of school extends to the in-class work connected with field trips as well.

Writing serves many functions

If you make reading and writing natural and important parts of your day in class right from the first day of school, students will come to see print as natural a part of communication as talking. Though they themselves are not yet writing, kindergarteners will begin to contribute to news time and use artwork and perhaps pretend writing as their way of communicating on paper. Modeling fluent writing that is meaningful and connects with the children's thinking will produce the same kind of learning that talking produces when baby is not yet ready to respond with real words. Messages are conveyed, patterns can be recognized, and babbling in print proves as productive a stage in written communication as oral babbling is in beginning stages of oral communication. So just as reading is for everyone, so writing is for everyone too.

COMPOSING AND SPELLING ARE MODELED IN NEWS TIME

The daily session of printing the news on the board based on open discussions and suggestions made by the children becomes a most important skill-building activity for everyone. Though guessing and quiet watching are very much the order of the day at the beginning of the school year, when neither kindergarteners nor most of the first-graders have a solid grounding in their knowledge of spelling and composing, they all observe and listen keenly as you model printing, spelling, thinking aloud, and reading back what you have just put on the board. From that beginning, your more mature students will quickly learn to participate, and they in turn will become models for their less experienced peers. If there is a wide divergence between the oldest and youngest children in your class, you may want to hold a separate news session for the older children when they first come in and another one for kindergarteners as they join the class. But at times all the children will work together, and all will listen closely to you and to each other as news time unfolds.

WRITING WORKSHOP TAKES MANY FORMS

The information offered during news time and the discussion of events or thoughts of interest to the children become the springboard for writing workshop. The open sharing of ideas helps students decide on topics for their personal writing. The less experienced children may simply opt to work on one of the favorite topics put forth by one or more or their older peers – wrestling, rainbows, Nintendo, and upcoming parties. And at the beginning of the year the younger children may spend most of their time producing pictures and then thinking of a caption that they can produce in pretend writing. But all children sit down to communicate on paper in some way.

As the year progresses, your more mature students will cover page after page producing stories, books, and reports. They will want to use every moment of writing workshop to expand their writing. To give them time to unfold their skills fully, expand the time allotted to writing workshop week by week without making unreasonable demands on the less mature writers. By setting (and constantly updating) appropriate minimum production guidelines for individual children – a picture and a caption, two lines of print, three sentences, five sentences, and so on – you will stretch their writing without pressuring them. Quite often they will show you that they are ready to extend their writing beyond their current minimum. But once they have completed their minimum, children are free to move to the various language arts centers available to them.

Center time is everyone's favorite

Very early in our joint in-class research we noted that discipline was far easier to maintain during center time than during more structured desk-bound activities. There may be more talking and interacting among children during those periods, but their talk is generally task-oriented. This means that when Margaret works with the kindergarteners she finds few occasions to admonish the older children to do their work, stop playing, or lower their voices. Similarly, during writing workshop, if more mature students continue to write, their less experienced peers will quietly and independently move to centers of their choice. At times the entire class engages in free-choice or center time, and collaboration among younger and older students is high.

Center time is another occasion when you will be able to make close observations of the choices that children make, how they interact with learning materials and with each other, who is opting to continue writing and reading, who needs more playtime or physical activity, and who is in need of special encouragement. While all students are busy with activities of their choice, you have the opportunity to engage individual children in a phonics game, an adding-and-subtracting activity, or some one-to-one reading or talking.

Math is for everyone

MAKING MATH CONCRETE IN EVERYDAY WORK

Providing pattern blocks, Unifix cubes, dice, playing cards, play money in the class store, and weights and measures for keeping track of science experiments makes math concrete and accessible to everyone. If you use every opportunity to incorporate number work into

"**T**UBBING" GETS EVERYONE INVOLVED   "Tubbing" is one way of getting all children involved in math activities despite the obvious differences in their levels of skills. Karen Abel describes her way of preparing clusters of math activities and placing them into six separate tubs, each to be used by four or five children. This kind of grouping could work for any math work such as measurement, work with fractions, and multiplication and division, but the graphic example she provided was working with money.   Karen began by doing some preparatory exploration to find children's levels of knowledge and expertise. While some children were busy with quiet desk work, she would sit with other children to observe their interactions with coins and with each other. Simply asking children to count money provided insights into who was quite proficient, who had a reasonably good idea about the numerical values and ways of working with money – grouping all nickels, all dimes, and all quarters – and who was still unsure about the values of the various coins.   From there she prepared the activities that went into each tub – some quite simple and others fairly complex. After showing the materials to the children, she discussed with them how long each group would want to work with the tubs. The students opted for two math periods with each tub. Before the next math period, Karen asked the children, "Who knows about money and can be a helper to others?" "Who would like some help?" After noting the names of those in each category on the chalkboard, Karen put together teams that had a mix of confident workers and students who still needed help.   As each of the teams worked with the activities in its tub, Karen observed how the work progressed, who was adding and subtracting effectively, who was regrouping money to make larger units, who was ready to move on, and who needed more practice. As the tubs rotated among the teams, she did some regrouping to give more proficient children a challenge and those in need of more practice plenty of time to work at their level.   Aside from learning math facts – adding, subtracting, grouping – the children also had wonderful practice in teamwork and being mutually supportive.

daily activities, children absorb their math facts within the context of interesting work, and learning math presents few problems. Such tasks as taking roll call in the morning, counting students, getting ready for apple sales to raise funds, keeping track of recipes during cooking sessions, and handing out supplies – so many sheets, colors, or whatever – give students that sense of using math for real-life purposes. Integrating math into everyday work becomes the incentive to learn basic facts and convinces children that they need those facts for something important.

Age is not necessarily the determining factor in proficiency. Temperament, learning style, insufficient practice, and overall maturity are all important factors. At times, based on a combination of these factors, a younger child will be far more proficient than an older classmate, who may, in turn, be particularly good in language arts or artistic work. As a result, children accept each other as equal classmates. With the collaborative work of "tubbing," even math gives all students the opportunity to work at the same activity.

What's left?

Once you consider all the possible whole-group activities, there is really very little left that requires separate lessons or special sessions to accommodate the various levels of maturity and knowledge your students bring to their learning. With math included in the hands-on work and special projects that incorporate work with money, weights, and measures or the need to graph observations, children of all levels of proficiency can participate.

If you adopt the attitude that all children will participate in the activities in class at their own levels and according to their own interests and experiences, you can stop worrying about having to teach separate lessons to each group in your class. The children's ability to work independently leaves you free to work with individuals or small groups to meet their specific needs - to help less mature students with their special needs and to extend the work of your most advanced students in reading, writing, math, or special areas of interest.

Starting the Flow
of Learning

Looking at ways of getting activities underway reminds us of the old saying, "You can lead a horse to water but you can't make it drink." A lively wag once pointed out that, while that may be true, "You can sure make the horse thirsty." That's what starting the flow of learning is all about: making the children thirst for more - getting them so involved they can hardly wait for the next story to be read, the opportunity to explore, the quiet time to sit down and draw or write, or the chance to run the next science experiment. Here is where the myth that "the teacher is not doing anything" is truly laid to rest. Setting the climate for learning, and infusing children with interest, curiosity, and enthusiasm is a big job, but a very satisfying one. As in so much of the "teacher's way," the benefits of making the children thirst for learning reward the teacher as much as the children.

No matter what their ages, children, like adults, work most effectively and enthusiastically when they pursue their own interests. And whenever they work in a context of activities that are concrete and meaningful to them, they learn in the same effortless way we do when we create inner maps. The process-oriented curricula found in most year 2000 documents give you lots of room to build on children's interests, while you use that rich context to help them learn all the essential skills. However, you are still left with the question, "But how do I get them started? How do I begin the flow of activity and learning?" In chapter 5 we talked about the importance of kid watching and its power to teach you more about children than did all your theoretical work at university. Here we want to provide some concrete examples of converting those observations into actions – actions that start productive work and the flow of learning.

Listening attentively gets activities started

Have you ever had the experience of listening attentively to someone who was holding forth on topics of interest to her and then having her thank you for "the wonderful conversation" you just had? You may have contributed little or nothing to her flow of ideas, but the fact that you were clearly attending to what she had to say was so encouraging that she felt you were actually in a dialogue with her. That feeling kept the flow of her ideas and talk moving right along.

Children respond in the same way. If you can let go of that inner voice that keeps reminding you of the plans you have for the day and the many things you have to accomplish, then you can focus your entire attention on the children and what they are saying. Like your adult friends, children will feel free to talk and will keep their ideas flowing when they sense that you are giving them your undivided attention. The unspoken message that you are interested in them and in what they have to say is the key to opening the flow of communication between you.

GATHERING INFORMATION AT THE BEGINNING OF THE DAY

Informal times are often best for opening lines of communication. The milling around as children take off their coats, deposit their lunch boxes, and say hello to each other puts no constraint on easygoing chatter. If you are greeting children, listening to them, and exchanging a few words with parents who have come in that morning, you are part of that informal talk that flows naturally from the children's need to communicate with those around them. Most will soon include you in their confidences and talk to you as easily and freely as they do to their peers.

Letting go of your mental agenda for the day will be easier if you tell yourself firmly that by listening to the children, you are gathering valuable information, not only about minor and major events in their lives, but more important, about their hopes, fears, concerns, interests, and special needs. As well as making the morning ritual of greeting the children a means of taking the temperature of the class, you are finding out that Luis is still deeply concerned about losing his father and likely will continue to brood when invited to think about writing, that Marcia is all excited about the arrival of a baby sister and needs to talk about that big event throughout the day, that Renu is worried about moving and needs reassurance, and that Garry still frets about leaving his mother to come to school but loves to go to his karate lessons (which will continue to be his topic for writing).

You have always known that feelings – both positive and negative – can greatly influence how children react to you, the children around them, and to any learning you want to instill. And now that emotional and social development are integral parts of many curriculum documents, you know that to pay close attention to these important aspects of children's lives is an acknowledged part of your role as a teacher. So listening attentively, not only to the words but to the underlying feelings and messages, takes on new importance and significance.

Rather than locking yourself into intricate plans, be prepared to adapt your teaching to fit the particular needs of the children that day. Listening with care will help you identify the teachable moments. By sensing the mood of children as they enter the class, you can make a quick decision about what to read to them that day – maybe something about moving, about babies, about being alone with one parent – giving some extra time to those children who have a special need for personal reassurance and encouraging those who need to share their special excitement or concerns during sharing or news time. Since you plan to make practical use of the information you gather as you listen to the children, you will have no problem being genuinely interested in what they have to say. Children are highly sensitive observers and readily spot a pretend listener whose mind is far away. But when they know that you are paying close attention to their every word, even the less verbal children become eager to talk. Since their teacher is listening to them intently, children say to themselves, "If she really listens to me, I must have something important to say." That kind of thought builds positive self-concept and shores up self-confidence.

ARGARET'S TIME CAPSULE When Margaret meets with the whole class first thing each morning, she shuts out the rest of the world and is present for no one but the children:

I feel totally involved in morning meeting. Nothing interferes! I feel as if the children and I are in a time capsule that admits no outside interferences. Any worries or concerns that I bring to school with me are forgotten as I get totally involved with the children, their thoughts, and their feelings. In turn, they feel acknowledged and important as we enter into our exchange of news and concerns, our planning, and our problem solving.

Children also seem to enter that time capsule and resent having the spell broken. For example, after one morning meeting had been interrupted several times and Margaret had to get up yet one more time to answer the door, five-year-old Jake loudly voiced his frustration: "Gosh! There she goes! Off that darn chair again!"

CREATING A FLOW OF TALK FOR GENERAL SHARING AND NEWS TIME

That readiness to talk carries forward into your morning session in front of the chalkboard. Sharing and news time evolve quite naturally out of the informal talk at the door. But with those children who respond with silence to your invitation to share their news, you may need to prime the pump to start the flow of information. You may want to ask Marcia to share her news about her new baby brother or invite Garry to tell everyone about his karate lesson. When all else fails, you might comment, "Well, while you are thinking of what news you want to share, let me tell you what happened to me!" and follow up with an anecdote about an incident that happened on your way home, while you were shopping, as you were walking your dog, when you went to a special show, or anything that is likely to elicit a "That's what we did [saw, heard]!" When children realize that you are simply asking them to recount something that happened to them or that they observed, and that you are interested in hearing about it, they will soon respond.

Often one child will start to talk about a TV show, a movie, a sports event, a visit to Santa, or a walk in the snow. Then others will start to chime in, and two or three of them will turn to each other to discuss their news more fully. At that point you become a moderator, making sure the discussion does not ramble on too long or becomes either a lengthy monologue or a small-group discussion that does little to involve the rest of the students. As the children talk, watch the rest of the group for restlessness and other signs of boredom. If a child monopolizes news time or rambles on for too long, intervene with a suggestion that he expand on the topic during writing workshop: "That sounds like a wonderful topic for you in writing workshop! Why don't you think about everything you can write about...." Or suggest that students continue their discussion during recess: "I can really see that the three of you are very interested in.... Maybe you can get together during recess and talk some more."

Since the aim of the morning meeting is to encourage children to talk, to express thoughts and opinions, to exchange information, and to interact positively, the tone and manner in which you intervene is of paramount importance. If you can recall childhood incidents when teachers cut you short or dismissed your verbal input in a hurtful way, you know the importance of guiding the talk in class with tact and sensitivity. And so, in redirecting verbal messages into more appropriate channels as suggested above, Margaret makes certain to acknowledge the value of and her interest in the information the children have volunteered. Just as she tunes in to the children's thought processes and concerns, so the children read her thoughts and attitudes, and they know that she will never simply cut them off, thus hurting their feelings or dampening their enthusiasm.

Starting the flow of talk and maintaining it at a level that works for everyone in the class takes some practice, but here, as in most of your teaching, modeling is the key to starting the flow of learning. And accepting the children's responses is the way to keep it moving right along. As children take turns giving their news for the day, Margaret acknowledges everyone's contribution, maintains eye contact, asks a clarifying question when it seems appropriate, and focuses all her attention on the speaker. If the news is quite personal - "My dad is going to take me fishing," "I got a doll for my birthday," or "We went to see *Snow White* last night" – she may comment, "That would be a great topic for your writing workshop" or "I have a wonderful story about.... You may want to read that today." Then she asks for some "news that concerns all of us." During the early part of the year, she may start the flow of news by commenting about special events, upcoming treats or projects, or information about the community or school. But very soon, the children need no further prompting and supply news items that will go on the chalkboard that day.

Shifting from more general sharing into giving information that concerns most of the group leads to a new burst of sharing. Then there is some sifting of topics to decide which news items should become part of the news of the day:

MARGARET: That sounds interesting. Shall we put on the board that we are looking forward to bicycle safety week?"

STUDENT 1: Yea. We could say, "Next week is bicycle safety week."

STUDENT 2: Maybe we could say, "We bring in our bicycles."

MARGARET: O.K. Do you all agree that we will write about bicycle safety week? [and after general consensus is reached] We have two good ideas already. Which sentence do you want first?

From there the children readily volunteer new sentences and advice on revising the ones already on the board. They know Margaret's question, "Shall we put that on the board today?" is genuine, because if the children decide that they would rather pick another news item for the board, Margaret accepts their choice, just as she accepts their decisions in editing. If Margaret's suggestion "Maybe we need to improve these sentences," is met with "Sounds fine to us," she agrees to their suggestions for improvement – as long as they do not violate rules of grammar.

That kind of listening and accepting assures that children will feel both safe and heard. They know that their ideas will not be rejected out of hand. As a result they continue to contribute news, and more important, they feel free to formulate and express opinions, secure in the knowledge that what they say will be listened to with interest and respect. Once they have been heard and their ideas have been acknowledged, children are quite ready to see some other news go on the board, but they never feel that *their* good idea has been spurned. Nor is there any pressure to come up with something! If a child has nothing to contribute or forgets what he was going to say just as Margaret asks for it, she will say, "That's all right, just think about it for a while, and when you remember what you wanted to say, let me know and I'll come back to you." So there are no command performances, no cutoffs, just genuine solid listening that never fails to start the flow of talking.

The genuine give-and-take between teacher and students sets a climate that encourages open communication and enhances spontaneity. If you can think back with pleasure to times when you had the warm feeling of being acknowledged and valued as an important contributor to a discussion or project, you will know how much that feeling enhanced your willingness and ability to be both creative and productive in your thinking and talking.

TRANSLATING INTERESTS INTO ACTIONS

As children reveal their special interests, encourage them to expand on them and share them with others. When Robert talked only about cowboys, Margaret encouraged him to continue talking, to look for books on the topic in the library, and to bring in his own books and pictures so that other children could look at them. As they, in turn, became engrossed, reading, talking, and writing became enlivened by the new content to be explored. Then the children decided to turn the playhouse into a ranch house, and a unit of researching life on a ranch was underway.

If you encourage expression and genuinely enter into the quest for new and interesting information, most children will join your exploration. Nor does it matter what the topic of interest is - pets, the disappearance of a young boy, war, death, books, field trips, family events. One of the keys to stimulating interest and imagination is to make your questions or comments open-ended.

Margaret recalls visiting a classroom and watching little Amanda rush in bubbling with excitement, "I saw the Goodyear blimp! It flew right over my house!" Her teacher turned to her, smiled and responded, "How interesting. I saw it too." Amanda's face fell. There was nothing to say after that response. The teacher knew all about the blimp and needed no further information. But looking around her for another chance, she approached another adult saying once again, "I saw the Goodyear blimp!" This time she was rewarded with, "Did you?! Tell me about it!" and the flow of descriptions and feelings rushed forward. Her teacher's answer and smile had been genuine, but the message cut off the opportunity to elaborate further, which Amanda was eager to do.

This incident underscores the importance of observing closely how children react to comments or questions when we are trying to foster open communication. In her own classroom, Margaret has done a lot of "wondering about" things to see what insightful or imaginative answers the children will come up with.

Once you look on your listening as a way to pan for nuggets that can become treasures of solid gold learning, you will find them quite frequently. You will develop a subtle sense for finding gold mines of information that will capture the imaginations of a large segment of your students. When you express your interest and ask the children's opinions about what might be done to find more information, all of you learn more about all kinds of topics – boats, sharks, Halley's comet, Hawaii, sea shells, gardening. As well as looking for books on a topic, you might muse aloud, "I wonder if that would make a new center" or "Do you suppose we could find some shells, butterflies, leaves, and other things to create a diorama?" or "Maybe we could visit the beach [a garden, the park] to check that out" or "What do you suppose *we* could do to help save the environment?"

Such musing is an open invitation to the children to take the subject further. As you develop a sense for the possibilities inherent in topics children raise, you will find that while direct questions of what,

CHILDREN BECOME TOWN PLANNERS   During news time, when one of the children commented that a lot of new houses were going to be built right next to his home, the children indicated a lively interest. To use that interest as a lead-in to a social studies unit on family living and town planning, Margaret encouraged the discussions and arranged for a visit to the site of the new housing development. Back in the classroom the children developed their own town. It was laid out on the floor and took up about a quarter of the floor space. Children made houses and service buildings out of Manila tagboard (and in the process learned about folding paper in squares and rectangles).   To plan the layout of their town, they discussed and decided where they would want to live – near a lake, a beach, a park, close to a friend. From there they decided where schools and banks needed to be located and where the center of town should be. As the children brought in their toy cars and pushed them around the town, decisions needed to be made about where the roads and highways should be. Pollution, traffic control, and safety became topics to be debated. As children added tiny dolls to people their town, pedestrian safety needed to be worked out. The project extended over weeks, and the custodian was greatly relieved when the children finally decided that they had exhausted all the possibilities of working with their model town.

when, why, or where can act to shut down discussion because they feel like tests in disguise, "just wondering" will elicit an enthusiastic response more often than not. Once ideas have taken shape, children will join you in a problem-solving session and they, not you, will ask the necessary questions: What is possible to do? What materials do we need? Who's going to help? Who knows something about this? Brainstorming will be rich and enjoyable, and there will be no hard feelings as the possible is sifted from the more impractical (though often exciting) ideas. Enjoy these sessions fully. Marvel at the increasing creativity both you and the children experience, in a climate that gives imagination free rein and is always open to input.

Along with sophisticated information supplied by outside experts, special field trips, and visits to the museum, reading, writing, researching, talking, listening, and problem solving will all be part of these spontaneous project-planning sessions. The basics will become part of the children's inner maps because they are learning them in the context of concrete projects that they have generated themselves. If you keep a scoreboard of your more pressing curriculum goals, you will find that you can not only check off the basics but will also have to add a lot of extra skills and knowledge because the learning has become so much richer than the basics alone imply. (See chapters 12 and 13, on the curriculum and buddies, for examples of scoreboards that relate the curriculum to what is happening in class.)

Drawing children to reading

Looking back to your childhood, do you remember the enchantment of bedtime stories, of sitting on someone's lap and having your favorite book read yet one more time, of knowing exactly what was coming next and eagerly chiming in? Children who come to school with that experience have little trouble relating to reading as an enjoyable and useful activity. But there will be other children who have no knowledge of the joys of story reading and are quite in the dark about what it means to read.

When we started our first joint research project, Margaret followed a structured approach to reading instruction by first teaching phonics and limited sight words. But close observation of children learning to read revealed that many of them had not yet discovered that reading is supposed to make sense. As they misread words, substituting others that did not fit the context, they showed no sign that they thought that meaning mattered. They were "saying all the words" and that was what it was all about. Some would read each word with the same emphasis, oblivious to the fact that phrasing draws words into meaningful units. Having just read aloud the words *here, we, go*, one young reader looked back over them, scanned them again, and suddenly had that bright *aha!* look as he exclaimed, "Hey! Here we go!" Once those disconnected words had made a pattern, he discovered that they actually conveyed a message.

We collected many other examples that attested to the fact that many children did not understand the purpose of reading. For example, they ignored the signals given by punctuation marks and read the end of one sentence and the beginning of the next as though they were a unit that formed a phrase. Thus, they might have read *go house Lucky* (when the text showed *go home, Lucky*) and looked thoroughly puzzled when the teacher asked them if that reading made sense to them.

We also found that the children did not use the phonics lessons in the way they were intended. When asked to make new words by replacing the beginning consonant of, for example, *mat*, they would produce non-words like *lat* and *gat* just as readily as real words. When Margaret offered *and* as the stimulus word for adding new consonants, the children found that what they had learned was the rule, "you take the first letter off, and put another one in front." They took the *a* off and produced *snd* instead of *sand*. No doubt you can look back on times when children's responses indicated to you that while they performed the task you set them, they did not necessarily learn the intended lesson. Though Margaret's students did the assigned work, the majority showed neither enthusiasm for reading nor desire to practice it.

To draw children into reading, the first and foremost task is to have them understand clearly that reading is meant to make sense, that it has many uses and can be very enjoyable. Like adults, children resist learning tasks that have neither utility nor appeal. But once they are drawn into the world of stories, learning to read becomes as natural as learning to talk – and fun too! (Learning about the alphabet and that stories and print are composed of letters is best conveyed during writing sessions, when children need that information to do their composing and spelling.)

THE STORYBOOK ROAD

Drawing children into reading and having them recognize what usefulness and joy it holds for them involves quite a different approach from the one Margaret used all those years ago. Beginning the year with lots of read-aloud sessions that give children that wonderful feeling of sharing fun and excitement will put them on the road to true functional literacy and give them the ability and desire to use reading throughout the day – and throughout their lives. As they listen to the stories, follow along with their eyes as you run your hand or a pointer along the lines in big books or on large charts, children are no longer in doubt about how reading works and how it is intended to make sense. Reading is for meaning, and there is a definite progression from left to right and from the top of the page to the bottom. So children's story time learning involves far more than just having a good time. It sets a pattern for reading practice and inculcates many skills, not the least of which is listening to more than words and their sounds.

CAPTURING THE MAGIC OF READING

To capture the magic of reading and instill a thirst for reading in your students, make every story session a memorable event. To add zest to your reading, pick books that *you* enjoy, that are fun, and that express emotions that both you and the children can enter into freely. Then put your whole being into that read-aloud session to draw the children into the story. Modulate your voice, create characters with your intonation, break into song when songs are included, and show the emotions of the characters on your face and in your gestures. As the children perceive that you are reading with your whole being, they, too, will invest all of themselves in the story.

From such high-energy read-aloud sessions the children learn that reading involves feelings and the stories contain messages that may relate to them personally – all without lessons, explanations, or tedious worksheets. Their map minds absorb the unspoken lessons about functional literacy effortlessly and eagerly. They easily absorb how much reading and books have to offer, how reading works, and how many different cues there are to help you extract information and pleasure from books and stories. No amount of phonics drill and worksheet fill-ins on rhyming words is going to instill the thirst for reading that your read-aloud sessions do. Without that thirst, all the phonics in the world will not produce lifelong readers who see books and reading as natural parts of their everyday lives.

THERE ARE GENUINE LESSONS IN ALL THIS READING

The read-along sessons also invite children to become actively involved with the story or text, to think, to expand their vocabularies, and to use their sense of language and rhythm to attend fully. Using predictable books with repetitive patterns - for example, *Brown Bear Brown Bear, I Was Walking Down the Road*, or *What Do You Do with a Kangaroo?* – holds the attention of the very young readers in your class and invites them to chime in. In the process of having fun and feeling competent as "readers," the young children learn an essential skill that fluent readers use so often – predicting what comes next. Healy (1990) has written extensively and persuasively about the vital importance of developing children's sense of language rhythms and patterns, and her research has revealed the dearth of such learning in homes where children spend hours passively watching television – an activity that invites no response from them.

Familiar nursery rhymes, songs, or the children's own writings serve the same purpose as predictable books and teach students the use of familiar phrasing and language patterns as a way to gain fluency and comprehension. Once they hear these books, they want more and ask to hear them again and again. They begin to make the stories their own, and if you leave inviting pauses in just the right places, a chorus of voices provides the next words or following line to everyone's great satisfaction.

As you model reading these familiar materials and then make them available for practice, children will emulate your reading right down to your body language and every nuance of intonation. At that early stage they may be drawing largely on memory, but they are also following your hand motions to trace the lines and words, picking up sight words and the rhythm and flow of book language.

Children in your class who have their own literature of legends, folk tales, or special songs that reflect their ethnic or cultural backgrounds will respond well to such special reading material. It not only draws them into reading in a natural and meaningful way, but also acknowledges and affirms their home learning and special culture. Because they can see their own lives in these readings – which they may not perceive in some of your favorites – they are drawn into the world of reading and accept it as a natural part of communication. Practice becomes voluntary, joyful, and prodigious.

The example of working with children from a different cultural background underscores the fact that personal relevance, interest, and enjoyment are the key to activating the children's map minds in reading. As you create a context of meaningful and useful reading, children are drawn into literacy in ways that not only foster good comprehension from the start but make reading so interesting, enjoyable, and easy that children are eager to practice and learn. At the outset they may tell you, "I can read without looking too!" as one of Margaret's kindergarteners did, but from that "memory reading" they move on to true reading using sight words, phrasing, and, yes, phonics to help them with unfamiliar materials.

The interesting aspect of drawing children into reading in these global ways is that they learn the advanced skills of phrasing, predicting, looking for patterns, and reading for meaning *before* they are quite sure about all the letters, their sounds, and the rules that govern their pronunciation. It is a case of many skills evolving simultaneously. The difficult, abstract, detail skills emerge from the more global, concrete work. Remember

MARGARET'S VISIT TO A FISHING COMMUNITY Margaret's experience in one of our northern communities shows the importance of reading material that relates to children's own lives:

I was visiting an aboriginal school when some unexpected guests arrived and claimed the teacher's attention. I offered to talk to the children and read them a story while she attended to the guests. So we talked, but my usual approach and topics elicited very little response and certainly no enthusiasm. Our conversation remained stilted and slow. To create a change I reached over to the library table where I had spotted a familiar book that I knew the children in my class loved to hear. The book Each Peach Pear Plum *is about characters – like Bo Peep, Tom Thumb, and Cinderella – who are very familiar to the children I usually teach. Not so here. While the children listened politely, they were obviously not interested. Sadly, my reading fell flat. Noting the signs of noninvolvement, I quickly reached for another book and was lucky to pick up* The Magic Fish *– an adaptation of the old story of "the fisherman and his wife." As soon as I showed them the pictures and began to read the story, the children came alive. They could relate to the characters and events, and we entered into an animated discussion about fishing and men's and women's roles in this industry. Suddenly there was no dearth of sharing and involvement. I had provided them with a story that touched their lives and they responded with their personal experiences.*

that this whole-to-parts sequence is the natural progression of learning that children experience in their home learning, and if you acknowledge that sequence and build on their innate desire to learn and evolve, learning to read will become both pleasurable and highly effective. To reassure yourself that you are not being derelict in your duty, you can always keep your own "scoreboard" of skills and goals on which to check off all the skills your young readers display as they enjoy their reading.

With your more independent readers you will want to select more advanced reading materials for read-aloud sessions, but always keep your eye on their reactions. If your own favorite does not charm them, don't read it through to the last page. Shift to something else instead. As you read with verve and expression, you will soon note that your advanced readers mimic you quite closely. Get them to lead readings using big books or sets of books so everyone can follow along. But keep reading choices flexible for all your students. If they want to use books that seem too advanced, let them find out how much they can extract from them – maybe next to nothing – but don't make books off limits by labeling them *too difficult, too easy, not part of our job*, or *already read too often*. As you observe children's choices, you will gain many insights into the ways they acquire reading habits and skills. Often these discoveries will run counter to your scope and sequence chart lists or structured curriculum guides.

Children enjoy taking turns leading unison reading.

UNISON, OR CHORAL, READING MAKES PRACTICE FUN AND EASY

Reading exciting stories in unison gives everyone a chance to read – or pretend to read – with gusto. The security of the group allows even your emergent readers and your shyest students to mumble along or to mouth the words to the best of their ability as you lead the chorus of voices, hamming it up. As you read the story with funny voices and lots of expression, you guide their eyes along the lines of print with your hand or a pointer. Like a sing-along these sessions produce a delightful feeling of being in harmony, and once you have a number of fluent readers (either because you taught them or because they learned to read before they came to school), you will find that they revel in being the lead readers. During center time, small groups will congregate around a big book, taking turns at leading – and often the leaders will not be your most advanced readers.

Modeling during unison reading and then making the books you have read freely available does much to foster extended practice of fluent, expressive reading. As with easy, predictable materials, unison reading gives students the sense that they are indeed readers. On that foundation of confidence and enjoyment they build the detailed skills of reading to flesh out the global learning they are acquiring so read-ily and joyfully.

BOOKS AND READING INSPIRE READERS' THEATER

Unison reading lays the foundation for readers' theater. Since you model your most expressive reading during those sessions, children get the message that reading lends itself to performance on a more extended scale. At first a small group of children may decide to share a poem or jingle that appeals to them and to perform it for each other. As you note the giggles and joint reciting as children bounce the sounds off each other, you can start the performance by inviting those three or four children to read their favorite to the whole class. During the early part of the year it might be a jingle like "Jelly in the Bowl" or small books like *There's a Dragon in My Wagon* or *The Carrot Seed.*

As they recite or read to their classmates, they will often emphasize the rhythms of their reading with body motions, and the foundation for readers' theater has been laid. That initial recital will invite others to spot fun materials that lend themselves to performance, and the children will come forward to give their renderings. When book time or other personal reading expands the repertoire, the recitals expand to performances with distributed roles and ultimately to complete plays with costumes and props.

As with the initial recitation, if you watch for that special glow of interest and the desire to reread a book again and again, that becomes your cue to remark, "Wouldn't it be fun if we acted that out? I wonder how we could do that." And usually you will be taken up on that prompting with alacrity. It is a good idea to begin such acting with simple stories in which only two or three characters interact briefly. Stories such as *The Three Bears, Chicken Little, Where the Wild Things Are* are ideal. But as children observe each other, they begin to look for drama possibilities in more complicated books and will start their planning without any prompting from you.

If the production requires preparation and rehearsal, remind them that choosing time will give them the opportunity to organize and rehearse their play. To help them along you may want to provide them with multiple copies of the story, enlist the aid of a parent to supervise rehearsals, and move the preparatory work into the hall or another available space a bit removed from the regular classroom. Children become wonderfully resourceful if you facilitate that kind of creativity. One year, Margaret's students decided to turn a story about a witch who didn't fit in with the other witches into readers' theater. They created the roles, the dialogue, and very ingenious costuming as they solved the problem of turning the witch into a fairy right on stage by making their witch's costume easily removable, with the fairy costume underneath.

At times it may take a lot of restraint on your part not to orchestrate and direct the show. But the real benefit of readers' theater lies in letting the children develop the play themselves. You act only as a resource person who will answer questions, help with suggestions for obtaining materials, and, of course, act as a very appreciative audience.

Observation will also show you the very different ways in which children proceed. You will find that young children and inexperienced performers create their costumes first. The concrete world of costumes draws students into the more abstract aspects of working out dialogue. Here again, if you stand back and let the children do all the negotiating and creating, you will learn much about their ways of thinking and functioning and will come to appreciate the sequence in which their learning progresses. While standing back may not seem like a very active role for you, it nevertheless gives children the necessary space and time to evolve their skills in their own way and provides a lot of learning for you.

That independence and practical work will stand the children in very good stead as they move along in school and then into the world beyond. You may need to remind yourself here that there are ground rules for behavior in class, so you know the rehearsals will not deteriorate into noisy, unproductive romps. As the observer you always have the option of reminding the children of the need to follow the ground rules for in-class behavior and for getting along with each other.

ADDING NONFICTION TO THE REPERTOIRE

Young children are insatiably curious. They love to explore and make new discoveries. If the books, articles, and magazines you make available in the classroom invite exploration and discovery, your students will accept them as eagerly as they accept storybooks. Building on the interests of some of your students - rocks, Egyptology, sharks, dolls – can be a starting point as you select nonfiction reading materials for your class, but you will soon learn that there are perennial favorites – dinosaurs, snakes, sports, space travel, pets, boats, and any number of others. Keeping a wide selection of books on a special table and inviting students to bring in books from home will kick off their nonfiction reading.

Of course, like adults, children seldom read nonfiction from cover to cover. Instead, they sample selectively – looking at pictures and their captions, listening to special chapters read aloud, and reading excerpts or summaries. If you make nonfiction material as freely available as storybooks, both boys and girls will delve into them. But a bonus will be the fact that boys in particular gravitate toward nonfiction if you cater to their specific interests. The myth that "boys don't like to read" will be roundly rejected.

Availability, time to use these books, and the clear understanding that the books may be used as intensively or cursorily as the students want or are able to do are the keys to drawing your students into nonfiction reading. Once again modeling provides a strong impetus. If you make it a point to include interesting nonfiction items in your read-aloud sessions and share thoughts or readings that are of special interest to you, your students will follow your lead and use reading to learn and to expand their own knowledge.

Students come to school with a vast stock of personal experiences and knowledge. Acknowledging that storehouse of information by reading them nonfiction materials that expand on their special knowledge or interests can unfold talents and extend their knowledge and interests as well as the development of their reading and research skills. Here again, higher-level skills and knowledge - reasoning, hypothesis testing, speculation, information gathering, and classification – are often at work and functioning well *before* all the basic skills are in place.

Interest, curiosity, and the innate drive to make sense of the world fuel your students' learning. For you, the teacher, it becomes fascinating to observe how children progress and how much they are able to accomplish. As their interests expand and they want to get more out of their research sources and develop better report-writing skills, they themselves become the ones who recognize the need for refining their basic skills.

Starting projects

Like drawing children to reading, initiating them into projects requires the same kind of lead-in activities – ones that will make them thirst for more information, more excitement, and more new activities. Lots

EVEN INDIVIDUAL PROJECTS NEED A SPARK TO GET THEM GOING
Even when a child asks permission to do a special-interest study on his own, there is still the need for a spark to give impetus to the work and sometimes draw other students into the project. So when Anne Peterson asked Margaret, "What do you do when a kid says he's not interested in the project all the other kids have decided to work on and wants to do a study about bears instead?", here is the advice she received:

The first thing you do is reassure the child. "That's all right. We can get you going on bears." Next you send him to the school library where the librarian will help him develop his research skills by showing him how to find information about bears in books, magazines, and reference materials. If possible, help him find some old newspapers and magazines so that he can cut out bear pictures, bear stories, bear anythings. If other kids in the class become interested and want to help, ask everyone to bring any models or pictures of bears they have. If enough students become involved, get home-school collaboration going and draw in parents and grandparents to gather stories of bears, bear rugs, claws, whatever. See if you can get real bear stories from older people, invite bear experts into your classroom, show videos about bears, and take the children to the local zoo to look at bears. All along read them stories about bears to lighten the research work. It may take weeks to assemble all the materials, but as long as the child is interested, he will continue to gather materials, draw pictures and charts, make his own book on bears, and set up his own mini-center. Even though his classmates will have given their input from time to time, the project will be uniquely his, and when he is ready, he can invite them on a guided tour through his very own bear center.

of talking
and careful lis-
tening, reading
appropriate stories,
sharing nonfiction materials,
going on interesting field trips,
hosting special visitors, and encourag-
ing knowledgable students or their parents to share a special topic with
the class are just some of the things that kindle the kind of enthusiasm required to get a project off and running. If you can recall the
drudgery of working on assigned projects that were of little interest to
you, you can understand students' reluctance and resistance to working on a project that has simply been assigned. The extra trouble it
takes to build students' enthusiasm for exploring new terrain pays off
handsomely. And you will have far more fun and involvement too.

Whether the project is small (lasting no more than two or three
hours) or large (extending over days or weeks) tapping your students'
map minds and connecting the project to what they already know are
crucial. Self-confidence, personal interest, positive feelings, and special
knowledge or experience combine to activate children's involvement
and dedicated work.

Something as simple and straightforward as creating valentines
takes on new life If you build on the warm feeling of doing something
special for someone you love. Picking up on the children's announce-
ment during news time that "Valentine's Day is almost here," Margaret
will tell the children about the wonderful valentines she has received
in the past, the fun she had in creating special ones as a little girl, and
the love that welled up as she received her own children's creations.

Older students created special valentines for their young buddies and presented them on a giant heart to the whole class. To share the fun, the young buddies came forward one by one to open their special cards and share the messages with the onlookers.

As her students watch and listen, her voice and expression draw them into a circle of caring and they begin to volunteer thoughts, ideas, and feelings about valentines they have received. In that broad matrix of feelings and memories Margaret injects the thought, "Maybe we could make special valentines. Who do you think would like to receive a valentine from you?" That extra input and the sharing of feelings and ideas lift what could be mostly a cut-and-paste session into something special and personal. (One small caution: if there is to be an in-class valentines exchange, figure out some way to ensure that all children receive the same number of cards.)

Storybooks offer interest and the promise of knowledge to start the flow of learning.

USING BOOKS TO LAUNCH A PROJECT

Selecting books and stories to serve as lead-ins enhances the teacher talk, ensuing discussions, and the many activities to follow. In chapter 16 we describe a school experience project that draws largely on books. Annual study units on special local industries or historical features offer many opportunities to build up a stock of books and articles to help you spark interest and set the tone for the children's work. To initiate her annual chick-hatching project and then keep the interest and information flow high, Margaret will draw on the books she has accumulated over the years – *Egg to Chick, What's Inside?, Too Many Chickens, Chicken and Egg, Good Morning, Chick,* and *Chickens Aren't the Only Ones.* (A trip to a farm to collect the eggs and see some chicks is the most exciting way to get this project underway, but it is not always feasible. However, books are valuable in any event.)

A Mexican unit and a Dutch unit each involving much artwork, crafts, and a culminating feast evolved on the basis of a wealth of reading about the two countries. (The lead-in might have been an even more general look at books and stories of faraway places and the customs and celebrations of different countries.) Book reading was enhanced by songs, dances, and special visitors who shared slides and personal tales of the countries, which added depth and reality to the written materials. In projects such as this, several of the children will invariably have special resources at home – relatives, friends, travel literature, artifacts – that add to the personal involvement in the projects. But reading is a fine lead-in and way of enriching interest.

Teaching children to see more in books than just the surface story can be a wonderful bonus of thoughtful book talk. It can also lead to mini-units such as the one that developed when Margaret invited the children to look beyond the story they were listening to to discover all the additional information available in the book. Reading the children the story of *Farmer Joe's Hot Day* she stopped to talk in a hushed voice about Farmer Joe's wife – who clearly is a force to be reckoned with on the farm. "You know, this is a story about Farmer Joe, but there is a *wife* in the story. Can you see all the things she is doing? Here it looks as if she is fixing the tractor. Does your mommy work on your car?" From that opening, the children took over to explore all the physical jobs Farmer Joe's wife was doing while Farmer Joe complained about the heat. They readily compared the work the farmer's wife was doing with their own home experience, and a mini-unit on the role of women in the home and on the farm was underway.

A DUTCH BREAKFAST One mother who had grown up in the Netherlands brought in a Dutch breakfast. To the children's delight she included what she termed "a Dutch staple" – rusks covered with chocolate sprinkles. She dressed her younger daughter in a traditional Dutch costume for the children to admire, and she brought in a whole round of cheese, which she had talked a deli owner into lending her. She used it as a prop to illustrate her talk about making cheese. Posters she had obtained from the Dutch embassy enhanced her descriptions of the country. All the children participated eagerly. They were particularly enthusiastic about the breakfast. So much so, that several mothers reported the following week that their children insisted on having chocolate-sprinkled rusks for breakfast.

Such thoughtful discussion following something read can also be seen as a way of teaching children to move beyond the surface aspects of stories they hear and read. Inviting reflection and a more thoughtful examination of the content of books is a marvelous introduction to reading that moves well beyond the superficial nature of the comprehension questions that were included in the antiquated readers Margaret used when we first began our joint work.

Today, she takes a very different approach as shown in Margaret's interaction with children in Anne Peterson's class as she read them

DON'T COUNT YOUR CHICKS UNTIL THEY'VE HATCHED ✳ The advice not to count your chickens until they've hatched certainly turned out to be sound when it came to Anne Peterson's replication of Marg's chick-hatching unit. Anne made a trip out to a farm and bought the suggested nineteen fertile eggs. As Mrs. Stewart, the farmer's wife, counted out the eggs, Anne noticed that they seemed unusually large, but she made no comment at the time. When it came to placing the eggs into the incubator, those large eggs would not all fit in, and two had to be left out. They served as research objects to be cracked open and examined minutely by Anne's students. ✳ Over the next twenty-one days (the normal incubation period) children took turns turning the eggs three times each day, and each weekend they vied with one another to take the incubator home to continue the care of the eggs. On Friday, at the end of the incubation period, everyone waited expectantly, keeping a close watch on those seventeen eggs, but not a single chick produced so much as a tiny crack in its shell. Faced with the question of whether to leave the unit as it was or take it home to discard the eggs, Anne decided to leave it at school over the long weekend. ✳ She had left the incubator plugged in, and on Tuesday morning, as the

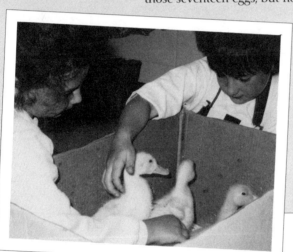

At times the chick-hatching project teaches unexpected lessons, such as, "Don't count your ducks until they're hatched."

Waters, a beautifully illustrated book written by a seventy-nine-year-old woman, Edith Newlin Chase, who clearly knows what will capture children's interest and imagination. Though most of the pages have only three or four words, their sounds and meaning combine with the wonderful textures of the unusual illustrations to provide much more than surface knowledge or cursory listening. As Margaret puts it:

> My goal in reading this book was to make the children think in creative ways. I wanted them to become immersed in the language of each page and experience how the words added to the beauty of the illustrations. I wanted them to wonder about all the little creatures

children rushed into class to see what had become of the chicks that were so slow to hatch, their excitement could hardly be contained. One by one, the eggs showed cracks, then tiny holes, and finally fluffy heads! It had taken a full twenty–four days, but now the little birds – ducklings! – were ready to emerge, much to the delight of the children and the utter amazement of the teacher. Hearing about the story, Anne's friends have decided to change the popular saying. In any situation of doubtful outcome, they advise her, "Remember not to count your ducklings until they've hatched!"

Division 13 Newsletter

Monday May 10
We think our chicks will hatch Tues., Wed. or Thurs.
The caterpillars have grown BIG and FAT.
Mrs. Vachon did a Draw-and-Tell story.

Thursday May 13
Our chicks' aren't hatching yet. We hope they will hatch today or tomorrow We're going to talk to them.

Friday May 14
Our chicks have not hatched. We're going to get a new incubator and try again.

Division 13 Newsletter

Monday We had a BIG surprise this morning !!!!
Our eggs hatched! But they're not chicks... they're DUCKS! Our caterpillars are in their chrysalids.

Ducklings provide a delightful surprise in the egg-hatching project.

hidden on each page. But most of all, I wanted them to think about the brook that gradually turns into a huge river. After each page I stopped to give them time to savor the words and to study the amazing detail of the pictures.

The following conversation illustrates how Margaret achieves this:

MARGARET: [Reading] "cunning baby brook"

STUDENT 1: What does "cunning" mean?

MARGARET: I wonder where we have come across this word before. Do you remember?

STUDENT 2: I remember! We were reading about a cunning fox!

MARGARET: That's right! Now I remember.

STUDENT 1: I think "cunning" means smart.

MARGARET: Good thinking. It also means crafty. [*Pauses*] Now I'm wondering what a "baby brook" is.

STUDENT 2: Do you think it means "young"?

STUDENT 3: Maybe it means it has a mother river somewhere.

STUDENT 4: Baby brook, baby brook [*rolling the words in her mouth and savoring the alliterations*].

MARGARET: [*Reading the next page*] "Joins a grown up river." Hmm, let's think about that. [*Repeating the words*] I wonder about "grown-up." What do you think it means?

STUDENT 1: I think it means a big river.

STUDENT 2: I think it could mean an old river.

STUDENT 3: I don't know what it means, but I like the words.

MARGARET: I wonder why the picture of the river is colored brown.

STUDENT 1: There's some dirt in the river.

STUDENT 2: Yea. It's turned into mud.

MARGARET: When you're on the ferry going to Victoria, have you ever noticed the brown parts in the water?

STUDENT 3: No. But I'll look next time.

Margaret continues:

What I'm looking for in book talk like this are creative, thoughtful answers. I want to probe how the children think and how they perceive the world around them. I don't want kids to have to put up their hands to answer. I want them to get excited about the book and their new knowledge. I want them to learn to dialogue in a group, to stimulate their curiosity about things, and to sharpen their powers of observation. They will probably drive their parents crazy next time they are on the ferry looking for the brown in the water.

The next time I go into their classroom, I'll tell them that I found some more information about young rivers and old ones. (I didn't elaborate further during my first reading because I was frantically thinking back to my geography classes and what I knew about the ages of rivers.) As we continue to talk and explore the beautiful detail of the illustrations, the children will probably want to produce a mural, and a river is sure to run through it.

Learning, creative work, discussion, and play with language were all part of our enjoyment of the book. That kind of interaction seems far away from the old who, what, when, and where questions that hampered the flow of creativity and all too often elicited that familiar "I don't know" response.

Modeling thoughtful questioning and demonstrating that books and reading can build on our own experience adds a much deeper level to children's reading than we used to observe in the primary grades. That kind of discussion certainly adds as much depth and interest to the teacher's work as it does to the students'. Books and stories that could become a bit tedious for the teacher after so many readings take on new life when you use them to marvel at the creative ways in which children think and talk about them. Their spontaneous reactions afford intriguing insights into their perception of the world and provide many openings for extending the depth and breadth of their reading comprehension.

OUTSIDE INFLUENCES CAN BECOME TRIGGERS FOR PROJECTS

Reports of violence in schools started discussions in class and an exploration of the feelings that might lead children to such violence. Collaborating with the school counselor, Karen Abel worked with her grade-two-three class to make them aware of their own feelings and possible thoughts of violence. To bring personal involvement to the unit, she and her students took time to brainstorm the physical signals they experience when they begin to get angry. They produced an impressive list (see the following page) and moved from there to find ways of dissipating or dealing with their growing anger before it reached the violence stage. Time, tactful acknowledgment of all expressions, and a calm and accepting attitude on the part of the teacher combined to add depth to the project. Parents became involved when Karen sent home the children's written self-expressions.

Name: _____ Age: _____ June, 1993

My Personal Plan for Managing My Anger

My body gives me clues that I am beginning to feel angry. Here is a picture of me when I am beginning to feel angry.

Red: I do this a lot.
Yellow: Sometimes I do this.
Green: I don't usually do this.

☐ 1. Bite my lip
☐ 2. Grind my teeth
☐ 3. Yell
☐ 4. Feel like hitting
☐ 5. Cry
☐ 6. Feel helpless
☐ 7. My heart pounds
☐ 8. I clench my fists
☐ 9. I suck in my breath
☐ 10. I feel hot
☐ 11. My shoulders hunch up
☐ 12. My neck feels tense
☐ 13. My eyebrows go down
☐ 14. My stomach hurts
☐ 15. I get a headache
☐ 16. I scrunch my eyes
☐ 17. My jaw gets tense

This is where and when I feel angry	This is my plan to manage my anger
At home	At home

This is when and where I feel angry	This is my plan to manage my anger
At school	At school
Elsewhere	Elsewhere

The diagram that is circled best describes my "Anger Mountain".
    A = feeling irritated. First clues of anger. Easy to manage
    B = harder to manage
    C = out of control

① Get angry quickly
Get over it quickly

② Quick to get angry
Slow to get over it

③ Don't Get angry easily

④ Slow to get angry
Quick to get over it

⑤ Slow to get angry
Slow to get over it

Thoughtful brainstorming and in-depth discussion produced the physical indicators of feelings of anger outlined here. To fill out their charts, Karen's students drew a picture of themselves and labeled those parts of their bodies that told them when their anger was growing. Next they explored when and where they felt angry and compared notes with other students before taking their personal charts home to discuss them with their parents.

STARTING LONG-TERM PROJECTS AND ALL-SCHOOL INVOLVEMENT

Deciding on and then launching an all-school project starts in the staff room with teachers and principals brainstorming the possibilities and logistics of the various projects under consideration. As in the classroom, personal involvement in the planning process is the crucial element that makes for success. At South Park School, having a voice, being heard, joining in the fun of exploring all possibilities, and forming alliances to lighten the workload for everyone are some of the features that emerged in planning all-school units.

As we discussed earlier in this book, to get an all-school astronomy unit underway, the South Park teachers invited the science consultant for the school district to talk to them about the possibilities and challenges inherent in such an undertaking. His skillful presentation and ensuing staff-room discussions captured everyone's imagination and enthusiasm. Teachers began to pool their information and resources and looked forward to learning a great deal themselves as they worked with their students.

Then each teacher invited the students to find as many sources of information as possible. They rose to the challenge bringing in books, magazine articles, and notes about TV shows. The teachers invited special speakers from the community to come in to speak to the classes and display such fascinating items as a rather large meteorite.

Perhaps the most effective feature of the learning associated with this project was making much of the information concrete - having children produce papier-mâché models of the planets to show their relative sizes, creating a planet walk that showed the relative distances between the planets, and having a stargazing night that involved parents as well as students. So once again, personal involvement, hands-on work and the connection between school and the world beyond it got the work underway and then kept it moving along with unabated energy. From kindergarten to grade seven and from the custodian to the principal, everyone had a part in the study. The climate of learning that affirmed adults as learners as well as children was a central feature of the project and impressed the students with the fact that they were genuinely collaborating with everyone involved – adults and students of all ages.

The teacher's personal interests get things rolling

Inherent in all the examples above is the fact that the teacher's own interest and enthusiasm provide the impetus that gets learning underway. She is the one who searches for more and more knowledge about children's learning, and that abiding interest in their ways of functioning opens the door to endless possibilities for learning. Children know intuitively that their teacher is totally absorbed in the work in class and they model themselves after her. Like their teacher, they become keen observers and good listeners who are always on the lookout for new and unusual opportunities to explore a topic in different ways. As the teacher leads them to new knowledge by being curious herself, by sharing her own interests, and by bringing a fresh approach to learning that moves beyond the acquisition of unconnected facts, they absorb learning eagerly and easily and are always ready for more.

10.
Spelling Does Count

Because many words in English have spellings that relate to their meaning or origin rather than strictly to their sound, spelling strategies need to change.... Awareness of the connection between spelling and meaning completes the understanding that spellers need to acquire (Tarasoff 1992).

"But they don't know how to spell!" is the remark we hear most frequently when we talk about the benefits of using reading and writing to help children learn the specific skills of spelling and sounding out. There is the myth that teachers no longer teach spelling, and researchers have commented that some "professionals at conferences state that the teaching of skills is antithetical to whole language instruction" (Gunderson and Shapiro 1988). Parents worry about their children's spelling, and it is obvious to them that their children are not being taught to spell as they were. The written work their children bring home often shows invented spellings without corrections filled in by their teacher, and there is no indication that spelling drills or worksheets are used in class. So they have the impression that accurate spelling no longer matters.

Of course, the facts are otherwise. Spelling is more important than ever. In the days when "spelling was taught as an end in itself rather than a means to writing" (Tarasoff 1990), spelling involved a lot of rote memory. Now that teachers use children's writing to teach conventions of print, letter–sound correspondences, and spelling patterns, spelling serves an important function in children's written communication. As a result, they work actively to evolve their spelling and to generate rules that they then update and revise, much as they did when they learned to talk. But with spelling, they require more detailed help, and teachers have not always known how to *combine meaning making with skill building.*

> To the extent that children are acting intelligently, they will be paying attention to the sense of what they hear and read, and not to the detail. Somehow, we must turn their attention to the detail. This would seem to imply that they have to turn off their intelligence while they do this. Indeed, that is the way "correct" grammar and spelling have most often been taught.
>
> Teacher's attitudes to conventions like this might be characterized as "running scared" – in the sense that, since there is only one right way, explorations of other ways must be avoided at all costs. But why not encourage explorations in these matters, just as teachers encourage explorations in other areas? (Duckworth 1987)

Why not indeed! Once you shift away from "correct ways" of teaching spelling and turn to explorations, then so many more avenues for learning open up – avenues that are natural to the children's ways of working and that invite them to become active researchers and hypothesis testers. Spelling becomes an intriguing puzzle as well as a way of communicating effectively in writing. It certainly does *not* require children "to turn off their intelligence."

It will take time and patience to make the shift to trusting learners to generate their own spelling. Based on the old logic of traditional teaching with its rote memorization of spelling words, it would seem that children "cannot generate what they don't know." But as you work with children to help them draw the basic patterns of spelling from the written work – much as they drew the basic patterns of grammar and phonology from spoken language – you will find that they respond to your modeling as you sound out words and refer to spelling patterns. In this interactive way of learning to spell, your input is highly important to the children's confidence and success and does much more for them than leading them in spelling drills.

The teacher's role in developing children's spelling

MAKING WORK WITH LETTERS FUN FOR EMERGENT WRITERS

Spelling is no longer a subject unto itself but is properly dealt with in association with reading, writing, and speaking/listening. Lists committed to memory for the Friday afternoon spelling test – complete with red marks, feelings of apprehension, and the occasional gold star – are a thing of the past. Margaret remembers her own fears over spelling tests. She also remembers her students' anxieties when she still used the weekly spelling tests.

Now that she incorporates spelling learning into the natural flow of written communication in her classroom, children use their map minds to absorb sight words, letter shapes and sounds, spelling rules, and conventions of English orthography. Skill building and mini-lessons are closely connected to reading and writing, as children's explorations respond to Margaret's invitations to turn their attention to detail. Margaret comments:

> As they begin to draw and write, I introduce children to letters, both in the context of spelling for them during news time and through games, puzzles, and hands–on work like tracing letters in the sand table or on large charts that show supersized letters. What I aim for most is making work with letters fun and playful. Children love puzzles and mazes, and they respond eagerly if I introduce letters as a way of playing guessing games: "How many letters can you think of [or print]?" "How can we put these letters together?" "Why don't you try finding all the letters you know in this pile of plastic letters."

SETTING THE SCENE WITH READING— BUILDING VOCABULARY

Reading exciting stories with language that is rich in interesting words expands children's vocabularies and draws them into the world of book language. As they read along with their teacher, their diction

TURNING KIDS ON TO WORDS

Reading stories with unusual words captures students' imagination and invites them to play with language, experiment with novel combinations, and test their spelling in many different ways. Reading Margaret Mahy's *17 Kings and 42 Elephants* offers just such opportunities:

TEACHER: [*Reads*]
"Seventeen kings on forty–two elephants
Going on a journey through a wild wet night.
Baggy little ears like big umbrellaphants,
Little eyes a–gleaming in the jungle light."

Hmm, I wonder why seventeen kings and why forty–two elephants.

CHILDREN: [*Offer all kinds of reasons and interesting conjectures*]

TEACHER: I love this sound: "Baggy little ears like big umbrellaphants."

CHILDREN: [*Repeat the line several times*]

TEACHER: I wonder why they have to go out on a stormy night.

CHILDREN: [*Offer their explanations*]

TEACHER: Have you ever noticed how small elephants' eyes are? [*Reads*] "Little eyes a–gleaming."

The children continue to talk about their own experiences with and knowledge of elephants. As the story continues, the teacher invites the children to make up words like "rockodiles" and to imagine what a "proud and ponderous hippopotamus" might look like. Children love to try out unusual words and make up new ones, and they love to repeat the words found in stories like this one.

becomes clearer, and the melody of rhymes and flowing prose draws their attention to the sounds of words. As Margaret encourages them to talk, they practice their newly learned vocabulary in all kinds of settings, at times with quite unintentional comical results; for example, Andrew told his dad to *constipate*, when the word he meant to use was *concentrate*. Children love to roll big words off their tongues, and for a time gloriously descriptive words like *radical*, *stupendous*, *actually*, *ridiculous*, or *extraordinary* will be freely interspersed in the classroom talk until some new discoveries take their place.

Interest in words and their wonderful sounds becomes the natural introduction to turning to letters and their sounds. Just as the children play with words once they have heard them in context, so they will play with letters once they connect them to interesting words they enjoy and want to use in their writing. Most will have been introduced to letters through watching television – "Sesame Street," in particular – or working with their parents at home, but the deliberate connection of letters to words of interest to the children adds a different dimension, particularly if you invite them to play with the sounds and guess which letters make up their favorite words.

SHOWING THE USES OF SPELLING

Describing how she draws kindergarteners and inexperienced first-graders into the world of letters and spelling, Margaret writes:

Right from the beginning of the school year, I make sure the children are constantly reminded that reading and writing are just as useful and natural parts of communication as spoken language – and just as important. We read stories together, compose and send notes to the office or their homes, make posters, or write to-do lists. And all along I comment on the practical uses of written language and the need to "write this down," "spell this correctly so people will understand," "use the right words, so we won't forget," or "get to know the letters so you can write to your grandparents."

Creating a menu for a restaurant provides practice in spelling.

Green beens $1.00
Eggs\ Sqrambld eggs $3.00
pees $1.00
Peech $2.00
Cofy\ tea $0.00
Ham $1.00
Chicen $1.00
Cookey $3.00
Meet $2.00
Bacen $3.00
Chips $1.00

CAPTURING THE CHILDREN'S INTEREST

Margaret describes how parents may comment when they bring in their five-year-old, "You'll never get David to sit down to write." Yet once she has shown a child like this the many interesting ways in which language and spelling can be used, he will sit or lie down with a large piece of paper to make his own design of letters and written messages. As Margaret explains:

Without any demand on children to do as I do, I draw them into the realm of written language, words, and spelling. By using non-threatening ways of stimulating their interest, I invite them to enter into this new world of communication. They join in with the anticipation of using their own ways of exploring and of having fun. Games like Word Lotto and self-checking phonics games – complete with audiotapes that provide the sounds – become favorites during center time.

When I see two children join forces to explore these games, I know that they are hooked on letters and ready to move right along

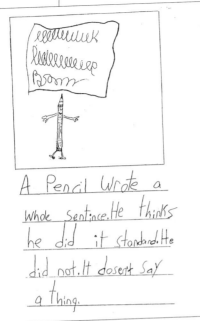

A Pencil Wrote a Whole Sentince. He thinks he did it standard. He did not. It dosen't say a thing.

toward spelling and writing. Later, those same two children may sit together while writing and talk to each other about which sequence of letters to use in their writing and drawing. Others may shift to making beautiful designs with their letters, adding curlicues and stripes or embellishing their names with flowers. I make it a point to admire their handiwork and to comment on the names or sounds of the letters they used to add an auditory component to their kinesthetic ways of working with letters.

OFFERING ON-THE-SPOT MINI-LESSONS

To bring spelling and phonics lessons into the flow of the overall language arts work, Margaret observes children's interactions to spot their specific needs, find teachable moments, and build on the interest of the moment. In addition to her special mini-lessons (described on page 50 in chapter 2), she uses center time to work with emergent spellers:

> As I join some of their games, I let my voice convey feelings of puzzlement, wonder, or awe at finding something new. In short, I enter with them into the intriguing world of solving very complex mazes. Solving a maze may sometimes lead to an impasse, but the maze can be retraced and then traversed with greater confidence. "Trrr-ophy, what on earth can we use to make that sound?" As I trill the r, I make funny faces to show them how my tongue is moving. They quickly join in, and one of them is sure to call out, "That's an r!" I get them puzzling over silent e's and how they affect the preceding vowel. I suggest that they hold their hands in front of their lips to see if they can feel the little puff of air as

Children are well aware that their invented spelling is not yet standard. They also know that standard spelling is important to communication.

INVENTED OR STANDARD SPELLING?
Brenda, age six, and Devan, age five, were doing their writing during writing workshop. Devan looked up to ask, "How do you spell *rainbow*?" Looking up from her own work, Brenda inquired, "Do you want that in invented spelling or in standard?"

they say *whistle*. Total concentration and any number of tries reward such invitations, and children will remind each other of the importance of the *wh* connection.

WATCHING FOR PROGRESS THEN USING IT AS A SPRINGBOARD FOR FURTHER DEVELOPMENT

With that kind of introduction to letters and their sounds, children find letters both friendly and intriguing. Instead of being barriers to moving along, they are bridges to more advanced work. Children's personal explorations spring up spontaneously during center time as they initiate games of their own, generate rules, and then try them out when working with the materials provided in the writing center.

As I observe how they interact with the letters and each other, I see the progress:

✴ Letters rather than pictures receive their main focus.

✴ Instead of cutting pictures out of newspapers, they select letters and then paste them up.

✴ As they write, they use sounds expressively: "Chooooo, said the train." "She screeeemed!"

✴ They overgeneralize spelling patterns – *yeer, soop*.

✴ As they talk about words and letters, they show much clearer understanding of how speech is segmented into sounds and words: "That's a compound word; that takes a soft *c*; here I need a finger space."

✴ Letters and spelling are becoming part of children's repertoire of communication.

As the children move along, I offer more advanced information: rules about vowels, irregularities that need to be committed to memory by "taking a picture in your mind," different ways of finding out how to spell a word.

MODELING SPELLING DURING NEWS TIME

As we have pointed out in other chapters, news time is Margaret's most concentrated time of teaching spelling and composition. As children gather in front of the chalkboard, Margaret helps them come to a consensus about what to include in the news that day and then invites them to "help with the spelling." On a day when the joint decision has been made to include three sentences – "There are two weeks until Easter Holidays!" "There are many birthdays in March and April." "Pat's birthday is tomorrow." – the exchange between teacher and students would be much as follows:

TEACHER: All right, help me spell. The first word is *there.*

CHILDREN: *t-h-e-r-e* [*Children remember this sequence early, probably because* there *occurs so frequently.*]

TEACHER: *T-h-e-r-e,* right. [*Prints the word*] There are....

CHILDREN: *r*

TEACHER: Right. There is an *r* in that word, [*Puts r on the board*], and to make it standard spelling we also need an *a* and a silent *e* at the end. [*Puts these on the board*] There are two....

CHILDREN: *t-o.*

TEACHER: Good. That spells *to.* [*Puts the two letters on the board*] I know you know that word, but in this case we need a *w* right in here [*Puts it in*] to change the word to mean the number *two.* Let me put those two words side-by-side down here. [*Puts them on the board*] And let me tell you something else that's really tricky. *To* can also be spelled *t-o-o.* When you want to emphasize the word *toooo,* you spell it with two *o's* like in the sentence, "I want to go too." I'll put that word down here with the other ones. [*Puts too on the board*]

CHILDREN: [Say *to, two, too* several times, experimenting with different intonations, holding up two fingers for one of them, and then intoning, "me too, me too!"]

The session continues along the same lines. When the children come to the word *birthday,* the teacher asks them what they know about the word. They will be sure to tell her that it is "a compound word because there are two words in it." (One little girl calls it a "pompom word.") There is a brief discussion about starting two sentences with *there,* but the class decides not to make a change. The teacher talks briefly about the possessive *s* at the end of Pat's name and then goes on:

TEACHER: Let's have some fun with Pat's name. [*She prints Pat on the board.*] See if you can give me some rhyming words for *Pat,* words that end the same way.

CHILDREN: Cat, hat, bat. [*They eagerly search their minds for more and vie with one another to be first in providing examples.*]

TEACHER: I'll leave these words on the board and if you can think of some more, just come up and add them to our list.

[*Quite often children will come back after lunch with a list of words and add others that they have thought up with the help of a parent.*]

At the end of the session, when all three sentences are on the board and children have had a chance to read them several times – first in unison and then individually with or without help – the teacher provides a cloze exercise. Children see it as a game and eagerly volunteer to participate, again with or without help from their peers.

TEACHER: I want you to close your eyes now and I am going to rub off some words, and then we'll see if you can put them back in standard spelling. [*Rubs off* two, Pat's, many *and* birthday]

The children eagerly volunteer and can hardly wait to get to the board. As four of them try to fill in the missing words, one or two may turn to the rest of the class to ask for help, which is generally provided in a good chorus of voices:

TEACHER: Good work. Now let's take a look to see if the words are really all standard spelling. [*One child may have put down* meny.] I really like the way you worked on that word and you have most of the letters right. To make it completely standard, we need to make one change. What do you think we need?

CHILDREN: [*From a number of children*] a

Describing one of the children's favorite spelling games (also referred to in an earlier chapter), Margaret goes on to say:

If the children are still paying attention, I'll say to them, "Let's have some fun! I'm going to put some blank spaces on the board. See if you can figure out what the sentence says:

_ _   _ _ _ _   _ _ _ _   _   _ _ _ _ _   _ _ _   _ _ _

_ _ _ _ _ _ _

Once I have put the dashes on the board I invite the children to fill in the spaces. They get *we* right away. Next they try *I* for the one space. So I tell them, "Good try, but it's not *I*." They keep trying, refusing my offer to put in the first letters. Pretty soon someone suggests *a* and then *will have*, and the mystery is solved: "We will have a party for Pat tomorrow." The children get very good at these guessing games using the length of the word as a starting point and their knowledge of syntax to fill in the rest. (During a demonstration lesson I gave in Calgary, I used a dash message to show how children will use their knowledge. Unfortunately, as soon as I had all the dashes on the board, one little girl blurted out, "It's snowing outside!" She was right and there went my lesson.)

Visiting teachers in my class are always impressed, especially if they have not been able to figure out what the message was. For the children it definitely is a way of using their intelligence to spell, and word length becomes one of the many strategies they use in working with words they need to figure out.

Often after a session like this, the children decide to offer me some fun, and when we return from recess there will be a dash message on the board for me to figure out:

— —   — — — —   — —   — — —   — — — —   — — —

Now this is in invented spelling so I often have difficulty. But with a little help I finally figure out that it says, "We want to have center time."

The role of the teacher expands

Taking that vignette of a news session and its spin-offs certainly shows the role of the teacher to be both more varied and far more interesting than someone who focuses largely on spelling drills. The interactions just described illustrate the teacher

* acknowledging right approaches and good tries
* recognizing overgeneralizations
* encouraging inference drawing
* using language to delight and intrigue
* being a willing learner who tries difficult jobs
* being ready to accept help when it is needed
* modeling pattern creation and awareness
* being systematic in producing a message

This list can be extended considerably if the session includes more editing and the opportunity to work with more complex words with prefixes or suffixes that can be commented on, or sentences that incorporate more complex sentence structure so that punctuation includes exclamation and question marks.

Margaret keeps these sessions fun, interesting, and free of stress. She encourages all children to participate and always assures them that she and the other children will help them if they come forward with suggestions for spelling or, later, the reading of board work. But she never puts any child on the spot to come up with answers. Her voice and manner clearly convey to the children that she is interested in their answers – as she truly is – and that she is as intrigued by the many possibilities as they are. Since she is always on the lookout for noting patterns, steps forward, and openings for new work in the children's ways of responding, her abiding interest and absorption in these spelling sessions conveys itself to the children. They know she enjoys these sessions too.

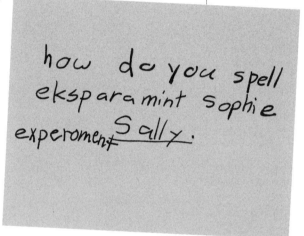

Exchanging spelling information moves partners closer to standard spelling.

LESSONS TEACHERS LEARN

Children are certainly not afraid to play with spelling and are soon ready to use their growing knowledge of letters and oral spelling during writing workshop. However, as we have pointed out elsewhere, knowing something in one context does not necessarily mean that that knowledge will be transferred. You will find that when the children do their own composing and writing, they generally revert to invented spelling even with words they have learned to spell orally. We call that "levels of knowing," but it is in fact an example of not "conserving" knowledge from one context to another. The two kinds of learning – oral and written spelling – eventually merge, but at first you will need to do a great deal of reminding to shore up children's knowledge.

DAVID AND *THEY* ☀ David went for months spelling *they* as *thay*. Margaret would remind him about the standard spelling, but nothing seemed to work. He was making progress in other areas and was learning to spell other words, but somehow it seemed that *they* did not make sense to him when there is *play* and *say* and *day*. Finally he accepted that *they* was one of those words you have to remember whether it makes sense or not, and after that David wrote *they* in his compositions.

Time, patience, and many repetitions are all necessary ingredients in spelling. During the oral spelling lessons of news time, Margaret will repeat the same comments time and again: "Here we need a capital letter because it's the beginning of the sentence." "That sounds just like an *s*, but we actually need a soft *c*." "At the end of the sentence we need a period." On and on the comments go, spoken in a matter-of-fact, information-giving voice. Often the more mature spellers will begin to provide those comments instead of Margaret, but emergent spellers and immature children need to hear the same message as often as they needed to hear words repeated at home when they first began to talk.

Once children develop a feel for the position of vowels in spelling, they begin by randomly using vowels as "placeholders." Here is one of Lauren's early efforts with vowels. Her spelling will move gradually toward standard use of vowels. The message was *Mom I love you. Mom please will you give me my money because it is chips day.*

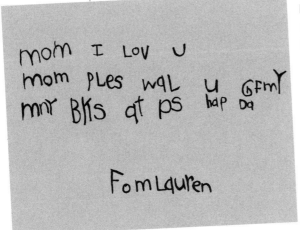

HONORING THE CHILDREN'S WAYS OF LEARNING

The kind of spelling work we are talking about may seem slower than the old spelling-drill method, but it honors the children's own natural ways of generating their understanding and their rules. It lays a foundation for spelling that runs deep and is broad at the base, and that kind of building takes time. Your role as the architect of that construction is satisfying and interesting. As you find more and more ways of encouraging the children's ways of using thinking and rule-generating skills in their spelling, you discover their natural sequence of learning - beginning consonants first, then ending consonants, then some frequently used words from their oral spelling, then long vowels – though not as yet accurate – and from there the sequence continues. Sometimes it varies, and that adds new interest as you observe the children's emergent writing and spelling.

Writing provides both practice and feedback for spelling

Spelling is *language*. It is *functional*. It is a system for recording *meaning*. Spelling serves no purpose except as part of the writing process (Bean and Bouffler 1987).

Writing for meaning becomes the impetus for spelling practice that is both personal and absorbing. Children who want to convey their messages practice as intensely to generate their spelling as they practiced making sounds when they began to talk. Their intent to convey clear messages keeps them focused on their writing, and, once they begin to acknowledge the needs of their readers, they turn toward editing and the move toward standard spelling.

Most young children accept that they cannot yet spell accurately and happily move through stages of scribble writing, producing strings of unconnected letters (babbling in print), and then beginning to represent the words in their messages by one or more consonants. But often it takes help from the teacher to create awareness of the first steps in spelling.

MAKING CHILDREN AWARE OF THE DETAILS OF SPELLING

Just as in babbling when learning to talk, children who are encouraged to follow their own natural sequences of learning will babble in print. And, like babies who play and experiment with many different sounds to find some of the right ones to convey what they want to express, so new writers produce strings of letters that – intentionally

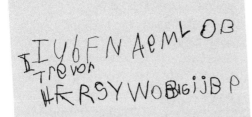

A seven-year-old ESL child is moving toward invented spelling. Though still babbling in print, he has copied his friend's name to give meaning to his printing. His message was *Me and Trevor are going to play GI Joe.*

or not – contain some of the right elements of print to convey their message.

To draw emergent writers' attention to their successes and to encourage them to become more intentional in their printing, teachers will ask the children to read what they printed aloud and will then comment on some of the letters: "Right, I can see that is a picture of the plane your dad took, and look, you have a *p* here, that's the beginning of *plane*. Here you have a *d* for your *dad*. That's great. I know you can sound things out as you write. Let's see what you can do tomorrow."

To develop a sense of sounding out that will also help them with their reading, children need to "huff and puff" their way through their writing words to generate their strategies and their own sense of letters and their sounds. As they do, they are moving through their own stages of learning, and hurrying them along does not work. Looking

SOL BEGINS HIS WRITING AND SPELLING ✷ Sol and Jessie were at the kindergarten news session, but felt more inclined to have a quick tussle on the floor than watch the writing too closely. When it came time to sit at their tables for writing workshop, Sol quickly produced a picture and then wanted to move to a center to play.

SOL: I've finished. Can I go to a center?

TEACHER: Let's see what you have drawn, Sol. Tell me about it.

SOL: It's a motorcycle.

TEACHER: Tell me what's happening in your picture.

SOL: [*Talks about the motorcycle his dad owns*]

TEACHER: Sol, I'd really like it if you wrote something about your picture.

SOL: I can't write.

TEACHER: I'm positive that you can. Let's think about it for a while.

SOL: I know. Let's say, "This is my dad's motorcycle." You write it for me.

back over years of being the spelling bee champion of his school, Richard Gentry (1987) recounts how the rote memorization of all those difficult words failed to build inner strategies that allowed him to spell unfamiliar words accurately. Once he entered university, he was faced with developing strategies that would help him generate spelling patterns that would make his college writing acceptable.

So the whole point of having children evolve their own invented spelling is to provide them with a repertoire of strategies for generating an understanding of the different ways of arriving at standard spelling and for internalizing the most common English spelling patterns. For example, over the years, Margaret has noticed how much easier it is for children to feel the consonants in their mouths than to hear them. So she models enunciating words and testing their feel with lips and tongue, and the children become quite creative in generating their own spelling. You may see some interesting grimaces as the children try out the "feel" of a word, but you will also see complete concentration and a readiness to try anything. At the same time, since they observe their teacher daily during news time as she thinks out

TEACHER: I'd like it better if you did it yourself.

SOL: But I can't write.

TEACHER: Let's think: *mmmmmmotorcycle.*

SOL: It starts with an *m.*

TEACHER: That's wonderful! How about you making the *m.*

SOL: [*Sits and squirms, then prints an* m]

TEACHER: [*Enthusiastically*] Sol, that's great. You *can* do it. Now you are a writer. Tomorrow you will be able to write lots more. Now off you go to a center.

After that kind of coaxing and encouragement, children like Sol generally begin to produce strings of print, and as their teacher helps them find the right letters to represent their message, they are on their way toward writing for meaning. By the time they enter first grade, many of them have started to segment their writing into words or word-like units, and they will evolve their spelling and writing from there with the same kind of encouragement Sol received at the very beginning.

Children follow their teacher's suggestion to try several versions of spelling to see if they can spot the right one. The words they are attempting to spell are *closed* and *everything*.

avreyThn avthine   avreyThing

Tara

loud, spells, and comments on letters and their sounds and spelling patterns, their own independent work is expanded and reinforced. They remember those difficult little words that are so frequent in everyday writing but have no content: *there, then, here, are.* Since words like these appear every day in their own writing or the daily news, children remember their patterns as sight words and use them correctly from an early point in their writing.

ENCOURAGING SELF-RELIANCE

When Margaret first shifted to more holistic ways of teaching, she provided the children with small copybooks in which they kept the most common words they needed and to which they added new words that they felt they wanted for their reference – their own personal dictionaries. But as she continued to observe children during their writing, Margaret found that they became too dependent on their dictionaries and overly concerned with being accurate. As a result, they limited themselves in their composing to words they knew or could find in their dictionaries. More important, they did not learn how to sound out words and to generalize spelling patterns. They relied on authority and outside help instead of generating their own spelling. Other researchers (Gunderson and Shapiro, Tarasoff) have commented on how too great a concern with accuracy early in children's spelling development will curtail both their writing and their spelling development. Having them use dictionaries too soon in their spelling development or at times when they are working on writing drafts (Phenix and Dunn 1991) is also counterproductive.

Children love to use big words and a variety of expressions. Naturally, the most interesting words, those that intrigued and delighted students as they listened to imaginative stories were often absent from those beginning, or self-made, dictionaries. But big words are far more satisfying than the carefully controlled vocabulary of one- and two-syllable words, and children revel in rolling big words around in their minds and off their tongues.

Commenting that children used to whole-language instruction "produced a huge volume of writing," Gunderson and Shapiro (1988) point out that the first-graders they observed produced about eighteen times the number of words they would have been exposed to in a typical basal reader. That rich vocabulary shows

A BIT OF SELF-CONCEPT BUILDING HELPS THOSE WHO ARE HOOKED ON ACCURACY. Talking about students who came to her class with a great need to be perfect in all ways, Margaret describes how a bit of self-concept building helps these children relax and realize that all work begins slowly. She tries to reassure them that, although everything is not always perfect to begin with, perfection will come with time:

Kids need to know that they are not born spellers. I have sat with kids who were new to my class as they cried and said they couldn't write and wouldn't try invented spelling, because it "was not right!" Most of these kids came from schools and homes that emphasized correctness. I talked to their parents and told them to back off on the spelling and acknowledge the content of the children's writing. Sometimes it took weeks for the kids to make the shift. Brodie and Daniel were two who held out for "perfect work only." Eventually they became good writers, but it took a lot of self-concept building and patience. Working on their overall performance gave them greater freedom to take risks. I emphasized what they did well and gave them credit for effort at every opportunity.

Working in a multi-age classroom helps the child realize that, although drafts and initial efforts tend to be messy, work can (and will) be polished later on. Convincing children that they have something to say and that their messages are interesting and valuable is the biggest help in overcoming the perfection block. As they feel good about their writing, they acknowledge that they are doing good work and that their spelling is moving ever closer to standard.

Three writing partners share information on spelling.

Sounding out has its pitfalls when children spell the way they talk. Here an ESL child has provided the model for a thank-you note for the other children at his table. Without questioning his personal version "Seng ku" that fits his way of saying "thank you," the other two boys include his version in their notes as well.

itself in their writing. If the teacher encourages them to "huff and puff" their way through spelling whatever they want to write and then acknowledges all good tries and rough approximations, the children develop a sense that they *do* have resources within themselves. And so they feel free to proceed with writing enlivened by interesting words and expressions.

Once they have moved beyond the early stages of emergent spelling and have acquired enough of a repertoire of beginning consonants and ways of sounding words out, children delight in referring to dictionaries to find what they need and to discover new words. To help them at that stage, the teacher models dictionary skills and looking up words as she works on writing or reading.

In Karen Abel's grade-two-three class, children use many reference works. When they write, she encourages them to consider the writing process first and to consider their first spellings as "temporary." Once the writing has progressed to the final editing stage, then the students turn their attention to accurate spelling. Like Margaret, Karen will offer mini-lessons as they are needed, and whole-class practice on spelling conventions that everyone needs to update.

Spelling Instruction That Makes Sense by Jo Phenix and Doreen Dunn (1991) certainly supports Karen's work. The authors advise teachers and writers to ignore spelling in their drafts and to focus attention on the composition instead, leaving the removal of "temporary" spellings until the very last stage. So "to think spelling always matters is as nonproductive as thinking it never does".

The correctness of that observation was recently borne out when a distressed grade-one-two teacher told Margaret of parents who had sought her help and advice because their children's writing in third grade was much below the level of the writing they had produced in her grade-one-two class. In talking to the parents, the teacher discovered that the grade-three teacher insisted on accuracy, the use of dictionaries, and careful printing, even in children's drafts. As a result, the students no longer used their imaginations or built on their spoken vocabularies to write creatively. Instead, they limited themselves to the words they could spell or could find in their small, self-made dictio-

SHOWING HOW DOESN'T NECESSARILY TRANSFER   Though it may seem more efficient simply to provide the correct spelling and have children do drills and exercises, time and again we find that even if a child has a correct model right in front of him, he will still use his own way of spelling, one that fits his stage of spelling development. If he has not progressed to hearing vowels, his writing will largely consist of consonants: "td w r gn...." (Today we are going....) When a class was working on a unit on bears, their teacher had bear poems, bear pictures with captions, and bear posters all over the classroom. Still, when the children did their own writing, their spelling showed *br, bar, bere,* and a number of other versions. They were focusing on the message they were creating, and it did not occur to them to look around the room for the right spelling.

naries. For them, the having of wonderful ideas was curtailed both in their writing and in their development of personal strategies for learning to spell.

When the grade-one-two teacher mentioned the parents' concerns to her colleague, she found that that teacher was not yet ready to combine meaning making with explorations in spelling. The grade-one-two teacher offered her own advice to the parents: "Encourage your children to write creatively at home. Make it a game to help them use imagination and pictures as part of their writing and show your appreciation of the wonderful words and fluent language. In short, be the admiring recipient of your children's creative writing."

Where do we go from here?

Spelling has taken on a new image, and teaching spelling has taken a new direction, one that is happier for students and teachers alike. We have shown some examples of the new role played by the teacher. The following four books will give you much more in-depth information about spelling development:

* *A Guide to Children's Spelling Development for Parents and Teachers*, by Mary Tarasoff

* *Spelling Strategies You Can Teach*, by Mary Tarasoff

* *Spell by Writing*, by Wendy Bean and Chrystine Bouffler

* *Spelling Instruction That Makes Sense*, by Jo Phenix and Doreen Dunn

These texts acknowledge both the nature of language and the nature of children's learning. They are filled with practical examples of how to teach spelling in ways that build on children's ways of learning. Use them as references and enjoy the delightfully inventive ways in which your students evolve their own spelling.

11

A Typical Day in Class

The two examples of "the day in class" that we provide in this chapter have worked successfully for two teachers and, like all learning, continue to evolve from day to day and year to year. We include them as general models that you may want to use as a reference for structuring your day to meet your personal needs, those of your students, and the requirements of your curriculum guides.

As we look back on Margaret's way of starting on her new path of teaching/learning and how she has evolved her approach, we see an ever-increasing sharing of responsibility with her students and with it greater satisfaction and enjoyment both for her and the children who flourish under her flexible class management. As her trust in children's ability to learn and to take responsibility has grown year by year, so has her confidence in letting go of more and more control-by-teacher structures for learning and for setting the social climate. (See also chapter 7 on beginning the year and chapter 5 on the importance of kid watching.)

A day in Margaret's kindergarten to grade-two class

MORNING

The day begins with only the older group of children in attendance. Later in the year some of the kindergarten children who have demonstrated their readiness to participate in a full day of school join their more mature classmates. But during the early part of the year, kindergarten children attend afternoons only.

Teacher establishes contact with children at the door, greets them, and connects with them each day. She greets them, makes eye contact, and exchanges a few words with each child. She listens to the children, acknowledges their messages, and laughs with them. She assesses the children's attitudes and moods and picks up ideas for interest studies. She also has a quick word with any parents who come in.

Students find their places at tables by looking for their name cards, which the teacher puts in a different place each day to give the children practice in reading and in getting to know the other children. They stay at their tables just long enough for roll call. They take turns taking roll call, which involves living math: for example, counting, adding, subtracting, and figuring out how many students are present, how many absent, how many boys, how many girls, and how many kindergarteners.

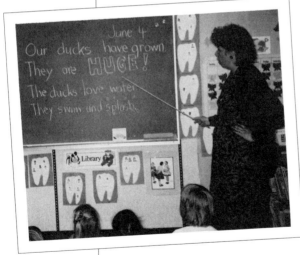

Morning Meeting *(with children gathered on the carpet in front of the chalkboard)*

Students interact with the teacher and each other, talking about things that interest or concern them.

Teacher listens, comments, expands, assesses – who is participating, who is speaking up for the first time, who is learning to take turns, who attends well. She picks up ideas for interest studies and possible news items.

Discussion

This leads to consensus about news items that will go on the board that day.

News Time

This is the most formal skill-building session of the day. Children observe, practice, and receive feedback on composing, spelling, patterns of English orthography, syntax and grammar, punctuation, and editing.

Teacher writes on the board and models spelling, editing, and composing. She thinks aloud for students: "*We. w-e.* I need a capital *w* here, because that's the beginning of our sentence. *Are* [Student offers *r*. Teacher puts the *r* down.] "That's right, we need an *r* here, and to make that standard spelling we also need an *a* at the beginning and an *e* at the end. Now I need a period here, because that's the end of our sentence."

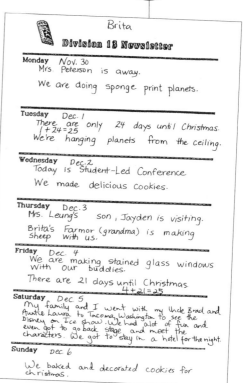

Brita

Division 13 Newsletter

Monday   Nov. 30
Mrs. Peterson is away.
We are doing sponge print planets.

Tuesday   Dec. 1
There are only 24 days until Christmas.
1 + 24 = 25
We're hanging planets from the ceiling.

Wednesday   Dec. 2
Today is Student-Led Conference
We made delicious cookies.

Thursday   Dec. 3
Mrs. Leung's son, Jayden is visiting.
Brita's Farmor (grandma) is making
Sheep with us.

Friday   Dec. 4
We are making stained glass windows
with our buddies.
There are 21 days until Christmas.
4 + 21 = 25

Saturday   Dec. 5
My family and I went with my Uncle Brad and
Auntie Laura to Tacoma, Washington to see the
Disney on Ice show. We had a lot of fun and
even got to go back stage and meet the
characters. We got to stay in a hotel for the night.

Sunday   Dec. 6
We baked and decorated cookies for
christmas.

Students observe, compose, spell, edit, reflect, discuss, revise, play around with language, make decisions, and learn about phonics. As the year progresses, the students chime in more and more to "help" with the spelling and then the editing, and to participate in discussions about such things as sound-alike and look-alike words.

Teacher makes sure all students have opportunities to participate at their own levels. She evaluates the students' performances unobtrusively, notes the skills that students demonstrate. She develops a sense of the natural sequence of learning. She watches the students' levels of participation, looks for signs of restlessness, and lengthens or shortens the session to fit that day's needs.

Daily news (far left) deals with topics that concern or interest the children. Each week, copies of the children's daily news make up the newsletter (above) that goes home on Friday and returns the following Monday with comments about the weekend, written by parents or students.

Reading the News

Teacher models fluent, expressive reading and runs her hands or a pointer smoothly along the lines of print on the board.

Students volunteer to read the news sentences (with or without help depending on their levels). Within a few weeks, they no longer need the teacher's modeling but begin the reading without such help.

Fun with Spelling

Teacher does such things as talking about sound-alike words: *two - to - too, four - for.* She invites play with spelling patterns –"Let's put down all the *ea* words [*wh* words, silent *k* words] you know." Then she erases a few words from the news on the board to have children come to the board to fill in those spaces.

Students volunteer to fill in the blanks (with or without help).

Teacher then puts a message on the board by simply drawing dashes to indicate the number of letters per word. She invites students to come to the board to fill in the blanks. (See also chapter 10 on spelling.)

Children (at top) delight in taking turns filling in blanks on the chalkboard.

Taped readings (above right) provide enjoyable practice in gaining fluency.

Students have fun trying to reconstruct the message. They use their knowledge of word length – two-letter and three-letter words first, then syntax (a sentence probably starts with *we*, not with *to* or *in*). Some very astute inference drawing happens with this activity.

First Story Time of the Day

Teacher reads fiction, nonfiction, poetry, newspaper articles - anything that is fun or interesting. She also tape-records her reading, including her interactions with students. The recording is then put into the listening center with the book she has read so that students can follow the text as they listen.

Students listen to the story, talk about it, look at the pictures, ask questions, relate the story to their lives, note familiar authors and similarities with other stories they have heard, internalize book language to use in their own writing, and, most important, develop a taste for literature. Some students listen to the story again at the listening center, following the text with their eyes as they listen to the taped reading.

Writing Workshop

Teacher invites children to talk about what they might like to write about that day. She encourages, probes, suggests, and listens as some of the children struggle to find topics.

Students discuss with the teacher and with each other what they plan to write, then go to their tables when they have topics that interest them. The youngest children nearly always start by drawing a picture.

Teacher sits down to write, then moves about the classroom encouraging students and helping to extend thoughts and ideas. She does not spell for the children at this time.

Everyone draws or writes, edits, proofreads, shares, and files finished writing in their writing portfolios. The amount of writing and length of time spent on it vary with each child's level of development.

Teacher conferences with individual students on conference day (usually held on Fridays or as requested by individual children).

Center Time

As each student finishes his writing, he chooses a reading/writing activity in one of the centers.

Children enjoy sharing their writing during Author's Circle and readily respond to suggestions from the audience.

Author's Circle

Students gather around a special "Author's Chair" to share, discuss their writing, encourage each other, offer constructive suggestions, ask questions, or otherwise influence each other's writing so that it begins to show concern for the reader or listener and becomes more expressive.

AFTER RECESS

Book Time/Sharing Time

Everyone selects books or stories and sits down to read. The youngest children may simply look at the pictures. Sharing time follows, during which children are invited to talk about their books, read sections aloud, or show pictures. Some share with the whole class, some with two or three buddies.

Math Time

Teacher puts out math materials and talks to children about the work they will do that day. She demonstrates ways of working with pattern blocks and other concrete materials. As necessary, she explains about grouping units into tens, tens into hundreds; introduces measurement concepts; connects math work to real work (using money, counting books, or supplies). She encourages children to work together to extend their number concepts and works with individuals or small groups to explain, expand on, and clarify math concepts.

Students work with manipulative materials at levels appropriate to their maturity or experience. They share, discuss, ask questions, work out answers, make discoveries, develop pattern recognition, and learn number facts. They transfer what they learn to real life – counting, measuring, dealing with money, producing simple graphs, solving problems, estimating.

Story Time (*ends the morning*)

Teacher reads a story aloud. She wonders out loud about content or interesting words, discusses connections to children's lives, enriches stories by adding extra detail, and enters into the feelings of the story with the children.

Students listen to the story, interacting with the teacher and each other. They comment on the story and what it means to them.

AFTERNOON

Kindergarten children join the older students, and the class has the full age-spread of kindergarten to grade two.

News Time

This is a modified version of the morning news with emphasis on input from the youngest children. During the first month of school the older children participate so that they can model giving news and help the kindergarteners with spelling. Later the older students almost always tiptoe away to attend to their own work, usually independent writing.

Writing Workshop (*for afternoon children*)

Teacher gives every child a piece of paper and tells them, "This is writing time. Draw a picture first and then we'll see what you want to write." She gets hands-on work going right away - drawing, pretend writing. While this is going on, she walks around, encouraging drawing and talking. She asks about the pictures – "What do you want to tell about your picture?" – and suggests they do pretend writing when the children say they don't know how to write: "I used to do pretend writing when I was a little girl." She helps with awareness of beginning consonants: "That's a beautiful picture of a sailboat. Tell me what it sounds like when you say *sailboat*." (The child manages to produce an *s* and prints it as a beginning.)

Catch-up Time (*for morning children, time to finish their morning reading or writing projects or to initiate new ones.*)

Teacher works individually with students who need extra help.

Students complete work, then mingle and talk. The older students enjoy talking to and working with the kindergarteners.

Story Time

Teacher selects stories particularly suited to the interests of the younger children, but everyone joins in and enjoys the session.

Choosing Time

Individuals or groups work at an activity: projects; math, reading, inventions, writing; library, games and toys; music, social studies, French; computers, physical education, science, art.

Story Time

Teacher draws children together for yet another story.

Active Time (outdoors if weather permits, indoors if it doesn't)

Looking Back Over the Day

Everyone discusses how the day went, what happened, what may happen tomorrow, what went well, what can be improved next time and how.

Day Plans are personal and varied. Anne Peterson provided this example, which is quite general and allows for the spontaneous changes that arise when the teacher takes advantage of teachable moments. But the Day Plan gives general guidelines and can be very useful to a substitute teacher who is unfamiliar with the usual sequence of activities in class.

Day Plan, 1992-93

8:40-9:30 **Greeting and Attendance.** Children enter, find name cards, and sit at tables. Attendance form is completed.

Move to Story Corner for Morning Meeting. Children are given the opportunity to express themselves. Class thinks of news of the day; recorded on chalkboard by teacher. (Use this for demonstrating phonics, spelling, capitals, punctuation, etc.) News from the week is written up as a newsletter and taken home on Friday.

Shared reading. Songs, poems, big books, theme-related books are read, re-read, and discussed.

9:30-10:15 **Writing Workshop.** Children have own choices of topic, which often come from news or stories just read. Each child conferences with teacher at least once a week. When writing is finished, date stamp and file or put in Author's Circle basket.)

Projects. Children move to centers where they choose their own projects or activities. (They can choose from writing, reading, language games, listening center.)

10:15-10:30 Recess.

10:30-10:45 **Author's Circle.** Children take turns sitting in Author's Chair to read the writing they completed that day. Audience may give positive comments or ask clarifying questions.

10:45-11:45 **Calendar/Math.** Complete calendar using math concepts - pattern counting, place value.

Math concept introduced or reviewed with whole group.

Math center. Children move to Center and choose materials to solve problems or demonstrate knowledge at their own levels of development. Teacher floats or works with small group.

11:45-12:00 Story.

12:00-12:40 Lunch.

12:40-1:15 **D.E.A.R.** (Drop Everything And Read)

Teacher reads for a while and then works with small groups reading together from multiple copy books.

1:15-2:15 **Developmental Play.** Children choose from Centers -

Writing   Science
Drama   Reading
Math   Construction
Creation   Games

Centers are designed to meet changing needs of students and changing interests. Curriculum requirements for Science and Social Studies are met through theme-related activities and Centers.

2:15-2:30 **Closing.** Discussion of day's activities with the following statements in mind:

–   The most interesting thing I read today was...
–   In Math I learned ... but I still wonder about....
–   The best question I asked today was....
–   My biggest frustration today was....
–   I especially enjoyed ... because....

Karen Abel's grade-two-three day

Karen Abel, whose comments pulled together the bits and pieces of our in-class observations with a synopsis of her grade-two-three day, said much the same thing as Margaret about the many changes she has made in the last few years – drawing children into problem solving, having them generate and enforce the rules that lead to harmonious in-class relations, changing her way of teaching math, becoming more of a co-learner with the children, leaving the structure of her day more flexible than ever before.

Like Margaret, Karen makes meeting the needs of her students the essence of teaching, and she looks well beyond the narrow confines of a grade-two-three class to the demands that will be made on her students in the community and later on at work. Her teaching is characterized by an emphasis on inculcating the ability to work harmoniously, to form teams, to negotiate, to settle problems and disputes in productive ways. Stretching the children's capacity to learn from day to day and month to month sets the changing pattern of her daily work. Keeping in close contact with the kindergarten-grade-one teachers, she builds on the foundation work the children have done during the previous years and gradually moves them into more and more challenging work as they grow and mature.

MORNING

Morning Meeting

Teacher greets students and makes herself available to those who want to talk to her alone.

Students move independently to the carpet to get ready for the morning meeting. As they wait for their teacher, they sit and talk to each other, play games (clapping, guessing), laugh together, make plans together, or read books.

Everyone looks at the list to see whose turn it is to sit on the couch and the beanbag chair. They talk over plans for the day, share personal stories and experiences, and air any concerns or problems.

Teacher reads aloud a chapter or two of a novel, if the class is not doing an assignment related to a particular book. She introduces new topics, works with students on developing social skills through role playing and discussion, and helps students plan for language arts period.

Language Arts

This varies from day to day but always includes reading/writing activities that integrate not only skill building but work on projects or special interest studies. During the early part of the year this period will include news time to bridge the newcomers' entry into class with familiar work; later there may be a two- to four-week blitz on hand-writing or on specific spelling needs.

Teacher provides a lead-in to the day's work. She discusses possible writing topics with the class. Then she reads a story to which students respond in writing or with a combination of writing and drawing. She gives special assignments for projects, encourages or approves students' special choices, and models the type of work she has in mind. She collaborates with students to set criteria for special projects or assignments.

Students read or write about their research project, write in their journals, make a written account of a field trip or a class visitor, do research on a project of their own choice, run a science experiment as a lead-in to writing, work on themes (Canada, the seashore, Pet Week), select ways of responding to themes (writing a report, making a poster, writing a story, doing a special research project).
Students' responses usually consist of a written report, a visual presentation, or a combination of written, visual, and oral elements. The oral element gives presenters the chance to tell of problems they encountered and how they solved them. The audience offers two or three "bouquets" for work they thought was done well. If they wish, the presenters can request one or two pieces of advice.

Teacher leads a group brainstorming session to generate ideas, words, spelling, facts, or memories for their writing. She encourages mature students to start on their reading/writing project right away. (They don't have to wait for less mature students.) She meets with small groups and individual students who need extra help to get started, helps students generate ideas for writing, places some sentence starters on the board, and encourages drawing to start the ideas flowing.

When that is complete, she conferences with students about their writing, provides sources and advice for research, models researching by extracting information from one or more sources and then pulling it together into sentences and paragraphs. At the same time she unobtrusively assesses students' work habits and progress.

Sometimes she plans special sessions based on her observations of individual students' specific needs; other times she will work with small groups on specific skills (groups are flexible, based on moment-to-moment needs, and change frequently). And she gives special assignments to stretch reading and writing for students who continue to work in one preferred mode – "Today I want you to write a story [report, poem] instead of working in your journal." Throughout she shares ideas and fun with the students as they work. At the end of each session, project, or theme she has a debriefing.

AFTER RECESS

Daily Draw

Students come in after recess and settle down with their sketchbooks. Usually they choose what to draw and what medium to use, but at times the teacher sets a specific task.

Teacher sometimes introduces topics for drawings that are connected with the research or theme the class is currently working on. Occasionally she will ask a student to work on a specific piece for three days – even longer if the work is still productive and absorbing.

Math Time

Students use a lot of concrete manipulatives and reality-bound work to learn basic facts.

Teacher introduces topics, groups children to work cooperatively. (See chapter 8.) She talks to children about the how and why of math, demonstrates that there are more ways than one to proceed, listens to students discuss their work, and elicits descriptions about how they solved problems. As much as possible, she ties math to the work the students do on projects; models problem solving, reflecting on errors; and makes risk taking safe, encouraging children to try different ways of solving problems.

Students work individually or in groups; share information; work at finding multiple solutions; talk about how they found answers; use manipulatives to learn about grouping numbers; use money, games, and cards to learn math facts; and make math facts visual by grouping, stacking, and building.

Story Time

If there is time before lunch, Karen will read to the children, but math will frequently extend to lunch hour. Karen's comment, "Everything always takes longer than I anticipate."

AFTERNOON

Super-quiet Reading Time

This starts right after lunch. To accommodate young students, reading time is only fifteen minutes at the beginning of the year, expanding as the year progresses to twenty-five or thirty minutes. The young students who still find it difficult to sit still for long stretches of time are allowed to get up and exchange their books, but must do so quietly.

Students come in and settle down to read books of their choice, select books to read from the wide choice available, and then sit quietly at their desks to read by themselves.

Shared Reading

This draws students together at the end of the reading period. Students may then share books with two or three friends and can sit anywhere they like. Many choose to continue their individual silent reading. The teacher sometimes listens to individuals read during this time.

Center, Special Project, or Choosing Time

This fills the rest of the afternoon. At times this part of the day is taken up with special subject teaching that could not be fitted into the morning. (Projects such as painting, print-making, or anything else that can be messy or require time to set up are usually begun in the morning in order to provide students with the opportunity and time to solve problems, reflect, and then try again.)

Topics or subjects include: social studies, science, music, computers; physical education, field trips, library time.

Centers provide many choices and open-ended activities. Options include: writing, listening, reading; imagination, math, discovery; games, seasonal or special-interest subjects.

By collaborating, children create elaborate structures during choosing time.

Teacher interacts with individual students, encourages practice on work that needs extra care, observes and makes unobtrusive evaluations, and participates in special activities.

Students work in centers or use the time to catch up on the reading or writing they want to do. Sometimes they join others in special projects.

Looking Back Over the Day

Everyone talks about what the day held for them, evaluates what went well or what could be improved, plans for the next day or the week ahead, catches up on idea sharing, and summarizes what has been learned.

The commonalities

Both Margaret and Karen are always open to change the shape of their days to fit in special events, field trips, or visitors or to work on themes and projects that occasionally demand more sustained efforts. But as we discussed before, a generally predictable sequence of events helps children work independently without having to be told what to do when all along the way. They know when it is reading time, drawing time, or gathering time for morning meeting or looking back over the day, and they begin whether the teacher is there or not.

Talking and listening are highly important parts of the day for both teachers. When children are truly concerned about something or the idea flow is rich and exciting, there is no question of watching the clock to terminate what is manifestly productive.

The climate of delight has an easygoing flow that provides comfort and security. Children and teachers know that they are not beset by time pressures and schedules that carve the day into predetermined blocks. Work flows naturally and productively, and at the end of the year teachers, students, and parents can look back with satisfaction on the wealth of learning that not only produced "the basics" but went far beyond.

12

To Be Accountable, Turn the Curriculum Upside Down

We have much to learn by using the child as our theoretical and curricular informant. "The child as informant" is our call to the profession to go beyond kid watching to the active examination of current assumptions about language learning and instruction (Harste et al 1984).

The real intent of curriculum documents has always been to ensure that students learn what they need to know – both in school and out. In the past, in an effort to make requirements more explicit, well-meaning experts dismembered the intended outcomes into minute skills and steps, and teachers were (or felt they were) constrained to follow all the steps in the sequence prescribed. The sad fact is that in dismembering the body of knowledge, "the experts" killed the life spark of learning, and both they and the teachers often lost track of the ultimate aim of that disjointed memory work. Reading, its joys and marvelous usefulness, was transformed into phonics drills and worksheets. Writing, the excitement of preserving and conveying thoughts and messages, became more a matter of penmanship and rules of spelling, grammar, and proper structure. Math, that wonderful and often mysterious tool, turned into a dull – or scary – routine of committing tables and rules to memory. Assumptions about language and how children learn had no place in these documents.

In the "eternal triangle of education – the *teacher*, the *child* and the *curriculum*" (Boomer 1982) – the traditional curriculum had disproportionate importance relative to the other two parts. It denied the professional expertise of teachers and ignored children's natural curiosity and effective ways of learning. One aim of exploring the role of the teacher in this book is to affirm the need to restore a balance among the three parts of the educational triangle.

When we talk about giving children choices, building on teachable moments, and being flexible in everyday planning, there is no intent to deny the importance of the curriculum as an authoritative guide to learning outcomes. In discussions of teacher autonomy and professionalism in making the multitude of decisions required each day in the classroom, there is no suggestion that the teacher should simply ignore the curriculum. On the contrary, her new role is to make learning come alive, "to see the curriculum as an overall plan that is shaped both by her and the children" (Peetoom 1992). That personal input by the teacher takes into account how children learn, and instead of skills being ends in themselves, they become the means of achieving the intrinsic aims of the curriculum.

Where does the curriculum lead?

Being accountable for children's learning means knowing the curriculum at a level that moves beyond sequences of skills and facts and coming to the true intent of the specified learning outcomes. At the primary level, all the language and communication skills are central and constitute what is referred to as "the basics." The main goal of the curriculum is to produce readers and writers who use and enjoy written language in all its facets. Learning letters, phonics rules, or spelling is merely one aspect of reading and writing to communicate. Communication also includes speaking and listening, and though they were often conspicuous by their absence in scope and sequence charts, they are part of the underlying goals of the curriculum. Teachers and children who collaborate to read and write, to tell and listen to stories, and to give and follow written descriptions and instructions are meeting the most important curriculum goals inherent in all the detailed skills and sequences that may be outlined: functional literacy and the ability and desire to communicate well. What could be more "basic" than that?

The basics in math are much more than memorizing times tables and doing exercises. There is no question that the intended goals of curriculum guidelines for mathematics are to produce an understanding of how math works, how it can be applied in innumerable ways in everyday life. Yet the skill exercises outlined in traditional curricula use only "route" memory instead of setting the work of learning skills into contexts that show children the everyday applications of math. That kind of decontextualized work "is similar to giving them a recipe to follow. In the end, the work may be completed, but they will not be able to deviate from the recipe in future situations" (Gamberg et al 1988). Here again, consulting the curriculum involves an exploration of where it intends to lead the learners. Unquestionably, the intent is to have children understand how and why to use math in the everyday world and to give them as many tools as possible to work effectively with numbers.

TURNING THE CURRICULUM UPSIDE DOWN

Looking at the goals toward which the curriculum intends to lead is a way of turning it upside down. It is a way of affirming that the ultimate goals are the most important part. However, in the scramble to deal with all the initial details noted in the curriculum, we often did not reach those important goals. "Many of us know of young children who learned to read by *working backwards so to speak*" (Schonell 1961, italics in original). It is an interesting commentary on our conviction about the rightness of our own course of instruction to have learning to read by reading referred to as "working backwards," or, as Schonell terms it, by "indirect reading instruction." It seems that curriculum experts created a mind-set that runs counter to what children do naturally and well – learning by doing and working the details out only after the fact.

Similarly, in math, Australian teachers have tested "using mathematics books backwards". They point out that mathematics books are often set out in a specific order that fits traditional curriculum documents well:

1. introduction and the rule(s) for a topic

2. some type examples

3. lots of exercises

4. problems for the better students, involving the application of the rules and routines practiced earlier

(Smart et al 1982)

The same teachers say:

> The end result is that many students do not get to the application stage and stay awkwardly in the exercise stage, with half–remembered routines being applied hopefully to the next example. This leaves those students vulnerable, because rote learning, which is not anchored by understanding, is often lost or misapplied and cannot be monitored for meaning. Thus we inherit the student behaviors we all know and love so well: the forgetting overnight, of what appear to have been well–practiced routines, the satisfaction with answers that are patently nonsensical, the confusion of types of problems.

That realization led these teachers to turn the sequence of math routines around, to begin by posing real problems – problems that extended beyond school and beyond mathematics lessons – and to "have students collaborate to develop possible solutions to the problems and their justification for them." With that approach, students become engaged in mathematical thinking – the true aim of the math curriculum – and they may actually be ready and willing to tackle other problems and even rules that traditionally are the first part of mathematics lessons.

And so we have come full circle. By turning the curriculum upside down, we are not denying the importance of detailed skills, but we begin our teaching with the most important aim – understanding and application of what is to be learned. Projects and themes, reading, writing, math applied to everyday tasks, and discussions that focus on real-life concerns of children become the means of teaching "the basics," the facts and skills children will need in the world outside of school. But since many curriculum guidelines still build their lists of requirements by starting with the component parts of learning, teachers need to rephrase the questions they ask when trying to determine whether their teaching is moving the children toward the intrinsic aims of the curriculum.

Finding the fit between children's learning and the curriculum

To maintain a proper balance in the educational triangle - teacher, child, curriculum – we look to the children to find the fit between their ways of structuring their learning and the sequence of topics in the curriculum guidelines. We used to check the curriculum to find out exactly *what* we were to teach *when*. Now we ask ourselves "*When* do the children learn *what?*" For example, research has firmly established that children are concrete, global learners. But instead of suggesting that teachers introduce children to literacy by reading to and with them to teach them what reading is all about, curriculum guidelines generally demanded (some still demand today) that teachers *begin* reading instruction by teaching the ABCs. This ignores the reality that children coming to school are concrete learners and meaning-makers. Abstract symbols have little or no meaning for them as building blocks for learning. To complicate matters further, ignoring that children perceive consonants first, curriculum scope and sequence charts traditionally start with drills on short vowels, which children find mystifying to say the least.

Once we acknowledge that children's natural learning moves from whole to parts and from meaning-making to more abstract work with sounds and letters, in-class observations of how children process information – rather than the scope and sequence charts of old - guide learning. With that change, instead of dictating exactly what is supposed to happen in the classroom and when, the curriculum becomes a scoreboard for checking off the children's steps forward, as well as a reminder of steps yet to be taken. The skills listed on scope and sequence charts will certainly be learned, but not in the sequence shown on the chart.

"NEGOTIATING THE CURRICULUM"

If the details included in the curriculum show the teacher what else the children need to learn in a given area, the children will show her how to build and expand their knowledge in ways that are meaningful to them. As they connect their learning to their own experience or interests, they give the teacher opportunities to build their vocabularies, elaborate on factual knowledge, and broaden their concepts of numbers. Such work often moves well beyond narrowly defined curriculum goals. Boomer (1982) speaks of "negotiating the curriculum":

> Negotiating the curriculum means deliberately planning to invite students to contribute to, and to modify, the educational program, so that they will have a real investment both in the learning journey and in the outcomes. Negotiation also means making explicit, and then confronting, the constraints of the learning context and the non-negotiable requirements that apply.

He points out that even the youngest students are able and willing to help shape what is to be learned in the classroom and how that learning takes place. Our own experience certainly bears out that, once children know they will be heard, they freely share their ideas. So it is you, the teacher, who sets the scene to create that balance in the educational triangle among curriculum, students, and teacher.

Karen's grade-two-three students are well accustomed to negotiating, debating, and then voting on issues of classroom work. They learn to work in teams, resolve disagreements, and come to consensus.

Being accountable is as important as ever

Turning the curriculum upside down and beginning work with the desired end rather than the usual small building blocks means that being accountable also gets turned upside down. The venerable custom of monitoring small incremental steps along a prescribed linear continuum does not work. Tests and worksheets need to be replaced by new questions about reading, writing, and using math:

* Is the child reading for meaning?

* Does he use books to find information?

* Does the student gather information for writing?

* Does writing spring from the student's interest?

* Can the student find topics to write about?

* Does the student discuss problems in productive ways that lead to a variety of solutions?

* Does he use math as part of his projects?

* Has he found ways to integrate his knowledge of numbers with his day-to-day activities?

Keeping the ultimate aims of the curriculum firmly in mind, ask yourself what indications the children are giving you that they are moving toward reading for meaning, writing to communicate, and doing math for practical purposes. Those moves will be different from the indicators of progress you may have used in the past, but they are generally more significant than the rote memorization of particles of language. To provide some more specific behaviors to look for and use when keeping track of children's progress, we include two checklists originally published in *The Learners' Way* (see figures 4 and 5).

As children progress in their moves towards literacy and numeracy, you will be able to use more conventional checklists and landmarks to note progress. As we suggested in earlier chapters, you may also want to construct your own checklists to fit specific jobs or children. In the meantime it helps to have a rough guideline of the sequence in which children's learning is likely to emerge as they learn "the basics" of literacy.

Figure 4

INDIVIDUAL PROFILE OF EMERGENT READING

Name of child

Teacher

Period of observation: from   to   Total observations

Marking: Checkmark = child performs   Minus = child does not perform   Blank = no opportunity to observe

Use of models   Date

Watches others to learn about reading behaviors
   Copies actions/responses of teacher or children
   Rehearses silently to approximate reading behavior of
     teacher or peers
   Begins to say some words when listening to others read
   Joins in to "read" a refrain or familiar passage

Imitates sequencing
   Leafs through book from front to back
   Tracks oral reading from left to right
   Tracks print with hands or eyes while others read
   Prints from left to right

Differentiating parts – language development

Develops oral fluency
   Communicates freely with teachers and peers
   Describes pictures or events accurately
   Dictates news items, picture captions, or personal
     messages
   Uses words learned from reading or classroom
     activities – expands vocabulary

Demonstrates knowledge of words
   Gives only one word when asked to say or read a word
   Recognizes some words on sight
   Leaves spaces between words when printing
   Gives one word at a time when dictating a sentence

Acquires knowledge of letters
   Begins to print letters instead of using wavy lines
   Names letters accurately when seeing or printing them
   Recognizes sounds of initial consonants
   Tries to produce/feel the sound of letters when writing

Integration

Uses the context or setting to aid reading
Uses illustrations as aids in recognizing printed messages
Uses familiar language patterns as aids to reading
Substitutes words that fit the syntax and meaning
when reading
Refers to familiar patterns or story lines to anticipate
what comes next

Keeps the focus on meaning
Relates books and print to story reading
Recognizes that print conveys the meaning in books
and stories
Relates stories to own experience
Provides appropriate captions or labels for pictures

Shows expanding cognitive development
Remembers stories or sequence of events
Anticipates or infers words from story line
Asks questions about stories or other printed materials
Attends when listening to stories, shows increased
attention span

Active involvement and social development

Demonstrates motivation and interest
Handles books, looks at pictures, or plays with books
Takes (brings) books (from) home
Enjoys and uses reading activities
Plays with word/letter games and puzzles

Develops independence
Does not cling to teacher for support or answers
Proceeds to next step in a task without help
Selects new activity when finished with a task
Chooses books or stories to be read

Shows growth in personal development
Relates well with teacher and peers
Uses learning materials appropriately
Accepts responsibility – for own belongings, cleaning
up, social interactions
Acts appropriately during book time

Listens attentively
Follows directions accurately
Hears necessary cues, screens out distractions
Discriminates sounds accurately
Demonstrates a sense of rhythm

Figure 5

INDIVIDUAL PROFILE OF READING DEVELOPMENT

_____

Name of child
_____

Teacher
_____

Period of observation: from   to   Total observations

Marking: Checkmark = child performs   Minus = child does not perform   Blank = no opportunity to observe

Date

Initial reading – gross performance
   Attends to reading
   "Reads" from memory
   Recognizes some words on sight
   Uses familiar phrases as guide to reading

Use of models
   Observes teachers and peers in learning situations
   Imitates reading/writing behaviors of teacher and peers
   Produces the same intonation patterns as fluent readers
   Plays teacher, using the teacher's actions and words

Use of feedback
   Listens attentively during reading/writing conferences
   Asks for comments or questions during authors' circle
   Asks questions about words, spellings, or story content
   Speaks up to give positive/constructive feedback to peers

Practice
   Reads/writes during center or choosing time
   Pays attention to books during book time
   Participates in plays or other presentations
   Helps with producing sentences during news time

The move from whole to parts
   Surveys stories before reading them
   Scans lines of print for meaningful units to aid fluent
      reading
   Thinks of message first, before worrying about words
      and spelling
   Uses familiar story lines as guides to story reading and
      anticipating words

Spelling – differentiating parts
   Recognizes/provides initial/median/final consonants
      when writing or spelling
   Converts spoken language to written symbols phonetically

Spelling – differentiating parts (continued)
   Invents own spelling patterns
   Begins to recognize vowel sounds

Use of letter-sound correspondence
   Comments on sound–alike words during news time or
      writing workshop
   Begins to use consonants as clues to sounding out
      unfamiliar words
   Notes similarities between words and their sounds
   Generalizes known spelling patterns to new words

Use of language patterns in reading and writing
   Reads in phrases instead of word–for–word
   Converts text to own language patterns
   Self-corrects misreadings to fit syntax and meaning
   Develops distinct writing styles to suit the different
      purposes of writing

Reading for meaning and enjoyment
   Relates books and stories to own experience
   Uses books to gain knowledge
   Reads aloud to other children or adults
   Deviations from the text during oral reading leave
      overall meaning intact

Independence
   Moves from completed task to new one without help
   Knows rules about use of equipment and supplies and
      applies them
   Generates ideas and initiates own projects
   Selects books and activities independently during center
      or choosing time

Motivation and interest
   Takes (brings) books (from) home
   Has favorite authors or reading topics
   Prefers reading/writing to playing when given a choice
   Talks about books and stories with others

Writing
   Writes to add meaning to drawings
   Composes complete sentences and messages during
      writing workshop
   Writes spontaneously three or more sentences
   Uses writing purposefully during or outside of writing
      workshop

THE "LITERACY CONTINUUM"

As your students work on more global understanding of literacy, you may find it reassuring to study what we term "the literacy continuum."

Stages of language development

1. Gurgling, squealing, crying, conveying feelings with sounds
2. Babbling, using and playing with recognizable language sounds
3. Adopting the intonation pattern of language spoken in the home; babbling speech-like sounds though not yet using words
4. Expressing meaning through intonation without using actual words: questions, requests, demands, protests
5. Using one-word statements and rudimentary diction to convey messages
6. Moving to two- and three-word sentences – primarily using nouns and verbs
7. Saying longer sentences using functor words and more accurate diction
8. Overgeneralizing patterns – "I bringed..."
9. Evidencing the internalization of rules: word order, sorting out pronoun references, accurate use of tenses
10. Moving toward greater accuracy of diction, language usage, and fluency

Stages of writing/composing

Note: Items I through 4 are "babbling in print." Children say message while "writing" or "read" it when finished. They intend to convey meaning.

1. Drawing pictures to convey meaning
2. Combining letters and numbers randomly on page
3. Placing strings of letters left to right, top to bottom on page
4. Segmenting letters into word-like units
5. Writing one-word sentences: *FLURS* – Read: *I planted the flowers*
6. Moving to two- and three-word sentences: *ALLISS BTHDAY* – Read: *It is Alissa's birthday today,* or *CAT DOG* – Read: *I have a cat and a dog*
7. Composing longer sentences, some compound. *I love cats Som KIDS in my class have TheaM anD I'm Gld to Be at School*
8. Generalizing patterns of familiar models: stories, poems, nursery rhymes
9. Evidencing the internalization of rules: placing periods at end of sentences; shifting writing style to fit topic; varying sentences
10. Writing fluently and coherently – continuing to evolve

Stages of spelling/printing

1. Pretend spelling, using letter-like forms and scribbles
2. Babbling in print, using strings of letters including some numbers
3. Grouping letters into word-like units, making word patterns
4. Using one-letter spelling: *UR* – Read: *You are*
5. Using two- and three-letter spelling: *W WNT HM* – Read: *We went home*
6. Using phonetic spelling based largely on consonants: *MM = Mom*
7. Expanding phonetic spelling to include some vowels: *We want to the Cirks*
8. Overgeneralizing known patterns: *BRITE, NOO = bright, new*
9. Evidencing internalization of rules: vowels are part of each word; double consonants change vowel sound; silent *e* affects sound
10. Moving toward greater accuracy and larger repertoire of spelling patterns

Stages of reading

1. Listening to stories, unaware of print and its function
2. Picture reading, describing pictures
3. Going through motions of reading: turning pages, tracking print with hands, rehearsing silently
4. Pretend reading: becoming aware of need to scrutinize print, making up story, or drawing on memory
5. Using memory reading, sometimes tracking print with hands but not eyes
6. Scanning for meaning and saying individual words (mostly nouns and verbs) during unison reading or while reading alone
7. Listening for repetitive parts of story and chiming in for a few words – usually nouns and verbs – while scanning text with eyes
8. Generalizing knowledge gleaned from practicing with familiar texts to unfamiliar ones: words, phrasing, style
9. Evidencing internalization of patterns of written language and rules of phonics. Using context, syntactic patterns, knowledge of subject matter, and letter and word sounds to derive meaning from print
10. Reading with fluency and expression (intonation indicates comprehension)

Our finding has been that there are close parallels between the stages of children's early language acquisition and their emergent reading, writing, and spelling. Being aware of this natural flow of learning confirmed for us that the children were making appropriate progress. It also reconciled us to the lateness of detailed skill development and gave us the confidence to concentrate on detecting the higher-level skills of comprehension, interest in literature, use of semantic and syntactic cues in learning to read, development of spelling patterns, and the evolution of composition *before* all the "basic skills" had fully evolved. Without fail, the details emerged once the children were ready to integrate them with their higher-level skills.

LOOKING FOR "THE BASICS"

The oft-repeated outcry for a "return to the basics" is not likely to stop. To satisfy concerned parents, administrators, and the media, it becomes important to define just what *is* "basic" in learning. Looking back to their own schooling, those who call for a return to the basics almost invariably have detailed skills and rote memory in mind. But if we look at the ultimate aim of school curricula, the basics deal with the kind of skills that students will need in the world of work. Those broad aims are echoed in a U.S. government report on what work requires of schools. Though it lists specific skills, what the report refers to as a "three-part foundation" sounds more like the end products of learning. Thinking skills and personal qualities are included, and even without a look at the much more detailed "five competencies" included, the report offers a sound, and very practical, guide to looking at the broad learning goals inherent in school curricula.

FINDING "THE FOUNDATION SKILLS" IN CHILDREN'S WORK

To satisfy those who call for a "return to the basics," you will find in the SCANS Report concrete descriptions that translate intrinsic curriculum goals into broadly based skills, skills that are frequently in the news and in discussions that call for school reforms and preparing children more fully for a world that requires lifelong learning.

As you observe children in your classroom you will find that, if you have set an open climate that fosters independent, responsible work, you can check off every one of the skills listed, even for your

Figure 6

SCANS REPORT: WHAT WORK REQUIRES OF SCHOOLS
A Three-Part Foundation

Basic Skills

Reads, writes, performs arithmetic and mathematical operations, listens, and speaks:

Reading – locates, understands, and interprets written information in prose and in documents such as manuals, graphs, and schedules

Writing – communicates thoughts, ideas, information, and messages in writing; and creates documents such as letters, directions, manuals, reports, graphs, and flow charts

Arithmetic/Mathematics – performs basic computations and approaches practical problems by choosing appropriately from a variety of mathematical techniques

Listening – receives, attends to, interprets, and responds to verbal messages and other cues

Speaking – organizes ideas and communicates orally

Thinking Skills

Thinks creatively, makes decisions, solves problems, visualizes, knows how to learn, and reasons:

Creative Thinking – generates new ideas

Decision Making – specifies goals and constraints, generates alternatives, considers risks, evaluates and chooses best alternative

Problem Solving – recognizes problems, devises and implements plan of action

Seeing Things in the Mind's Eye – organizes and processes symbols, pictures, graphs, objects, and other information

Knowing how to learn – uses efficient learning techniques to acquire and apply new knowledge and skills

Reasoning – discovers a rule or principle underlying the relationship between two or more objects and applies it when solving a problem

Personal Qualities

Displays responsibility, self-esteem, sociability, self-management, and integrity and honesty:

Responsibility – exerts a high level of effort and perseveres toward goal attainment

Self-Esteem – believes in own self-worth and maintains a positive view of self

Sociability – demonstrates understanding, friendliness, adaptability, empathy, and politeness in group settings

Self-Management – assesses self accurately, sets personal goals, monitors progress, and exhibits self-control

Integrity/Honesty – chooses ethical courses of action

Reprinted from *What Work Requires of Schools*, prepared by the Secretary's Commission on Achieving Necessary Skills and the U.S. Dept. of Labor, 1991 kindergarten children. As you have modeled attentive listening and open-minded discussion for the children, their communication skills, creative decision making, analyzing, and reasoning function freely. The climate of independence and self-reliance in your class has established the personal qualities, and involving them on an ongoing basis in evaluating and then upgrading their own work has put them on the road to self-management as described in the report.

Like the petals of a flower, the five primary program goals of the British Columbia Ministry of Education surround a child who is actively at play. The shape of the logo symbolizes the unity and importance of all five goals in fostering intellectual, career, and human and social development.

FOLLOWING BROADER CURRICULUM GOALS

Across North America, states and provinces are replacing the traditional curricula for the primary years. These new curricula express requirements in much broader terms. Here in British Columbia the Ministry of Education has developed five broad "Primary Program Goals" that are given equal weight in the overall program. To help teachers decide whether children are progressing toward those goals, the Ministry has issued sample questions that teachers can use as a starting point:

Artistic and Aesthetic Development

Does the child:

* demonstrate an interest in and enthusiasm for art, drama, and music?
* demonstrate a willingness to participate in a variety of sensory experiences?
* demonstrate an ability to imagine and visualize?
* use materials appropriately?
* use a variety of materials/media to explore/learn/represent what is known?
* respond to performances (drama, plays, dance, musical performance, other children's work)?
* demonstrate confidence in and acceptance of his or her own creations?

Emotional and Social Development

Does the child:

* cry easily/show anger/use physical force/give in/negotiate?
* act on impulse?

* consider the feelings of others and interact appropriately?
* take emotional risks?
* deal appropriately with the emotions of others?
* express and receive empathy?
* demonstrate play (independent, parallel, cooperative, or organized)?
* choose appropriate peer models?
* accept responsibility?
* make alternate choices when necesssary?
* cope with change?

Intellectual Development

Does the child:
* attend to the task at hand?
* demonstrate curiosity?
* ask questions?
* apply new information?
* exhibit listening behaviors?
* apply problem-solving strategies (define, gather, analyze, solve)?
* use language to explore/learn/represent knowledge and under-standing?
* use language to communicate effectively?
* involve self in processes of reading and writing?
* represent knowledge in a variety of ways?
* apply thinking skills, strategies, processes?
* demonstrate reflective thinking?
* show joy in learning?

Physical Development

Does the child:
* show interest in and participate in physical activity and movement?
* show body and spatial awareness?

* control physical movement (freely, hesitantly, awkwardly, age-appropriately)?

* practice good nutritional habits?

* demonstrate awareness of the importance of physical fitness?

* work cooperatively and collaboratively in a physical activity setting?

* handle toys/tools/implements/equipment appropriately?

* demonstrate an awareness of the need for safety in a variety of settings?

* show care and respect for own and others' bodies?

Social Responsibility

Does the child:

* show sensitivity to other living things?

* show a tolerance for differing opinions, feelings, and points of view?

* accept differences in others (appearances, customs, and habits)?

* appreciate cultural differences?

* take appropriate action without adult reminders?

* lead, cooperate, and follow as appropriate?

* participate in decisions made by the group?

* assume responsibility when given directions?

* care for classroom equipment?

* show flexibility when dealing with change?

* appreciate and respect the environment?

(British Columbia Ministry of Education 1991)

There are remarkable parallels between those questions and the items on the SCANS Report shown on page 257, and it is reassuring that government departments of education are responding to real needs in the real world. As you can see, life skills and broadly based competencies predominate. If your district or supervisory body has issued similar documents to those we have in British Columbia, you may want to abstract questions from them to serve as your guide in monitoring children's progress.

As you observe your students at work, we suggest that you make notes on the specific learning you observe. Generally we find that it becomes both simpler and more rewarding to wait until the end of the day to reflect on all the learning that has come out of the exciting unit on pirates, the absorption in the science experiments, or the field trip to the museum. (See also the scoreboard of skills on page 283 in chapter 13.)

Inherent in all these activities is "finding the curriculum in the children's work." They are invitations to broaden the perspective of monitoring progress, and they are also invitations to stop and reflect on the significance and breadth of the children's work. In the past, we have found that focusing too closely on the minutiae of specific skills created tunnel vision. Now we find that looking for the curriculum in the children's work is a way of widening both the focus and the appreciation of children's learning.

If you draw the children into self-evaluation with the use of a drawing, they will help you generate impressive lists that document just how much learning arises from the fun and excitement of a unit such as this one on pirates that the children themselves initiated. But with or without their help, you can always draw up a checklist of special skills you want the children to acquire at a given point and mark down how their participation in projects helps them learn facts about spelling and printing, conventions of sentence structure, rules about capitalization, or specific number skills.

SOURCES TO HELP YOU ASSESS PROGRESS

In both our previous books we have provided examples of non-conventional ways of assessing progress. Since they have been published, a number of excellent guides to assessment have appeared. Here are three we recommend:

* Braun, Carl. *Looking, Listening, and Learning – Observing and Assessing Young Readers.* Winnipeg, MB: Peguis, 1993.

* Davies, Anne, Caren Cameron, Colleen Politano, and Kathleen Gregory. *Together Is Better – Collaborative Assessment, Evaluation, and Reporting.* Winnipeg, MB: Peguis, 1992.

* Picciotto, Linda Pierce. *Evaluation – A Team Effort.* Toronto: Scholastic, 1992.

Finding the learner in the curriculum

Harste et al (1984) suggest that we see children as "curricular informants" and that we reconsider the nature of the ways they learn language. Garth Boomer (1982) made a strong case for giving children ample opportunity to "negotiate the curriculum" (see page 248), but there is also the need to build children's ways of learning right into the curriculum. Brain research, linguistic studies, and direct observations of learners all confirm that natural learning moves from whole to parts, from concrete to abstract, and from gross processing to fine discrimination.

Turning the curriculum upside down honors that progression. But why not start with the children's ways of learning in the first place? The SCANS Report and the British Columbia curriculum goals offer fine examples of coming right to the heart of what students need to learn. Without denying the importance of detailed skills, both documents focus on the true end results, the deeper learning we want for our students. Keep your focus on the larger, more important goals and see the building of detailed skills as positive steps in the right direction, rather than as ends in themselves.

13.

Buddies–Power in Partnership

There's power in a good partnership. When you tackle a job with the help of your favorite partner, you become instantly aware of the wonderful boost in energy both of you experience. As you talk and work together, you stimulate talents, special skills, and best efforts in each other to an extent not always possible when you work on your own. Your skills, abilities, and personal qualities will complement each other, and the job at hand will become fun. You may find your partner laughs at problems you thought overwhelming. There is the warm feeling of companionship and mutual support as each of you try out new ways of working under the eyes of a friendly observer who is as keen as you are to see what will work and what and how to improve.

Adding a buddy system to your teaching brings that kind of power into your classroom and can turn buddy sessions into the most rewarding time of the week. The kind of buddy system we are talking about results from two teachers making definite plans and setting regular schedules for joining the work of their two classes. The aim is to give students of different ages and levels of maturity a chance to work together on a regular and ongoing basis as "buddies" so that they can form close friendships with one another and derive learning and benefits they are unlikely to find working solely with their own class.

We have observed a few of the important factors that lead to successful buddy work:

* Classes need to be at least two years apart in age/grade level to assure that there will be mutual enhancement and support rather than competition.

* Teachers must be committed to collaborating and sharing the responsibility for setting up and then running the buddy sessions. One of the great benefits of buddy work is the teachers' modeling of animated interactions, mutual support, and close collaboration for the students of both classes.

* Sessions have to be regularly scheduled and predictable – not haphazard or on-again-off-again events.

* The planning of activities has to be sufficiently flexible to make room for spontaneity and student input.

* Teachers must prepare their students for working with buddies through discussions and the open airing of concerns, hopes, and ideas. The more mature students need to give serious thought to the importance and value of the leadership, nurturing, and personal support they will offer their young buddies. The young students need to explore what they will gain from the meetings and what, if any, worries or fears they have. They can also explore how they can involve their mature buddies in their favorite activities and think about the fun of working with their buddies at the many interesting centers available.

* Every student should have a definite say in the selection of his buddy – although teachers will help him choose – and once settled to that choice, make a commitment to stay with his buddy during the joint sessions for the rest of the term.

* Teachers and students need to take time to discuss what transpired during a session – what worked well, what created problems, what was fun and exciting, and what should be improved. Relationship problems need to be ironed out, and students need the opportunity to get the input and advice of their peers about how best to work with their buddies the next time around.

When you observe these guidelines and launch a buddy program, both you and your students will experience a surge of new energy as you all work with a compatible partner and share the excitement of working and learning in new, more creative and productive ways. From the start, working with their little buddies brings out qualities of leadership and caring in the older students, confidence-building and new learning for the younger ones. Over time, there is wonderful growth in creativity, enjoyment in learning, and organization skills for everyone, including the teachers whose close collaboration with a teaching partner is such an essential component of successful buddy work. After all, joining two classes for a few hours or an afternoon is *not* a convenient way to "get a spare"; instead it involves the melding of two talents, two mutually enhancing personalities, and two catalysts for lively interactions to tap that power inherent in partnership.

Getting started

SELECTING A PARTNER FOR TEACHING

In his fable *ZAPP! in Education*, Byham (1992) talks about zapping people's energy to make them glow with an inner light. Having the freedom to make decisions, interacting positively, and being acknowledged are high on the list of ZAPP! power. In selecting a teaching partner, ask yourself the following questions:

* Can we share decision making easily?

* Will we work together harmoniously?

* Do we appreciate each other and feel free to acknowledge the contributions each makes?

To be fairly certain about the answers to those questions, it helps to join forces with someone you know, someone who shares your outlook and has similar ideas on classroom management. If you each share the same vision for your students, you will find it much easier to create a mutually enhancing working relationship that ZAPPs the energy for everyone.

TEACHERS EXPLORE POSSIBILITIES

It is important to create a climate of delight for both young and mature students from the very start. To accomplish this, the two partner teachers need to develop

PARTNERS ENHANCE ONE ANOTHER
Margaret found that she and Marne St. Claire thrived on their joint work. Marne helped Margaret unlock her spontaneity and, in turn, Margaret made it safe for Marne to give full scope to her bubbly personality and prodigious artistic talents. As they became co-creators of the work in class, they also became close friends, and their students thrived on the harmonious, relaxed ways in which the two partner teachers interacted.

some broad guidelines within which each will feel free to move beyond the conventional limits of structured teaching. They must also feel comfortable enough to model the free-flowing give-and-take they hope to instill in their students' interactions. To that end it helps to explore aims and hopes and to reach agreement about the logistics of the joint sessions, including setting the time, place, and duration of each weekly or biweekly session.

Despite the need for some planning and for agreement on the overall aims, it is best to keep guidelines to a minimum and deal with questions as they arise – once actual sharing has begun and you are building on the spontaneous ideas that are bound to pop up when two groups and their teachers interact.

EXPLORING AIMS, HOPES, AND PRACTICALITIES

 What do we hope to achieve for our students?

 How can we make the sessions both enjoyable and productive?

 How much scope will we give to students to shape the sessions?

 How much direction will we give in the selection of partners?

 How permanent will the buddy pairing be?

 What guidelines for conduct and caring will we need?

 What types of activities are likely to enhance learning?

 How will we create a climate that fosters social and academic learning for both buddies?

 How will we encourage buddies to form playground friendships as well as to support each other in classroom work?

 How will we help an only child to enter into a buddy relationship?

 How will we build on our (the teachers') special talents – music, art, science, literature, math, whatever – to foster buddy work?

 How will we share responsibility for the weekly sessions?

 What special gains do we hope to derive for our students and for ourselves?

 Which will be the host and which the visiting class, or should they alternate?

 What is the best day and time of day to hold the sessions?

 How soon after the first week in September should we start?

SETTING THE CLIMATE FOR STUDENTS

Once the two teachers have done their own preliminary explorations and feel comfortable about the overall direction of their joint planning, they prepare their students for the first buddy session. Student input and genuine choices are once again the keys to ensuring that the sessions will be harmonious, free of anxiety, productive of learning, and enjoyable for both the young students and their older buddies. So to prepare, each teacher holds one or more group discussions with her students to describe what is planned and has the students think of ways their interactions with their buddies will be productive for everyone.

Marne made sure her mature students understood the important job they were undertaking in becoming mentors to their younger buddies. She wanted them to know they were doing something worthwhile and that joining the kindergarten-to-grade-two class was not a case of doing "baby stuff." To reap the full benefit of the buddy work, the older students needed time on their own – away from their young buddies – to talk over what they were gaining, the solution to leadership problems that might arise, plans they could make, and special skills or treats they could offer their buddies.

Margaret worked at preparing her young students for all the interesting work they could do with the help of their big buddies. Stressing the fun and excitement of new work, she made sure the children had ample opportunity to voice any fears or worries they might harbor in connection with having a whole class of older students join them. She also reinforced lessons in hospitality and sharing since their class was generally going to host the joint sessions.

ASKING FOR STUDENT INPUT

Help with planning and genuine sharing assures that students enter this first phase of buddy work with enthusiasm. When they know that their ideas are valued and listened to, both young and mature students eagerly respond to the teachers' prompting, explore how buddy work relates to them, and generate plans and ideas for making these get-togethers a success.

The following are some of the questions to explore with the children:

* What do you do at home to help your brother/sister?

* If you don't have any brothers or sisters, how would it feel to have a younger/older sister or brother to talk to?

* Do you remember special fun times when you played/worked with an older/younger buddy?

* Did you ever feel afraid or embarrassed playing with younger/older kids?

* How many of the students in the other class do you already know?

✳ Would you like your buddy to be a boy or a girl?

✳ How can we make sure the buddies feel welcome when they come in to our classroom?

✳ What special activities could we plan?

✳ What do you have to offer your buddy that's special?

✳ How many ways do you know to make your buddy feel comfortable working with you?

✳ How can you make our buddy work a real success?

Any number of other topics may come up in the discussion, as the younger children look at their expectations and concerns about working with older buddies, and the older ones examine the "mature" status they will have when they become mentors to the younger students. If you listen with care, the students themselves will let you know their concerns, hopes, and plans. Any prompting you need to do will be minimal and will probably be limited to active listening and then confirming what the students are saying.

Making buddy work successful

Commitment is the first priority for teachers and students alike. If you stop and start and stop again, keep the schedule too open, or give the sessions little energy, your students get the message that buddy work has little value or importance. To generate the full, positive energy and productivity of buddy work, make a strong commitment to it. The guidelines that follow have worked well for us and a number of teachers who have embarked on a buddy program.

Teachers need to

✳ be compatible, kindred spirits with a desire to work together

✳ practice a division of labor based on their preferences; for example, some like to plan, while others prefer logistics and cleanup

✳ plan together, debrief, evaluate, and watch children become supportive of each other

✳ work hard but reap satisfying benefits (insights into the work and the ways of learning of different levels can be illuminating)

* laugh together, have fun, and let students see their enjoyment
* build up anticipation and excitement for getting together and for each activity
* have interesting projects ready to suggest and implement if the group fails to generate its own plans
* both be present throughout each buddy period
* present and discuss reasons for working with buddies
* separate two buddies who do not work well together
* build on the children's emotional and social needs:
    * liking to be around older/younger children
    * wanting to help/be helped
    * needing kindness, gentleness, compassion, caring
    * thriving on laughter and fun
    * wanting to work together
    * wanting to work with a boy or girl
    * wanting a sibling
    * reducing fear of older or younger children
    * glorying in taking the lead (both young *and* old buddies)

Students need to
* have time to get to know one another before choosing buddies
* have some lead-in discussions to define their roles
* see and feel the commitment and energy their teachers put into the work
* be at least two years apart in age to gain maximum benefit from buddy work

General guidelines

* Designate a regular day and time each week as buddy time.
* Brief and debrief each time to reap full benefits of buddy work.
* Don't worry too much about noise and mess; when fifty to sixty kids get together, their interactions are bound to be noisy.
* Give students enough time to finish projects. Extend the activity over several sessions if necessary.
* Find enough space to spread out work. Use a multipurpose room, a gym, or hallways.
* Give buddies time in their regular classrooms to create cards or gifts for each other on special occasions.
* Put your whole heart into buddy time and enjoy the work.

KNOWING THE GAINS TO BE MADE

Your confidence in the value of buddy work, enthusiasm for its ways of involving kids, and commitment to doing the work will be the main factors in setting the climate for success.

More surely than words or exhortations, your own conviction that buddy work has real value for both the younger and the more mature buddies will set the climate. Students are sensitive to your feelings and are guided by the unspoken messages you give. As they watch the confident, relaxed, and enthusiastic manner in which you and your partner share the preparations and warm–up for each session, they will enter the spirit of open, natural learning and fully savor the pleasure of interacting freely.

You will find that the social learning alone can make the sessions worthwhile. As you progress through the year, older students become very caring and protective. Their young buddies look up to their mentors and model themselves after them; they learn communication skills and lose their fear of interacting with older children. Many bond for the rest of elementary school and form friendships that extend beyond school.

The interactions also spark creativity in ways that enhance both groups. The freedom to be playful, to laugh a lot, and to work with toys and centers generally thought to be "too immature" for the older students frees up their spontaneity and imagination. Having scribes and models helps young students become authors and more effective problem solvers. And the general goodwill that grows with each session extends beyond the classroom, as buddies meet on the playground to carry on a project, play together, or seek protection if the young ones ever feel the need for it. For you, there is the stimulation of interacting creatively with another teacher.

SELECTING BUDDIES

For some years, Margaret's kindergarten–to–grade–two class formed buddy teams with Marne St. Claire's grade–four–to–six students, and the two teachers settled into a routine that worked well for both groups of students. Margaret's own account speaks for itself, but also echoes what other teachers have experienced in similar work.

During the first few days of school, Marne and I would get our stu–

dents together to choose buddies for the year. We felt that a year's commitment was better than asking students to switch halfway through the year. We have found that buddies grow very fond of each other and giving up a buddy becomes too much of a wrench.

Marne's students usually came to our classroom, and, at the beginning of the year, both classes sat down together to talk about what it means to be buddies, how personalities have a way of meshing or getting in the way, and how you need to select your buddy with care to make sure you are just right for each other. The students joined in to talk about loyalty, caring, bonding, helpfulness, friendship, modeling, getting along, problem solving, what to do if there was a disagreement, and how to handle bossiness or overcome shyness. They discussed independence, the importance of helping (but not too much), and the difference between holding your own and being selfish. When there were children in the group who had experienced buddy time the previous school year, these discussions took on amazing depths. The experienced students also injected the enthusiasm of their personal experience with buddy work into these early get-togethers, and some of the more timid newcomers watched with rapt attention as the old-timers told them of the fun they had had during buddy time the previous years.

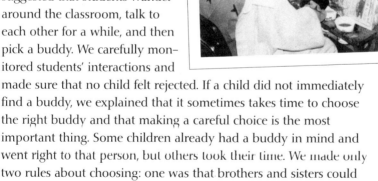

After the group discussion we suggested that students wander around the classroom, talk to each other for a while, and then pick a buddy. We carefully monitored students' interactions and made sure that no child felt rejected. If a child did not immediately find a buddy, we explained that it sometimes takes time to choose the right buddy and that making a careful choice is the most important thing. Some children already had a buddy in mind and went right to that person, but others took their time. We made only two rules about choosing: one was that brothers and sisters could not choose each other as buddies; the other was that the initial choice did not have to be final.

Artwork draws young and mature buddies together at the easel.

AT TIMES THERE CAN BE A MISMATCH   Most students pick well when they select their buddies, but there are occasional mismatches:

Two strong personalities may clash if both are strong–willed and neither is willing to give an inch when it comes to negotiating the how and what of joint projects.

Two "silly" children in a buddy team can disrupt the whole group. Each needs a more sober-minded partner.

Two self–assured buddies don't always work well together. Each does better when paired with someone shy who needs to be nurtured and who will use the strong–willed child as a role model.

As in all work with students, negative comments and chiding –"You're too bossy!" "You don't keep your mind on the work!" – accomplish nothing. Instead, we found that sitting down with each pair of buddies to discuss how things were going, what was working well, and where there were problems elicited honest comments from the students and genuine listening to teacher comments. When we commended their strengths, they were quite ready to respond positively to a question like, "Since you are both really strong and your opinions clash, don't you think it would be better if you worked with a more easygoing buddy?" And as they had participated in setting guide-lines for mutual respect and getting along in class, they were also open to our com-ments that their horseplay was disrupting other students' work and were willing to make a change without sulking. That kind of discussion and negotiation gave students the opportunity to practice the cooperative spirit that is the essence of buddy time.

We also pointed out that you sometimes need to spend a little time together to find out whether the partner you picked is going to be just the right buddy for you. So during the next two or three ses-sions children had the option to switch if they wanted to. We occa-sionally made suggestions for change if we felt that two children were not going to work well together. But most buddies bonded very quickly, and only a few had to have help getting along and over-coming differences in personalities.

STARTING OUT GENTLY

Margaret goes on to say:

During the first part of the year we started out with easy, familiar activities. Students read together, shared choosing time, went for walks in the park, or played flag tag on the playground. From there we moved into more complex activities – watching films together and then having a follow-up activity, doing artwork such as tracing hands and then turning those drawings into some kind of design such as a friendship circle or a tree with hand leaves. The kids became pretty imaginative. Sometimes our students selected their own activities, but usually we decided on the day's activity, did a lead-in, and then let the kids make decisions about how to handle the job.

But before every activity the students joined in the idea sharing, and we always accepted their input. Marne and I modeled a quick give-and-take in idea exchanges or lead-in activities – one day we joined hands in a dance – and the kids saw us get so enthusiastic about the activity that the feeling spilled over to them. The idea-sparking, concrete modeling, and follow-up "debriefing" are essentials to success. Even simple activities like reading together or making a special get-well-quick card need that lead-in modeling to kindle interest, enthusiasm, and imagination. For example, before having the buddies settle down to a shared reading session, Marne and I would start to reminisce, putting a lot of feeling into an exchange:

MARGARET: I remember the fun of getting together with my sister to read our very special favorite. Did you have someone to read with Marne?

MARNE: Did I ever! My best friend Sally and I had our very own secret place in the garden where we would read together and laugh and cry about the stories we shared! Did you have a special reading place?

With that the children would chime in to talk of the pleasure and excitement of shared reading, and the session would be off to a flying start. Children talked about their favorite books and stories, about special places to snuggle down to read, and about exciting stories they found on the special library table. Then the noisy scramble for books and a space to read settled into the most intense reading and sharing you could ever wish for. So simply telling students "Here's what you are to do today" is not enough. You need a lively give–and–take exchange between the teachers – and then among the children – as a lead–in to breathe life into the day's buddy work.

From mundane materials favorite activities grow

With two teachers keeping their eyes and ears open for good ideas for sharing, planning flows quite easily from one week to the next. The trick is to invest everyday occurrences and mundane materials with the magic to spark activities:

* An oversupply of breadcrusts? Aha! Duck feeders!

* Extra plastic cups? Great for doing a building project!

* Listening to a poem? Wow, let's make masks!

If you think you no longer have that childlike spontaneity and imagination to see the possibilities inherent in everything around you, here is the wonderful pay-off buddy work delivers: as you relax into the easy give–and–take of interactions with your partner and observe the creativity the students bring to these encounters, you will find that you *are* tapping that vast reservoir of your creative mind. Like the mature buddies who often draw their most creative ideas and artistic inspiration from the kindergarten children, so you will find yourself inspired and drawn into the flow of childlike imagination.

What you are modeling for your students and for each other is discovery learning at its best. As the excitement of an *Aha!* discovery rises in you, your students will find the atmosphere contagious. The ideas will bubble up amidst a lot of laughter, and you will find that you never become tired on buddy days. Excitement and energy will carry you and your students right along.

As you give free rein to imagination, both you and the children reexperience the intense learning of early childhood when all senses are at their most acute and when there are no taboos about turning a shell into a boat, a pile of sand into a castle, or a stick into a lively charger. Problem solving is a matter of trial and error, and everything around you is material for learning and exploring. The power of "the beginner's mind" is functioning fully.

So instead of preparing a year's outline ahead of time, Marne and Margaret relied more on looking for possible themes to emerge from their students' interests and work, special events, or materials that happened to come to hand. Margaret was always able to get her classroom ready for projects and special activities with little lead time. Often she would suggest an interesting project her students could pursue at buddy time, and Marne would come flying in at the last minute to add her creative ideas. Since there were no rehearsals or fixed plans, the two of them would present those ideas to the students in fresh and spontaneous ways, with Marne bringing her verve and artistic talents to the exchange. As a result, the teachers had as much fun as the children, and the relaxed atmosphere set the tone for working together harmoniously and joyfully.

IKEBANA AT THE ART GALLERY BECOMES THE LEAD-IN

After a trip to the art gallery to see Japanese flower arrangements, the students – with a bit of creative prompting – decided to create their own *ikebana* arrangements. At this point creative scrounging became helpful, as one parent found a whole bunch of discarded flowers in a dumpster, another teacher volunteered to bring in vines from her garden, and the students created their own bases for their arrangements. Using these materials, each buddy pair produced a creative design, and the finished *ikebana* were put on display in the hall so the entire school could enjoy them. Once the idea of making their own arrangements had taken hold, children's powers of observation took over and their research and memory skills got a good workout. During the creation phase, planning, discussing, designing, problem solving, and creative cooperation flourished. The joint trip to the art gallery was definitely more than "time out for fun."

POETRY SPARKS ARTWORK AND MORE

During one buddy session, a local teacher came in to read a poem he had written in which he brought problems of the environment to life through images of the "good river" and "the polluted one." As he read his poem, he took on the personalities of the two rivers, using his voice, movements, and two different masks to add life to his words. The students were entranced by his presentation, and the heightened visual imagery helped them identify with the personification of the two rivers. So, when the writer told them that he needed a lot of help to get his message out to the people in the community, the students readily entered into a brainstorming session to find ways in which they could help. The idea of making more interesting masks for the writer's use captured their imaginations, and they set to work to make a large variety of masks for his future presentations in the community.

As with so many buddy activities, the excitement and fun of that one session had carry-over effects for both classes. Some produced large murals showing the clean river and the polluted one. The poet's vivid presentation inspired some of the younger students to put on mini-plays in which they invented their own dialogues between the good river and the bad river. Their more mature buddies used the method of dialoguing as a way of calling attention to other types of pollution of the environment.

> Margaret was surprised, that after all the choices generated during brainstorming, the consensus of the children was to turn the playhouse into a mansion and to develop the topic into an interest study.

petting zoo ●●
hotel
restaurant
candy shop
hardware store
bank
video shop
bakery ●
mansion ●●●●●●●● ●● ●●
Easter bunny house ●●
library
toy store
clothing store
pet shop
shoe store ●
balloon store
office
club house ●●

WHEN YOUNG BUDDIES BUILD MANSIONS

When a teachers' strike created a short interruption in teaching, Margaret, on her return to the classroom, felt that students did not show their usual enthusiasm and energy for learning. To infuse the classroom with new energy, she invited the students to help her come up with a new and interesting project. First they looked around to see what was missing: no mini-centers to reflect students' special interests, no interesting displays of students' artwork, a playhouse that stood empty.

Starting with a look at interesting uses for the playhouse, the students offered a long list of suggestions, ranging from a petting zoo to a candy store to a balloon store. Margaret created a chart of all the suggestions and then invited the children to choose one. (See the chart on the previous page.) They indicated their preference by placing a colored sticker next to the heading of their choice, and to their teacher's amazement the largest number of stickers showed up next to "mansion." Somehow the idea of creating a mansion had captured the children's imaginations, and they set to work to do the conversion job right there and then. Their playhouse was transformed over several days, and the low energy was a thing of the past.

Always ready to follow up on teachable moments, Margaret built on her students' interest in mansions. They looked at pictures, visited some heritage houses, researched mansions in literature, and read stories like *The Fisherman and His Wife.* The school's secretary brought in a huge old key that came from a house in Ireland, and the children brought in clothes and trinkets so that they could dress up as children a hundred years ago. They used their artwork to enhance their study with drawings and cardboard mansions complete with towers, covered on the outside to simulate stone and papered inside with wallpaper scrounged from samples.

Oona brings a purse
think of a name
Sarin, Philip, Jessica, Lia } bring fake money
make gold out of paper
put the stove in
make paper windows
Jared brings mirrors
Taigen brings doll stroller
make outside + inside
silver + gold outside
Eliza brings baby
cut out money
make a bed
horses
Taigen brings safe
Jared, Sol, G.P., M.R. } make a roof
Lia
Mihaela brings paper for clear windows
G.P., Lia, M.R. } bring dress up clothes
mansion
Sarin, M.R., Sol, Cody, Lia } bring crystals
M.R., G.P., Lia } bring stuffed animals

To implement their mansion project, children decided on specifics and volunteered for special jobs while Margaret recorded their input on a mindmap.

The older students were fascinated by the work their young buddies were doing and decided to make some smaller-scale mansions during their joint sessions. They gathered all the materials they could find, made mansions out of boxes, and found material to make curtains, cushions, and wall hangings. Then they furnished their mansions with furniture fashioned from cardboard and scrap materials. Each buddy team created some kind of mansion. The young buddies made figures to people the homes, played imaginative games, set up scenes to create estates around their mansions, and held little plays and puppet shows. They had definitely set the project in motion, and for several sessions the work totally absorbed their more mature buddies, who would have been "too cool" to start such a project on their own. Once the young buddies had initiated the project, the older students felt they had "permission to play" and plunged in with enthusiasm and interest.

Turrets and stone
facing adorned the
"Amazing Mansion."

The mansion project exemplifies the core of buddy work. Though the teacher provided the impetus for brainstorming, the children themselves generated the idea. Their teacher honored their special interest and then fanned the spark of interest with suggestions, solid background information, and special field trips. The young students' work inspired their older buddies to let go of their "mature dignity" and drew them into an absorbing learning project. The students set the time frame to allow full development of the idea exchange and creative work. The project certainly confirmed Sylvia Ashton-Warner's words about the creative vent of the child's inner volcano narrowing the destructive vent. Here were over fifty students working together in fairly confined areas with limited resources, yet they all collaborated happily and productively with almost no fussing or fighting.

Turrets and stone facing adorned the "Amazing Mansion."

GIVING THANKS OVER A SHARED MEAL

As Thanksgiving approached, the two teachers talked to the children about being thankful and had their usual quick exchange of ideas. This modeled for children how many interesting things there were for which they could be thankful. They talked about the origin of Thanksgiving as a holiday, some of the traditions surrounding Thanksgiving, and some of their own memories of Thanksgivings when they were little girls. They exuded excitement as they shared happy or funny memories and, once they had the students brimming over with eagerness to share their own memories and ideas, they asked them how they would like to celebrate Thanksgiving and show their thankfulness for each other and all the good things around them. After such a rousing introduction, brainstorming generated a wealth of ideas and then easy consensus. What students wanted most was to fix special lunch treats for their buddies and to eat them together.

On the assigned day, students packed something special for their buddies into their lunch boxes. They decorated the wrappings in unusual ways with flowers and leaves, drawings of fruit, and beautiful bits of cloth. After they shared their special treats, they went out to the playground to play together. The thoughtful ways in which they all interacted certainly gave rise to thankfulness and a deeper feeling for the holiday and its traditions.

CHRISTMAS OFFERS MANY POSSIBILITIES

After Margaret's class had celebrated some aspects of Hanukkah with the kindergarten-to-grade-two class at South Park School (see chapter 15), the children decided to work on a Christmas project with their older buddies. To share in the whole-school effort to decorate the gym for the winter concert, the buddy teams worked at decorating giant Christmas trees. Margaret had provided large tree-shaped cut-outs made of green construction paper, and when the two classes got together, she and Marne fanned the enthusiasm by reminiscing about the wonderful old-fashioned ornaments they used to have on their trees. The children joined in the talk and proceeded to create imaginative tree ornaments from the materials available in the room.

To surprise their young buddies, older students made individual presents for them for Christmas.

As a special project for the mature buddies, Marne suggested that they study the personalities and interests of their young buddies and to make each a special gift for Christmas. They talked about their buddies, compared notes on their interests and talents, and then produced very personal Christmas gifts. There were Ninja Turtles, dolls, boats, cars, teddy bears, koala bears, planes, houses, and all kinds of other objects made of clay, Plasticine, and scraps of cloth. Margaret's students were delighted, and the gifts truly reflected the interests of the young buddies.

Christmas recaptured a lot of its magic of sharing and caring in the course of these special sessions. The secret work done by Marne's class added the element of surprise for the students' little buddies. And the winter concert was enriched by the wonderful artwork the buddy teams had done with their tree decorating.

ARTWORK BLOSSOMS IN THE SPRING

Victoria has a wonderful abundance of flowering trees that herald the beginning of spring – cherry, plum, and almond. South Park School is right across the street from a beautiful park, so nothing could be more natural than taking the buddies out for a walk on the first sunny day of spring when the trees had come into blossom.

As with all the buddy activities – even something as straightforward as going to the park across the street – Margaret and Marne infused the event with special excitement and interest. They and the children talked about spring, the reasons for the blossoms, their beauty, the shapes of the petals, the leaves, the trees themselves, and all the colors that made the park beautiful. Both teachers showed their delight in the colors and shapes and joined the children in their explorations of all the signs of spring.

When they got back to the classroom, the teachers had art materials ready to capture those impressions in pictures and collages. There were huge sheets of black, blue, and yellow paper, pots of paint, and many sponges and paint brushes. The children lost no time in setting to work. The older students seemed to be in charge of tree trunks and branches, and their younger buddies dabbed on the blossoms with

Trees in blossom covered an entire wall of Margaret's classroom after buddies had captured their view of spring in the park in a joint art project.

paintbrushes and sponges. Many children decided to put grass and flowers at the base of the trees, and some of them added cut-outs of flowers to their artwork. The large paintings graced the halls and classrooms of the school to everyone's pleasure.

In a project like this where a finished product is involved, you will see concrete evidence of the mutual enhancement that buddies derive from their joint sessions. Artwork takes on a new quality that might not be present in work done by either group alone. The collaboration encourages both younger and older buddies to move beyond their customary boundaries. For the teacher it may be necessary at times to persuade the older students to relinquish control of the production process and give free rein to the creative input of their younger buddies. Showing appreciation for the cooperation and teamwork between buddies goes a long way toward inculcating the pleasure and pride that develops as students work together.

A session of having older students evaluate the physical skills of their young buddies generated caring, pride in accomplishments, and tactful reporting as well as careful observation and record keeping.

SHARING HANDS-ON WORK TEACHES MATH

A surplus of plastic cups set the scene for a rich and varied math session. Each of the children was given five of the small cups and the teachers challenged the students to use those cups to build the highest towers they could create. The children set to work in pairs, and it took only a little while before some of them decided that it would be more productive to join together into teams. With that, they really moved along, and together they built huge towers.

Next the teachers gave each child five playing cards, asking the children to incorporate the cards into the design of their structures. That generated renewed discussion, problem solving, planning, negotiating, and more teamwork. Working in teams seemed to give an extra boost to creativity and ingenuity. Dexterity, spatial planning, negotiating to get more cards, and admiring and then copying another's design were all part of the work. The teachers then provided measuring sticks and demonstrated how to measure the towers to see which one was the tallest. That inspired the students to measure every part of their towers, and as a final activity the whole group graphed the different sizes and shapes of towers to make a record of all the work.

Culminating a session that to a casual observer may have looked like just so much fun and games was solid learning in geometry, measurement, comparison of numbers, graphing, and record keeping. There was practice in problem solving, negotiating, and creative design. And there was the practical lesson of the benefits of teamwork. For the teachers there were the joys of standing back and observing the process, letting the students do their own problem solving, and rejoicing in their ingenuity and persistence.

THERE ARE LESSONS EVEN IN FEEDING THE DUCKS

(far right)
Time spent on making floating duck feeders may seem like the proverbial "basket weaving" when students should be "working on the basics." But checking the variety of activities involved against the curriculum goals produced a score-board filled with a multitude of skills and achievements. Here is an impressive example of discovering the curriculum in the global work children do.

For the South Park buddy teams, the all-time favorite buddy activity was the production of floating duck feeders. Margaret had a lot of bread crusts left over from cutting sandwiches for a party and brought them to school with the thought that the students would make a trip to the park to feed the ducks. It was buddy day, and as the discussion about the trip to the park took shape, the students' planning thoughts moved from feeding the ducks to making bird feeders to producing floating duck feeders. They set to work with enthusiasm and concentration and used every bit of material available in the classroom. They built trimarans, tugs pulling rafts, round and square floaters, two-level ships, sailing vessels, and houseboats. Their teachers extended their usual session, and the children worked in pairs all morning.

Then came the moment of truth. They loaded the bread into their floating structures and marched off to the park with great anticipation. At the pond, ducks and seagulls watched the launching, but to everyone's disappointment only one seagull – no ducks at all – lunched on the bread provided in the feeders. After much discussion the children concluded that for some reason the birds were frightened of the structures. So it was back to the drawing board.

The greatest fun of the day came when the children tried to retrieve the boats. They made waves to move the boats toward shore. They reached for them with sticks, threw rocks to propel them along, and even tried blowing to move the sailboats. Eventually they retrieved

Goals	Making Floating Duck-Feeders with Buddies	Planning the use of stale bread	Planning Floating Duck-Feeders	Constructing floating duck-Feeders	Launching Duck-Feeders	Observing Duck-Feeder Birds, Ducks, etc	Retrieving Duck-Feeders	Evaluating Debriefing
Intellectual Development	using curiousity	•				•	•	
	thinking	•	•	•	•	•	•	•
	listening	•	•	•	•	•	•	•
	reading	•	•					•
	writing		•					•
	researching		•					•
	planning	•	•		•		•	
	organizing		•	•	•		•	
	problem solving	•	•	•	•		•	
	analyzing		•		•	•		•
	synthesizing		•		•			
	making connections		•	•	•	•		•
	drawing inferences		•			•		•
	using arithmetic		•	•				
	learning science concepts: ballast, wave action		•	•	•		•	
	tides, water displacement		•	•	•			
	studying birds/animals		•	•	•	•		
Social / Emotional Development	sharing	•	•	•	•		•	
	working with a partner	•	•	•	•		•	
	planning	•	•	•	•		•	
	organizing	•	•	•	•		•	
	risk taking	•	•	•	•		•	
	verbalizing	•	•	•	•	•	•	•
	learning leadership		•	•	•		•	•
	following directions		•	•	•		•	•
	using teaming	•	•	•	•		•	•
	taking initiative	•	•	•	•		•	•
	making choices	•	•	•	•		•	•
	learning from others	•	•	•	•		•	•
	negotiating	•	•	•	•		•	•
	co-operating	•	•	•	•		•	•
	collaborating	•	•	•	•		•	
Aesthetic / Artistic Development	using fine muscles			•				
	drawing painting			•				
	building			•				
	using graphics		•	•				
	using spatial awareness		•	•	•			
	exploring media		•	•				
	observing		•	•	•	•		
Social Responsibility	responding to different opinions	•	•	•	•	•	•	•
	responding when others need help		•	•	•		•	•
	cleaning, tidying							
	working without supervision	•	•	•	•		•	•
	interacting with partner	•	•	•	•	•	•	•
	respecting others	•	•	•	•	•	•	•
Physical Development	using fine motor skills			•				
	using social skills in physical activity			•	•	•	•	
	using large muscles			•	•		•	
	learning water safety			•	•		•	
	learning boat safety			•	•		•	

twenty-nine boats, but one kept eluding them. So off they went to find a park worker who assured them he would get out the rowboat to rescue the last boat.

There was no dearth of learning in the project, but above all there was fun, excitement, and creativity. The fact that the duck feeders did not serve their intended purpose only momentarily dampened their spirits. Then children were off into the next problem-solving session; the fun of devising ways of retrieving their boats managed to overcome their initial disappointment.

Assuring there is closure

Throughout the year most of the buddy sessions were marked with the production of some finished work – a piece of artwork, a poem, a joint piece of writing, plays produced and critiqued constructively. That closure of performing or displaying the co-productions of the buddies was always augmented by an in-depth debriefing.

Since Margaret generally set up her classroom for the buddy sessions, Marne was in charge of cleanup. Although students were conscientious about putting away materials and cleaning up as they shifted from one activity to another, Marne would supervise the final job of putting the classroom back into its single-class order. After that she generally held a separate session with her students, commenting on what she had observed and asking students to air their feelings and concerns. Along with acknowledging successes, steps forward, and ingenious ways of working with the young partners, at times the debriefing sessions turned to problem solving and idea sharing to figure out better ways of interacting with younger buddies who need extra encouragement or who tend to be strong-willed or unforthcoming. The students themselves often provided the best suggestions. Here again Marne took the role of a facilitator and catalyst who made certain that thoughts and feelings could be expressed freely. Margaret held much the same kind of debriefing sessions with her students.

Talking over how many new things students discover and how much learning those fun activities produce reassures everyone – including parents and supervisors – that along with all the fun and excitement, there is solid learning and that the buddy sessions are of real value. Buddy time is certainly a wonderful way of socializing students and enhancing that feeling of community that can be so productive for teachers, students, and their parents.

Closing the year—saying goodbye

With all the special projects punctuating the buddy sessions throughout the year, saying goodbye had to be a highlight for the buddies at South Park School. Sharing their own goodbyes and mutual appreciation in front of the students, Margaret and Marne suggested that each pair of buddies celebrate their year together in some unique way. Brainstorming together for one more time, they generated a list of possibilities:

Buddies not only said good-bye to each other but to their teacher too, and they did so in the way they knew best— by producing a book of pictures to mark Margaret's retirement.

* writing a poem to each other

* reading favorite stories one more time

* making goodbye cards

* creating a memory book

* making gifts for each other

* creating a remembrance painting

Each pair set to work to capture the spirit of their partnership and their time together. Deep attachments had been formed over the year and their caring

Marg teaches her children to read.
Louis Stroud

See Marg brainstorm with her class.
Zoë Hartley

ways of parting were deeply moving. The ZAPP! power of being acknowledged, of having freedom to act, and, above all, of interacting positively had indeed infused everyone with a glow of inner energy.

Students and teachers gave concrete expressions of their appreciation and yet one more time acknowledged one another in positive ways.

Marg loves books.

David St.Claire

14.

Parents as Co-Creators of Learning

When I became a parent, I thought that my teaching had taught me a lot about being a good parent. I was wrong. Instead, I found that being a parent taught me a lot about being a good teacher (Steve Bialostok 1993).

Parents have always been the co-creators of their children's learning. Though we have not always acknowledged them as such, they are their child's first and most effective teachers and help establish the natural learning strategies that work so well. As baby learns to walk, talk, and make sense of the world, parents know intuitively how to foster the child's natural ways of learning. We are now basing our school approaches to teaching on those effective home models – providing a physical context for learning, modeling what is to be learned instead of lecturing, valuing all steps forward no matter how small, giving feedback that expands and acknowledges what the child is saying or doing, and making room for endless voluntary practice.

The learning that takes place at home has also shown us how to recognize the effectiveness of peer teaching and the effortless learning that results from peer interactions. Parents include all their children, regardless of their age or level of maturity, in family activities. The recognition that "family grouping" works equally well in schools has become the foundation for multi-age teaching. Most important, parents have modeled their abiding trust that children are going to learn.

Parents don't question whether their babies are going to learn to walk or talk; they know they will!

As Steve Bialostok puts it, "parenting teaches us a lot," and so does opening our minds, hearts, and classrooms to the parents of our students. By acknowledging their vital and effective role in the children's learning, we turn "parent power" to good use and unleash a fount of energy that not only empowers parents but lightens our own loads in highly positive ways. In fact, inviting parents to participate more fully in their children's first school years creates the same open learning atmosphere they have provided in the home – trust, confidence, good feelings, and a sense of being part of a cohesive team.

Margaret's way of drawing parents into the circle of learning

Reflecting on her years of working with parents, Margaret comments that when she began teaching, she used to dread parent interviews but now looks forward eagerly to those meetings. Gone are the days when nervous parents came to meet that remote and somewhat ominous figure – the teacher. Ever since she began to reach out to get to know both parents and children on a far more personal level, she has tapped the deep caring and concern parents feel for their child's entry into school and has laid to rest many of their doubts and fears.

Letting parents know her genuine appreciation of the wonderful job of teaching they have done – and continue to do – lays a solid foundation for her interactions with parents. They know they are appreciated and respected and they respond in kind, trusting the teacher and actually becoming her friend. As Margaret opens the classroom to parents, she finds that her unorthodox ways deepen and broaden the relationships that evolve. Much as she becomes involved with each and every student's needs and achievements, so she becomes involved with the joys and worries of their parents. They confide in her and talk over their thoughts and feelings, secure in the knowledge that Margaret cares about them as she cares about their children and that she always treats any information she receives as confidential.

As Margaret describes her way of working with parents, you may want to ask yourself to what extent you would feel comfortable following her model. You may already have strong parent input into your class. But if you are just beginning to build such liaisons, then, like Margaret, you may want to start gently, try out whatever feels O.K., and then build on your successes. Margaret's ways are presented here only as suggestions. Just as curriculum guides are no longer prescriptions for lock-step linear progression of work, so our examples are not step-by-step recipes to be followed. Instead, we invite you to sample and savor whatever suits your taste and needs.

THOUGHTS THAT GUIDED ME

Looking back a few years, Margaret tells us:

> When I was invited to speak at a whole-language institute on the topic Parents as Partners, my first thought was, Why me? I break all the unwritten rules when it comes to involving parents. Instead of keeping a professional distance, I make good friends of parents – I sometimes lend them money, get them jobs. And they help me – like Jerry who prepared my income tax forms and Mona who cut my hair. I visit their homes and invite them to mine. We share personal concerns and have fun together outside school as well as in. So why ask me to speak? There are plenty of teachers who know just how to interact with parents in "the right way."
>
> As I reflected on my topic, it occurred to me that I treat my students' parents as I do my students. I make the classroom safe for them, so they feel it's O.K. to take risks. They know I won't criticize them and that mistakes are as much a part of learning for them as for their kids. They also know I will treat them as positively as I treat their kids. They feel they are welcome and needed in the classroom, they can ask for special job assignments, and what they do has value.

Reading to kindergarten children and sharing the joys of stories are among mothers' favorite jobs in the classroom.

To get parents started when they first come to help, I model the kinds of behaviors I want from them – both in the way they will interact with the kids when they help them read or write and in the way they will use the materials. Over the year they get lots of practice, and I acknowledge their work as positively and fully as I do the children's. They know I trust them to make a positive input to the classroom, and I value their ideas and their help. In short, I make sure they know I accept and appreciate them as co–creators of their children's learning.

PARENTS BECOME FACILITATORS OF LEARNING

Margaret continues:

Having parents help with special events or field trips has always been part of classroom work. But as I changed my teaching and moved more and more to holistic ways, I found my interactions with parents changed too. Just as my role shifted from information giver to facilitator of learning, so the role of parent helpers in the classroom shifted from dispensing facts or advice toward facilitating learning. I managed to persuade parents it is to the children's advantage when the teacher and parents assume a let–the–kids–do–it–themselves attitude. Then I pointed out that with the independent work that kids do, I needed parents' help in class more than ever. And so parents reclaimed the role of facilitators of children's learning that they had filled so well at home.

PARENT ORIENTATION IN SEPTEMBER

Margaret goes on to say:

As we described in chapter 7, I like to meet the parents of my new students early in September to let them know what to expect in my classroom. I like to give them some idea what holistic and multi–age teaching are all about, and in the process I tell them about invented spelling, drafts of writing, concrete work with math, the gradual emergence of reading, and the whys and hows of new ways of reporting. Usually I show slides of previous years' classroom routines and projects so they can get a feel for what goes on in the classroom.

As I talk to them over a cup of tea about their children, I prompt them to tell me about their children's special interests. I then make a mental note to include books about model airplanes, special pets, the seashore (or whatever has come up) on my library table of books. I also encourage the parents to let me know of their concerns, and I always write down anything specific they tell me about their children or their needs – special likes or dislikes, allergies, the fact that a child still needs to be reminded to go to the bathroom, or needs extra encouragement in a group. Seeing me jot down what they say assures parents that I am taking them and their concerns seriously.

Keeping this orientation meeting informal and friendly sets the tone for the year. By breaking bread together we seem to invoke the ancient law of hospitality – safety, goodwill, and mutual respect. After that beginning, parents know a pot of tea is always ready for them, and they begin to relax and enjoy the easy give and take. As they bring their children to school, they often stop to chat with me, and several may congregate around the teapot to get to know each other better, to exchange ideas or even recipes. They stay to talk, to help, and to observe. Occasionally they become so engrossed in their visiting that I have to ask them to quiet down a bit, but generally they are more interested in what goes on in class than in their socializing.

One mother, Krisha, stayed for morning news time each day. She would stand with her arms folded and seemed riveted on how the children volunteered information to be put on the board and then "helped" spell the words I was putting on the board. Toward the end of the year when I once again commented on Krisha's interest and persistence in watching each day, she confided that all year long she had been learning to spell along with the children.

SCHEDULING HELPERS

Elaborating on her way of organizing parent help, Margaret explains:

I ask one parent a year – usually one who has worked with me the year before – to be my parent coordinator. During the orientation, we talk to the new parents about the value and importance of parent help and then send a note home early in the school year to invite parents to help in the classroom. We ask parents to indicate on what days they would prefer to come in, and we begin to build

August 29, 1994

Dear Parents:

I would like to invite you to become involved in our classroom activities. Over the years I have found that we all gain a lot of enjoyment and learning by having parents come into the classroom to participate in our projects and learning activities. Not only do children gain much from having their parents come in, but parents tell me that they too have benefited in many ways and enjoyed being in the classroom.

Our studies and activities this year will be many and varied, and having parents help in the classroom makes them that much more successful. Most of the jobs in class require just the everyday skills you use at home all the time, but if you feel that you have special expertise in some area and would like to share that, please let me know. The children and I would enjoy and appreciate your special input. And remember that you are welcome to bring your younger children into the classroom as long as they will not cause a disturbance.

If you feel that you can work well with children on a one-to-one basis, you would be very welcome in the classroom. If your talents lie in doing such things as making charts or models, many are needed throughout the year. If you cannot come to class during the day but would like to help, there are many important ways in which you can contribute. Typing, sorting materials, collecting props or making costumes for plays can all be done at night.

The following are examples of some of the classroom activities that benefit particularly from parent help:
-reading to and with children
-talking to children and telling stories
-transcribing children's own stories
-typing
-preparing and setting up materials for math
-helping with arts and crafts work
-supervising cooking
-participating in field trips and special events
-putting on puppet shows
-making up our book order and collecting money for it.

There are many more possibilities, and I know you will feel comfortable working on them with the children. We will have an orientation meeting early in September to discuss ways of helping. For anyone who would like to become more deeply involved, I will provide some special training in working in positive ways on children's learning.

I very much appreciate your support and look forward to seeing you in the classroom. Please feel free to come in any time whether you can stay to help or just want to drop in for a visit.

Sincerely,

Margaret Reinhard

our schedule on that basis. Except for September, we send out the completed parent–help schedule a month ahead of time, so that parents know well in advance when they are expected.

We ask parents' permission to include their telephone numbers on a parent–help list so that if a volunteer can't make it on any given day, that parent can phone another parent to take the shift. We also tell them to feel free to come into the classroom at any time, whether they are scheduled or not. If they have an hour or two they can spare, their presence and help are always welcome. We encourage them to bring in a younger child on their help day if the child is able to be in the classroom without causing a disturbance. The students love to welcome the toddlers and babies and learn a lot about caring and social responsibility by helping to look after them.

The personal contacts I have with parents helps with volunteer recruitment. Some are shy about working with a teacher and need special reassurance that they can work in their own best way, simply drawing on their knowledge of raising their own children. In our note we make it very clear that to come in to help they do not need to have any special skills, but I encourage any parents with some area of expertise – music, art, marine biology – to share these with

Once the parent coordinator has filled in the main events and bookings for parent help, the children decorate the monthly calendar, and it is posted outside the classroom. Regulars like Joan, who make a definite commitment early in the year, are in their chosen space each month. Others, who have less time available, feel free to add their names to any blank spots on the calendar or simply drop in when they can spare a bit of time and energy. All are welcome guests and helpers in the classroom.

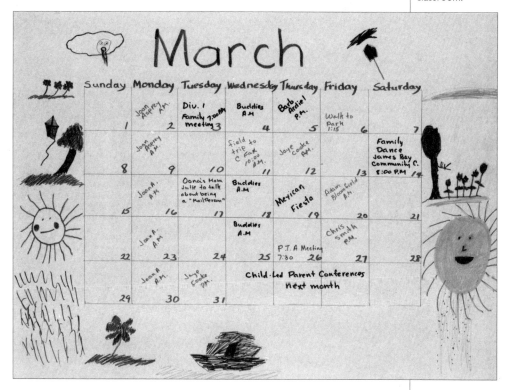

the class. I have had many mothers who did not yet speak English come in to work on art projects and other physical work, and both they and their children quickly became integrated into our group. In the process, their English skills improved considerably.

MOVING THROUGH THE DAY WITH THE CHILDREN

Providing specifics about starting parent helpers in their support work, Margaret describes how she sets parents at ease while making sure that the help they provide fits the philosophy and intent of her own teaching:

Bringing baby along to class makes it possible for a mother to visit the class and to do some reading with the students. The notebook for parent comments on children's reading behaviors is open and ready so she can record her observations after reading with the students.

I like parents to come in a little ahead of class so I can give them some instructions before the kids come in. Usually I like parents to work directly with the kids, but if one parent's way is too directive or focuses too much on negative statements about the children's work, then I give that volunteer some other work – making charts, creating big books, working on covers for the children's published books. In making that shift in assignment, I make sure not to give any negative feedback to the helper. Instead I thank the parent and suggest that I like to vary the assignments to give everyone a chance to do different jobs. If at a later time the parent wants to resume working directly with children, I again stress the importance of being positive in prompting children and may even model with one or two children what I would say as I work with them.

As my day begins with talking to the children and then news time around the chalkboard, the helper has time to set up what-ever work we agreed on for that day – selecting books for reading, preparing a chart for keeping track of who has read what, listening to the discussions that lead to personal writing in order to formulate some ideas about reinforcing what the children will be doing. As the children go to their seats to begin work on their writing, the helper starts circulating among them to talk about their plans, to encourage them to move from drawing to writing, and to listen to them read finished work.

I caution the parent helpers not to spell words for the children, explaining that I want the kids to huff and puff their way through the words themselves. In their orientation, I explain to parents that the children need to reinvent writing themselves so they can make it their own, and the only way to do so is to encourage them to try spelling without help. If I explain the pedagogical thought behind use of invented spelling, parents will usually accept the fact that merely giving children the correct spelling of words does not help at all at this stage of emerging literacy. So I encourage my assistants to help the children spell words by saying each word clearly, by asking how they think the word starts, how the sounds feel in their mouth, and what sound they hear at the end of the word. At times parents find it hard to accept that at the early stages of writing, words without vowels are O.K., but they generally begin to take a keen interest in the children's ways of evolving their spelling and writing. (See chapter 10 on spelling.)

As we progress through writing workshop, the next task for parents might be to help with the publishing of children's writing. Once a piece of writing has passed through the draft, edit, rewrite, and polish stages and is ready to be published, a parent helper can type the text. I have a typewriter set up in the classroom, and as the parent types, the child usually hangs around close by to watch the process. (This typing takes very little time and no special typing skills as most beginning stories are quite short.) The finished story is then put into a special cover and handed back to the child to be illustrated.

Another job parents often do during the morning period is listen to children read. While I am working with small groups of children, the parent helper works with individual children asking them to read aloud independently, to read along with the helper, or, in the case of nonreaders, to listen to a story and follow along with hands and eyes. The child will usually read whatever we have just read in story time, but sometimes chooses something else that seems more interesting.

I have an exercise book in which the parent helper records the date, the name of the story, the child's name, and any pertinent information that seems useful. The ongoing record gives me an overview of what has been covered. At times it is surprising how observant some parents become. They may note something that I had not noticed before, and most of them readily agree to accept the children's reading without undue prompting or correcting, so long as the general meaning of the text is preserved. At first I have to do a bit of modeling, explaining, and coaxing to convince parents that even fluent readers do not give word-perfect readings but focus on meaning when they make minor substitutions or omissions as they read.

I encourage parents always to stand back and let kids do things for themselves. If, for example, I have a very efficient mother in the classroom, she may feel that in the interest of getting things accomplished she should take on some of the work. But I want my kids to be as independent as possible, and I know that parents are often inclined to give too much help. Children know that, and when they are looking for shortcuts, they make a beeline for a likely looking parent and ask for help they really don't need. So I really encourage parents to let kids make decisions and do things on their own.

After writing workshop and reading time, the children have center time. Here they are free to choose their own activities and mate-

PARENTS OFFER SPECIAL TALENTS AND KNOW-HOW   At times parents will offer to come in to share their special ethnic or cultural heritage. Usually, the children respond with interest and enthusiasm to the visitors' presentations.   When a mother of Danish background offered to come in to show the children how to make beadwork pocketbooks, all the girls in Margaret's class were eager to try. Since the boys showed far less interest in the project, Margaret asked a father to come in to make model boats (Danish designs, of course) with the boys while the girls did their beadwork:

Mrs. B. offered to get the supplies such as the beads, felt, and backing. When she came in to start her lessons, I was horrified to see how small the beads were. I thought the little girls would have a terrible time keeping track of the tiny beads. But I underrated the children. Mrs. B. had the different colored beads in small medicine vials and provided very fine needles to work with them. The girls had a wonderful time designing the patterns and then sewing the beads on the black felt. Several of the boys looked on with interest and decided to join the beading group. The beadwork developed into a unit on Denmark that was very successful, and we ended the interest study with a display of the pocketbooks, model boats, and other project work pertaining to Denmark.

rials. I ask parent helpers to interact informally with the kids: to talk to them, to enrich their activities with suggestions or comments, to be sounding boards for ideas, to act as general helpers, to play games with the children, to help them find appropriate materials for art projects, to answer questions, to do some wondering for the children to help extend their thinking, or simply to be an appreciative and admiring audience for the children's work. The children are used to generating their own ideas and jobs, but thinking and creativity are always enhanced by having a listener who is willing to reflect with the child on the many possible ways of working.

About once a month I set up a cooking center. I usually choose a cooking activity that the children can do unaided, like making trail mix, open-faced sandwiches, baked apples, or "ants on a log." Here I really have to watch parents, because they want to jump in and do most of the work themselves. Kindergarten children may need a little more help, and so I usually have a parent stationed at the center for the duration. But I still caution them to intervene only if a child can't do the job or is likely to hurt himself. When they are trusted to act on their own, children become quite independent and even

Sharing fun in the gym gives a father a chance to show off for his young admirers.

keep track of those who have had their turns. Next to the cooking center I place a feltboard with pictures of the children tacked on it. As the children go through that day's cooking job, they remove their photo, so I know who has gone through and who still needs to complete the work.

After recess we have book time, and while the children are settled down with their books, my parent helpers sit down with a book or magazine that interests them to model silent reading. I am particularly pleased when fathers come in during book time. I want to be sure that children see men too become engrossed in books and reading. So often they see only women reading in class and some of the boys – particularly those whose fathers are nonreaders – may decide that reading is not for them.

Math comes next in my day, and parents help set up equipment, give out supplies, and oversee project work on such jobs as pattern making or counting with Unifix cubes. I ask parents to make lots of manipulative materials, particularly for kindergarten children. An example of this is the Christmas number line that I use in December. The parent helpers cut twenty–five small Christmas ornaments out of paper for each child in the class, write the numbers one to twenty–five on them, and string them together one above the other. Each day the child takes home one of these paper ornaments and starts making a number line at home.

The impressive array of Christmas number lines teaches children a great deal about the number 25—and parents a great deal about much higher numbers as they conscript neighborhood helpers to cut out 750 paper ornaments.

Put in bowl 1 spoonful.

Eat by handfuls

As the days go by, the number line gets shorter at school and longer at home. The children really have a feel for "25" by the end of this project.

Afternoons in my classroom usually begin with a story. After that comes work on a theme in progress, a field trip, center work, individual projects, reading, invention day, music, or physical education. I have found parents' help invaluable in carrying out this work. In fact, they often make an activity possible by being there to supervise, to drive, or to work with the children.

Learning to follow directions not only produces delicious trail mix to enjoy in class, but becomes a lesson in reading and taking turns. Parents who like to be in charge often need special cautions from the teacher not to intervene unless it is absolutely necessary.

FIELD TRIPS

Field trips are built into Margaret's program, and whenever possible she has one small – or not-so-small – outing per week. Here again, the presence of parents is invaluable to ensure children are safe and all goes according to plan. These outings are also a relaxed way to continue to build rapport between teacher and parents and to have them share the children's fun and excitement exploring the world outside school. After many years of working with parent helpers, Margaret has evolved efficient ways of organizing these field trips:

I take the children on field trips as often as possible. To get started I send notes home asking the parents' permission for the children to participate. At the same time I also ask for parent volunteers. When I know how many parents are available, I divide the class into as many groups as I have volunteers (ideally about four to six children in each group) and give each parent a list of the children in her or his group.

If, for example, we are going to the beach, I also give the volunteer a list of the things I want the children to look for – crabs, sea anemones, starfish, clamshells, interesting rocks. The same kind of instructions are given for a

Dear Parents:

On Tuesday, June 2, our class is planning a train trip to visit the Forest Museum in Duncan. While there, we will watch old-time logging equipment, see a logging camp, and look at pictures and artifacts of another time. There is an old steam train on which the children can take a ride, and we will share a picnic lunch. In the afternoon we will return by train and will get back to Victoria before dinner.

We will need parent volunteers to join us on this trip to help supervise the children. Each parent will be responsible for a small group of children throughout the day, and we encourage parent volunteers to bring along their younger children. They, too, will enjoy the trip. Would you be able to join us?

Field trips like this one add much learning and enjoyment, and we are planning this trip to enhance our special interest study on transportation. Having parent involvement on such a field trip ensures that we will have a really successful day, and we very much appreciate the contribution of time and expertise you make.

Please contact me if you can help with this trip to the Forest Museum.

Sincerely,

Margaret Reinhard

P.S. Our train leaves at 8:00 a.m. and arrives back in Victoria by 5:00 p.m.

trip into the woods. There we would be looking for the local flora and fauna and for special viewpoints that could be described or drawn later in class. We always take picnic lunches on these trips to add to the fun. The parents get a chance to meet each other and become friends. They also get a chance to work with and talk to the teacher on an informal basis. To foster that informality I always bring along a large thermos of tea for all the parent helpers.

SPECIAL PROJECTS NEED EXTRA HELP

Some of the special projects Margaret and her students have undertaken have become so popular that she makes them annual or biennial events. For example there are always new and interesting facts to be discovered about the different countries that have been studied before, and the chick-hatching unit, which we discussed in an earlier chapter, offers excellent opportunities for science lessons about anatomy, reproduction, the development of embryos, and conditions needed to protect the young. Margaret frequently uses these projects as examples in her orientation or in-service presentations because they are not only popular but offer a lot of learning for both children and adults. At times parents expand their vocabularies and their abilities to observe and measure things accurately along with the children. Word about the projects is passed along from parent to parent from year to year, and Margaret finds that when she is ready to embark on one of her projects, she can always count on solid support and help from parents.

> Parents are always willing to help with special projects and seem to get as much out of them as the children. For our annual egg-hatching project, a parent is usually the one who obtains the fertile eggs from a farmer he or she knows. Once we begin the project, the eggs in the incubator need to go to someone's home on weekends so they can be rolled three times a day. Children eagerly ask to take the unit home, and once parents agree, a letter goes home with the incubator giving instructions and asking for tender loving care for the eggs over the weekend. After the eggs have hatched, a birth announcement is sent home together with a request for a weekend home for the chicks. There are usually many positive responses brought back to class, so they are put in a box and the lucky letter is drawn out. The parent comes to school on Friday to pick up the chicks and then returns them on Monday. Yes, we have had some casualties over the years. One parent spent the weekend combing farms in the area for three-day-old chicks to replace the ones killed by a neighbor's dog.

CONCERTS

The fun of special events and concerts lends itself well to drawing parents in to become stagehands, costume designers, and makeup artists as well as being an appreciative audience on the big day. Margaret has always counted on parents to offer their special talents and general help as she and the children plan, rehearse, and produce the show:

Concerts, of course, require a lot of parent help. Usually a creative parent will coordinate a costume–making session or will make patterns and enlist more parent help. One year the children were involved in the school operetta *Sky Happy*. Parents made boater hats out of cardboard and ribbon and bought dowels at the hardware store, sprayed them black, and created walking canes for the children's song–and–dance routine. Makeup is put on by parent helpers just before the concert. They join me in supervising the kids and then, of course, in enjoying the concert.

Five-year-old Lauren and seven-year-old Andrew produce personal invitations to ask their parents to attend the parent appreciation tea.

> Pavent Appreciation
> Ted
> Mondd y
>
> 10:30 A.M.
> KAMTooMI KLAS
>
> Fom Lauren.

PARENT APPRECIATION

Like their children, parents thrive on having their efforts acknowledged, and a year–end special appreciation event not only provides the opportunity to demonstrate concretely to parents that their help and support are valued, but also makes for closure. Children need to have a model for showing appreciation to people who support them, and they also need to develop a sense of the life drama of openings, rising action, dramatic high points, and closure. Their map minds absorb those concepts without special lessons when they observe parent involvement with the opening orientation, the warmth and good feelings of the ongoing support, the high points of concerts and extra-special events, and then the closure of a par-

> Dedr Mom and Dad,
>
> please come to our classroom. A Parent appreciation tea will take place on Monday
>
> 10:30 A,M.—12:00 P.M.
> We have made lots of refreshments and there will be lots of activities to.
>
> From Andrew

ent appreciation day. Margaret makes sure the children play an important role on this special day:

> At South Park School the Parent Appreciation Tea has become a tradition. It is a way of involving the children to show how much we value all the time, effort, and help parents have offered throughout the year. To get ready for this special event, the children in my class bake cookies in several sessions over a period of weeks, and the goodies are stored in someone's freezer Doing all that preparation in advance leaves lots of time to think and talk about ways in which we can show parents that we notice and appreciate all their help.
>
> As the year draws to a close, we send notes home inviting all parents to come to our tea, which is scheduled for an afternoon about a week before the end of school. (At South Park School many of the parents with small children and those on shift work find the afternoon to be the best time. However, you may want to hold such an event in the evening.) One parent comes in at one o'clock to set up cups, plug in the coffee, and make the tea – the children handle the rest. They decorate the room, make beautiful paper tablecloths, bring in flowers, move the desks out of the way, set out their goodies, and then wait impatiently for their parents to come. Such excitement! The children serve the refreshments and then settle down for a slide show of the year's events in the classroom. Judging by the comments people make as they leave, the guests really enjoy the afternoon. A lot send thank-you notes the next day, which I put on display to be read and reread by the children.

THE CYCLE STARTS AGAIN WITH A NEW PARENTS' TEA

The ritual of opening and closing the year with a positive, well-marked event begins again as the old school year ends and new school year approaches. Parents who have worked closely with Margaret and the children are more than willing to introduce newcomers to the school. Though it may seem just one more chore to crowd into an already overcrowded year-end schedule, Margaret finds that it pays solid dividends in easing the entry of newcomers – both children and parents – into the school and the new year ahead. This event is fully discussed in chapter 7, "To Start the Year – Begin at the Beginning."

The benefits of positive parent involvement

The benefits of parent input into the day-to-day classroom work extend well beyond the welcome help parents provide. The mutual trust and respect that characterize the interactions between parents and teachers model positive, courteous relationships for children. At the same time, parents learn a great deal about the pluses of a safe and courteous learning climate and sound reasons for teaching in new, holistic ways. Many have commented their parenting skills have improved after their year in Margaret's classroom.

Forging a closer connection between home and school also reinforces the real-life aspects of much of the learning and invites input from the community – visits from people who have special expertise or information, family heirlooms sent or brought to school, the sharing of traditions or special holidays by families of cultural or ethnic backgrounds different from the majority of the children, and the demonstration of special handicrafts or skills used outside of school.

The home-school connection also fosters practical work on the part of the children. For example, gardening, fishing, and caring for the environment have become subjects of mini-units or centers initiated by children who developed those interests at home. Some children have worked on science experiments and brought in equipment and supplies to put on demonstrations for the class. In the eyes of children – and parents – learning is not confined to the classroom or to teacher-prepared lessons when the connection between home and school is so strong.

There may be times when the presence of a parent creates specific problems – Julie becomes whiny and dependent when her mother is present; Charles shows off more than usual; Tony and Chou make every effort to get the parent helper to do their work for them in spelling – but on balance, the benefits far outweigh the drawbacks.

When parents bring in their younger children, Margaret's students always enjoy the opportunity to make these youngsters feel welcome and to play with them for a while. One year, children in Margaret's class traced the growth and development of a baby from the time she was in the womb to the end of her first year. Margaret recalls the interest and excitement that was generated as a parent shared her pregnancy and then the new baby with the children:

Denise was an excellent parent helper. When she told me that she was pregnant, we discussed the possibility of giving the children the opportunity to learn about the progress of her pregnancy through the months ahead. The children were entranced when we talked about the new baby coming. Denise talked openly to the children about her condition. She let them feel her belly and the movements of the fetus. We followed her – their – progress by weighing Denise regularly and measuring her girth. We also talked about proper nutrition and about getting ready for a new baby in the house.

Building on the obvious interest of the children, I invited another parent helper who is a midwife to come into the class to talk to the children about birth. She brought in books, charts, and plastic models to demonstrate concretely how the birth process evolves, and the children listened and watched in rapt attention. Their excitement mounted as the day of birth neared, and each day they came in wondering if the baby had arrived yet.

When baby Ashley was born, the children created and sent out birth announcements to let everyone know of the arrival of the baby girl for whom they had waited so long. Denise brought Ashley into the classroom when she was just a tiny baby, and as she continued to bring her to school, Denise fed, bathed, and changed Ashley right in the classroom. The students watched as the baby was introduced to solid food, and all along they kept a journal of Ashley's first year of life with photos, drawings, and copious notes. Denise told the class that when Ashley is grown up, she will present her with the wonderful "Baby Book" they prepared.

Having Denise bring baby Ashley for an in-class bath was one of the high points of the children's ongoing study of Ashley's growth and development.

The keen interest in family life stimulated by the presence of infants and toddlers quite naturally led into the required study of family life. Toward the end of the year, as the children prepared snacks for the upcoming parent appreciation tea, reading and talking about families developed into a full-scale unit on family life. Appreciation for the love and support parents give was a lead-in topic, and even at that young age, students gained a real sense of the care and love their parents give them that so often remains largely unacknowledged. Reading about stepparents and talking about personal feelings developed a depth of discussion that required a great deal of tact and sensitivity on the part of the teacher to acknowledge students' feelings and keep their personal needs and concerns in perspective.

Perhaps the best and most important part of parent involvement in class is the genuine sharing of responsibility for the children's growth and learning. That feeling of real collaboration is enhanced by keeping parents informed in positive ways through notes sent home, three-way report cards that include input from parents and children as well as the teacher, student-led parent conferences, and portfolio evaluation that gives a graphic picture of the ongoing progress of learning and skill building. As parents share your joys and concerns about their children's growth, you make them co-creators of learning in school as well as at home, and in the process you learn a great deal that helps you become a better teacher.

15

Networking– Teachers' Lifeline

Embarking on new ways of teaching can be intimidating and full of uncertainties. Even though you know that you can trust children to learn, the weight of tradition holds you in check until you can find some kindred spirits and like-minded peers to help you expand on your first tentative steps in the new direction. Looking back on the early years of our work, memories of collaboration and networking stand out clearly. That mutual support helped us build on our early experience and move on from there. Talking to one another, comparing notes, and sharing ideas shored up our confidence and then built certainty that we were on the right track.

We recount our experience here because as you embark on new and unfamiliar ways of teaching, you may have many of the same doubts and fears that haunted our early work: "Is this really the best way to foster learning?" "Am I being derelict in my duty by changing?" "Will the children really learn everything they need to learn?" "Can I convince parents that their children are learning in their very own ways?" Later you may agonize – as we did – over the "right" amount of input to make, when to stand back and when to step in with lessons or specific help. And as we did, you may find that creating a support group, a network of like-minded colleagues, will be your life line to overcoming those doubts and building the confidence you need to trust your own observations of children's work and their ways of growing and learning.

THE TEACHER–RESEARCHER CONNECTION

Our own work began as a two-way network between an experienced teacher, Margaret, and a not-so-experienced but very curious researcher, Anne. Interest in how children learn from and process classroom teaching was the link that started our partnership, as we compared notes on our in-class observations and mused about what they meant in terms of effective teaching/learning. That search for better ways and the desire to fit teaching to the children's ways of learning gradually expanded our two-way network to include supervisors, parents, other researchers, and like-minded teachers. Looking back to those early days, Margaret says:

> As Anne and I began our shift to a learner–based approach to teaching, we felt very alone, so we supported each other. At the same time, I made sure I kept my principal informed of all the ways in which I was changing my teaching – adding lots and lots of story reading, getting kindergarten children involved in learning to read, augmenting center time to include more listening to stories, abandoning round–robin reading and the use of worksheets, encouraging the use of print for all messages and notices around the classroom, covering every free surface in the classroom with books and familiar stories to immerse children in print, encouraging children to write and compose, and above all shifting from lecturing or information giving to modeling, practice, and feedback as the main avenues of fostering learning.
>
> Gradually, as we implemented these changes, parents began to notice the difference in their children's attitudes to learning. The children were bringing home lots of books and were enthusiastic about reading. As they learned from listening to stories, their fluency and expression was far different from their earlier, halting efforts at sounding out each letter and word. They were also writing at every opportunity and eagerly looked forward to coming to school. Based on those changes, parents wanted to become part of our network. I made them welcome in the classroom, and they took pleasure and pride in their children's learning. Many of them reminisced about their own school days and sharpened our awareness of what had helped or hindered them as they were learning. They also became our staunch allies and eventually demanded that open learner-centered teaching be expanded into grade two.
>
> All along, we continued to compare notes. As I was shifting my

teaching step by step, Anne would come into the classroom to observe and then discuss how children were responding, what their actions told us, and how I could best move further along to meet their ways of learning.

We shared the excitement of discovery and shored up each other's confidence when doubts assailed us or outside complaints threatened our confidence. The best one came from a grade-two teacher who remarked, "Your kids sure can read, but they don't know their long and short vowels." On reflection we agreed that the ability to read with fluency and expression (denoting good comprehension) was far more valuable than the ability to distinguish between long and short vowels. We had already discovered that phonics is learned most easily and effectively during writing and spelling work, but having someone who shared my concerns for creating the right learning environment was very reassuring in face of that specific complaint.

From talking, planning, and reflecting together, our partnership moved into writing, and giving workshops. Since we first began to work together, the value of our joint work has come out of our open sharing of thoughts and feelings as well as valuing and respecting the contribution each of us makes to the partnership. Collaborating has deepened the theoretical foundation of our work and broadened the practical application year after year. There is definitely reciprocal learning in the researcher-teacher partnership as we spark each other's ideas. But to us, the greatest joy lies in the close friendship we have built as a result of our joint work.

Soon after Margaret began to turn her teaching upside down to correspond to the ways children learn, we began to find researchers who were writing about the same thoughts and interests that moti vated our work. Holdaway, the Goodmans, and David Doake were among the first to become part of our researcher-teacher network. We read their research reports, talked to them at conferences, shared our own findings with them in joint conference presentations, and reveled in the knowledge that we were becoming part of a larger network. Now that so many more researchers are observing learners at work, that research network has broadened tremendously. By now, thousands of teachers are joining the network, either as partners to researchers or as partners to each other. They share not only their own in-class research but their ideas, practical work, and personal

NETWORKING HAS MANY FACES *

Over the years, we have participated in and observed many examples of teacher networking:

TEAM TEACHING with teachers in the same school who are working with children in the same grade levels:
- sharing resources
- sharing themes
- joining together on special projects or field trips
- doing joint planning for plays or concerts
- transferring the enthusiasm of special work from one class to the next – "We're having such fun! Come and join us!"

TALKING PARTNERS:
- meeting daily to talk about the day's events
- walking home together to get exercise and sharing time
- discussing plans or events during breaks
- sharing worries and frustrations openly
- becoming friends

TELEPHONE NETWORKS:
- having a whole list of people to call on
- providing reassurance when worries arise
- asking advice
- sharing joys and breakthroughs
- comparing notes on students' work
- laughing together

doubts and achievements. They derive much mutual support and co-creative learning from these networks and continue to expand and deepen both their theoretical and practical knowledge.

Teachers are networking with each other

When you spend most of your time alone in your classroom with your students and all responsibility rests on you, reaching out to create a network of like-minded supporters opens many avenues for support and information sharing. These connections not only reassure you but enhance your knowledge, understanding, and enjoyment of new insights and practices that shape your teaching. The most wonderful aspect of networking is that the enhancement is mutually stimulating and supporting. As you share ideas, feelings, plans, and concerns, your network partners gain as much as they give.

Margaret's networking experience

Margaret tells us how much networking has added to her life – both in and out of school – over the years:

As I changed my teaching to learner-centered ways I had several teacher partners who added other dimensions to my work. Having someone to share with added immeasurably to my joy and satisfaction in working with children. At one point a partner and I taught fifty kindergarten children in one large room. We had a large ratio of boys, and often our ears buzzed with all the activity. So we discussed our problems, encouraged each other when things got tough, and often found that our thoughts were so similar that we came up with the same idea at the same time.

THE EARLY DAYS

Looking back to the early beginnings of working in new ways with children, Margaret remembers fondly how much support she and her partner-teacher June Domke gave each other:

During the early days, June and I taught kindergarten and grade-one classes in adjacent classrooms. Instead of following our pattern of alternating teaching kindergarten one year and grade one the next, we decided to form two multi-age classrooms in which we each had both kindergarten and grade-one children.

From the start, we found that June was the organizer and implementer, who not only worked energetically at setting projects in motion, but was also the one who would see the principal, talk to parents, and run interference for both of us as we launched into our new ways of working with children. We talked and planned together, exchanged ideas, provided moral support as it was needed, launched a newsletter, and organized the year-end picnic for our two classes of multi-age children.

As I was evolving new ways of teaching, I felt that June looked after me when the going was rough and I felt unsure. In turn, June was inspired by the new ways of teaching and at one point commented that "teaching phonics and structured lessons had started to be a real drag," just when we began to shift to holistic methods that infused the class and the two of us with new energy.

A STUDENT TEACHER EXPANDS THE NETWORK

Like students in multi-age classrooms, so teachers find that teaching someone else becomes a source of stimulation, fun, and new learning.

Margaret certainly had that experience when Diane Cowden joined her classroom as a student teacher. Diane came well prepared to work in holistic ways, as she was drawing freely on her years of experience in a cooperative day care center where parents and teachers worked together to foster children's development. Her entry into Margaret's classroom added a new partner to the network of like-minded teachers looking for better ways to fit their teaching to the children's ways of learning.

In class, while working together, each teacher found opportunities to observe the children while the other was teaching. There was also time to talk things over, to compare notes on observations, and to draw on the different experience each brought to the job. Laughing together, sharing new discoveries, and talking over concerns or musing about different ways of working made their interactions far more than a learner–mentor connection. They were partners, and together they were stronger and more sure of themselves than when either worked separately.

Once Diane was teaching her own class, phone networking added another dimension. As Diane puts it:

> We would be on the phone for hours. I'd tell Marg, "Here's what's happening in my class. What about yours?" and she would confirm that the same thing was happening with her children. Boy, that was reassurance! The next day I'd go back into my classroom knowing, "Yes, I'm on the right track. Children *will* shift from memory reading to actual reading, and their writing *will* become more accurate." As soon as parents understood what I was doing, I rarely had any complaints or pointed inquiries. Mostly they came in, looked at what the children were doing and said, "Oh, I like this. This makes sense!" But some of my peers were not so sure about these changes from traditional ways, and so having an outside network was very reassuring.

THE WEDNESDAY CLUB

From those beginnings, networking moved into what became known as "The Wednesday Club." For an entire year, a group of teachers met over potluck suppers or at one of their favorite restaurants every Wednesday evening to share ideas, talk over new plans, discuss the latest publications, and, later on, watch each other on the local educational television network, as their classes were shown as examples of holistic ways of teaching/learning.

These get-togethers captured the excitement and interest of doing new things in new ways and gave the teachers the opportunity to share with peers who knew what they were thinking, who acted as a sounding board, and who gloried with them in their successes. In the safety and good feeling of the Wednesday Club, creativity and imagination blossomed for everyone.

When we asked the participants to reminisce about those meetings, each one in turn pronounced without hesitation, "good food, fun, friendship!" And those were the key ingredients that drew those teachers together. They became close friends and established bonds that now extend far beyond the Wednesday Club. Like the students in their classrooms, who drew new energy and excitement from the social climate, the teachers thrived on the excitement and fun of exchanging ideas informally over dinner.

The Wednesday Club fulfilled a strong need during those early years, and the meetings were enjoyable, relaxed social events with no agendas. They continued for well over a year, produced untold enjoyment, and gave much-needed support to the club's members. As Carl Braun (1993) puts it when talking about the need for and benefits of peer networks, support groups "become professionally supportive. They result in a kind of optimism, a feeling of hope that 'what I'm doing is significant' – a feeling that change can and should come from within."

The Wednesday Club achieved just those aims. As we watched the more structured, sober attempts to network that other teachers started in later years, we found that these networks rarely survived the first meeting or two. Like students resisting structured lessons that offer little or no fun and precious little laughter, teachers rejected those formal occasions, and networking reverted to the time-honored personal contact system of mutual nourishment. From our experience, forming a Wednesday Club is a much surer, more enjoyable way to successful networking.

There is also the question of need. In the early years, we felt an urgent need for mutual support, for sharing ideas; and for discussing why ideas might or might not work, what else we could do to build learning, and what we could learn from the children's reactions to our new ways of working. Once our own experience and that of others confirmed that we were moving in the right direction, the number of our meetings was reduced to one or two a month and then became even more sporadic. Still the bond we forged through our time together is as strong now as it was in the past, but we no longer need those weekly meetings to shore up our efforts. We know that help, sympathetic ears, and kindred spirits are always right there if we need them.

NETWORKING WITHIN A SCHOOL

When you have like-minded peers teaching right next to you, then networking within a school can be wonderfully productive. Margaret found that support when she moved to South Park School:

> By the time I began working at South Park School I had experienced the support a network brings. But I also remembered my early partnership with June Domke and was convinced of the benefits of working with a teacher who shared a similar

Children are quick to pick up on the climate of sharing. Since the two teachers obviously considered it worthwhile to share each other's fun, Thomas decided he would follow suit and joined Margaret's class to work with two of her students on a project that seemed more inviting than what was happening in Linda's class at that moment. He blended in so well during that period that Margaret did not discover his presence until she showed her slides of the projects and noticed that one of the children was not her student but Linda's.

CELEBRATING THE EIGHT DAYS OF HANUKKAH ✳ Drawing on Linda's knowledge of the Jewish holiday Hanukkah, the two classes joined to hear her tell the story of Hanukkah and to learn some of the traditional songs. Then the two teachers shared their classrooms to get children involved in some of the ways of celebrating Hanukkah, and for days afterwards children continued to talk and read about the celebration, to produce artwork based on their learning, and to work in the math center practicing the challenges they faced in learning about the *menorah* and the *dreidl* game. ✳ As Linda worked with one group of children teaching them the *dreidl* game, a math activity that involves spinning a small top with Hebrew letters printed on its four sides, Margaret helped the other children prepare *latkes* (potato pancakes) – a traditional Hanukkah food. She had arranged for a parent who celebrates Hanukkah at home to come in, help supervise the cooking, and talk to the children about Jewish cus-toms. ✳ Both classes learned about the *menorah* and either drew or created the tradi-tional candle holders from Plasticine. (See page 89 in chapter 4.) On buddy day, Linda led all the children in dancing the *hora*. Three classes joined hands in a huge circle in the gym, and what they lacked in precision dancing the traditional Jewish dance, they made up in enthusiasm. ✳ As Linda puts it, "Parents often tell me that they appreciate such things as our Hanukkah study. Non-Jewish parents are happy that their children are given an opportunity to understand more about another way of life in such an enjoy-able and meaningful way. Jewish parents are happy that their children have a chance to feel proud of their heritage" (Picciotto 1993).

philosophy and outlook. At South Park School, Linda Picciotto was teaching at the same level – kindergarten to grade two – and we found that we sparked each other's ideas and complemented each other in ways that proved very productive. One of us would get a great idea – let's not just read about castles, let's build some! – and the other would help implement it. The children liked working with both teachers and both classes. Sometimes children would see something interesting going on in the classroom across the hall and would want to join in, and whenever possible we fostered that inte-gration, to everyone's delight.

We found safety in numbers in such endeavors as introducing student-led parent conferences and continuous entry for incoming students. That safety factor also worked for the children who knew both teachers well and could always find one of us to get help or comfort. On the other hand, we would gang up on our principal if we felt strongly about a problem or idea and wanted to talk him around to our point of view.

Throughout our work we made it a point to share our expertise. Linda has talents in music and likes to use different methods of assessment. My strengths are in the language arts and holistic ways of working. As we joined forces, we found that we both gained by relying on the other in specific contexts. If we prepared together for an assembly, Linda might focus on teaching some songs, and I would handle poetry recitals or general organization for the two classes. That same mutual enhancement flourishes between teachers who have different kinds of experience. The combination of an enthusiastic novice with lots of ideas and an experienced teacher who can implement them is wonderfully productive and enjoyable.

Linda and I also shared exercise time. Every day we would walk together after school, and as we strode along the seashore in just about any weather, we would talk over the day. That informal recap at the end of the day gave us time to discuss our concerns about children, mull over problems we were having with parents or supervisors, and compare notes on the successes children had achieved. That sharing often generated new ideas for extending activities or creating new beginnings.

> Even students sense that networking is at its best when done informally and in ways that are enjoyable.

See Marg and Linda power-walking along the breakwater. Vanessa Marsh

Again, it was the informal nature of the joint work that created the wonderfully productive benefits. As Linda puts it, "Our walks are what I remember most clearly. We didn't always talk about school, but simply enjoyed each other's company. As we got into our stride, we might talk about possible plans for the following day, and even though we did not necessarily do all we talked about, we had a chance to think out loud knowing that we had a sympathetic ear and a supportive friend."

Talking about their joint classroom work, Linda comments on having that rare pleasure of working with another adult in a primary classroom: "The company of other adults is lacking in a primary classroom, and that's one of the joys of working with staff who will enjoy being together and having fun. Margaret and I would do spontaneous things like dash into the other's classroom and say something like, 'Hey, there's something really neat going on in my room. Why don't you come and join us!'"

The children captured that spirit of enthusiasm as they observed how much interest the two teachers took in what was going on in class. They certainly noticed that the two teachers found the work the students were doing really absorbing. They benefited from sharing two teachers, two talents, and two sets of interests.

Margaret's wealth of experience and love of language arts added much to the team work. Linda not only brought talent in music but also her interest in assessment, science, and math to the team effort, sharing her supply of mealworms or a math project in which her students learned so well, they became teachers for Margaret's students. Joint field trips, art projects, and spur-of-the-moment joint projects such as building castles enriched both classrooms and delighted students and teachers alike. In all the joint endeavors, the two teachers appreciated and acknowledged the freedom their principal accorded them to do such spontaneous work. And so the network extended to administrators and support staff as well.

Networking confirms and stimulates

Now that holistic ways are much more solidly established, you may not feel the need for a support team, but since you are working with your students in ways that continually stretch and enhance their ways of learning, you do need the stimulation of peers. Whether you find a research partner, a team teacher, or a group of parents to act as your sounding board and be your partner(s), keep your association as unstructured and easygoing as possible. Just as your students flourish in a climate of delight that is safe, relaxed, and pleasurable, so you will grow and extend your knowledge and expertise as you make friends with those who share your interests and concerns.

16.
Pulling It All Together

To punctuate the end of your day, the end of a project, or the end of the year, go out on a note of excitement. Look back on the many accomplishments and look ahead in anticipation of things yet to come, of visions of new and better ways to work. A satisfying closure that accentuates successes and positive steps forward is as important as a good beginning and equally productive. It is also an integral part of the teacher's way of pulling together all the elements of achievement and of shaping a vision for the steps ahead for her students and for herself.

Celebrating successes

Cultivate the habit of reflecting on work just completed, making notes of everything positive you can think of. For example, looking back over the chapters of this book, give yourself full credit for everything we have discussed that you already do – fostering independence and sharing power, getting work started on a note of excitement, providing lead-ins that make children thirsty for more knowledge, finding the curriculum in the children's work, and doing research in your classroom to become still more attuned to the children's ways of learning.

When reflecting on the work in your classroom, focus on the positive steps you take each day, just as you focus on the positive steps forward in the children's work. Allow yourself to be carried along by enthusiasm for learning, and *celebrate your successes.* "I'm getting much better at hearing underlying messages when the children talk to me. Morning meeting was great this morning!" "Making participation voluntary has paid off. Now *all* the children participate in spelling and composing at news time." "Giving students more independence and sharing power for decision making have changed the climate in the classroom. I have no more discipline problems!" "I learned as much as the children in our seashore project."

Whether you share those positive musings with colleagues, your students, or just your diary, putting them into words helps reaffirm the direction of the teaching/learning in your classroom. That sense of closure, of work completed and well done, builds your confidence as much as that of the children and puts into perspective any minor (or not-so-minor) problems that arise. Children will take their cue from you, and that unfortunate propensity of assessment to dwell on errors and negative aspects of work becomes a thing of the past.

Looking back, looking ahead

At the end of the school year, good closure sees students and teachers go out on a high, looking back with pleasure and satisfaction on the months just past and looking ahead with eager anticipation to the summer holidays and the new year. Converting the usual late-spring slump into rising excitement and energy that stays high until the last day of school takes planning and flexibility. As in all the work, the teacher's input is key. She is the one who floats the ideas, breathes life into them, and then relaxes to ride the crest of excitement as the children capture the spirit of the suggestions and soar ahead to expand and shape them to fit their needs.

As you and the children look back over the high points of the year, you draw the children into the magic of shared pleasures and achievements, of work done joyfully and cooperatively. Providing that kind of closure for the year entices children to work together enthusiastically until the last day of school. For you, the teacher, it becomes a time to remind yourself of the many steps forward taken by you and the children. Looking at the successes opens a window onto new vistas: "What else can I do?" "How much further can I move in fostering independence?" "What new ways of creating learning opportunities are inherent in the projects we enjoyed so much?" "What can I learn from the children's reactions and favorite memories?" "How can I stimulate greater awareness of the warm feelings engendered by more subtle gains and treasured moments?"

The example of working for year-end closure we provide below has been equally successful in a number of classrooms. Teachers have found it both easy and exciting to shape their own year-end closure to fit their students and the work they have done together throughout the year. We provide concrete descriptions here to encourage you to plunge in and create your own way of bringing your school year to a close.

REMEMBERING HIGH POINTS AND ACHIEVEMENTS

When "spring fever" – the need to be active, the beckoning sunshine, thoughts of summer vacation – diverts the children's thoughts from school tasks, asking children to reflect on the joys and successes of their school year draws them back into the classroom. Talking about the fun that lies ahead in the summer months and the plans to be made for visits to special places and people becomes a fine lead-in to reminiscences about the fun and planning that has shaped the school year up to this point: "What was it we really enjoyed?" "What do you remember best?" "How many places did we visit?" "What was your very favorite activity last year?"

Margaret joined teacher Anne Peterson in modeling a fast-paced idea exchange about fun-filled memories of special field trips, the joys of intriguing stories, and the satisfaction of jobs well done. With that lead-in (which could just as easily have been an exchange between the teacher and some of the more experienced students), children captured the spirit of looking back over the year to talk about all the things they remembered: field trips and special events, favorite stories and readers' theater, projects that had involved them over a number of weeks, writing workshop during which they produced their own books, buddy work that grew and expanded in unexpected ways. Perhaps the lead-in modeling of the two teachers set the tone, but whatever the reason, all the memories evoked during the project were positive. No one talked about failures or hard feelings. The children looked back fondly at the work that had captured their imaginations and memories.

Acting as scribe, the teacher recorded the children's recollections on large charts and continued to add to them over several days as the classroom work brought even more memories to the surface. Next she invited the children to select one of the items on the chart to write and talk about. Again there was a lot of talk and lead-in modeling by the teacher to elicit more than "we went to the zoo and we had fun." As she and the children compared notes on all the things that had happened, all the work they had put into a project, and all the feelings that had been evoked, their writing moved to a new and higher level. Sharing with each other added to the lively exchange of ideas, enhanced detail, and enriched language and artwork. If two or more children decided that the trip to the beach or art gallery or local farm had been their favorite, they pooled their memories to produce a special account of the event.

While the children enjoyed their reminiscing, sharing, and writing, the teacher stood back to note just what the favorite activities had been, to what extent children recollected special learning, and what had made a lasting impression. Quite often, the specific lessons intended are not the ones that are foremost in the children's minds. A trip planned to experience life on a farm, to learn about the animals and the jobs, to understand the need to work within the seasons, and to learn the use of equipment in harvesting overwhelmingly produced memories of the trampoline that had been available for each child to use. Yet later on, there will invariably be evidence that a great deal of solid learning took place – learning that has been tucked away in the recesses of the children's minds to be called on when needed. The fact that the recollections are anchored by memories of "fun on the trampoline" only enhances the map-memory quality of the learning.

TURNING MEMORIES INTO THE CLASS ANNUAL

The suggestion that it might be fun to publish all the writing and illustrations in the form of a class annual to be shared and taken home by each child at the end of the year, infused the work with extra energy. Editing, proofreading, and polishing descriptions took on new meaning. (After all, when you publish something, you have to use standard spelling and produce specially good artwork.) Margaret volunteered to type the finished descriptions, and then the children took over to arrange, rearrange, and finally place the work on pages. The

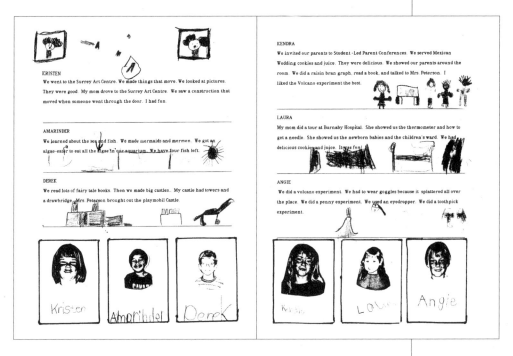

KRISTEN

We went to the Surrey Art Centre. We made things that move. We looked at pictures. They were good. My mom drove to the Surrey Art Centre. We saw a construction that moved when someone went through the door. I had fun.

AMARINDER

We learned about the sea and fish. We made mermaids and mermen. We got an algae-eater to eat all the algae in our aquarium. We have four fish left.

DEREK

We read lots of fairy tale books. Then we made big castles.. My castle had towers and a drawbridge. Mrs. Peterson brought out the playmobil Castle.

KENDRA

We invited our parents to Student-Led Parent Conferences. We served Mexican Wedding cookies and juice. They were delicious. We showed our parents around the room. We did a raisin bran graph, read a book, and talked to Mrs. Peterson. I liked the Volcano experiment the best.

LAURA

My mom did a tour at Burnaby Hospital. She showed us the thermometer and how to get a needle. She showed us the newborn babies and the children's ward. We had delicious cookies and juice. It was fun!

ANGIE

We did a volcano experiment. We had to wear goggles because it splattered all over the place. We did a penny experiment. We used an eyedropper. We did a toothpick experiment.

Kristen   Amarinder   Derek   Kendra   Laura   Angie

idea of including a photograph of each of the authors came about after an annual was brought in by one of the children, and the layout job took on yet another dimension. Math entered the picture: "How many students?" "How many pages?" "How many descriptions can be fitted onto a page without looking crowded?"

APPRECIATING WORK WELL DONE

The project not only infused the classroom with energy and enthusiasm, it also called attention to all the learning and solid work that had taken place throughout the year. The children looked back with satisfaction at what they had accomplished, and parents were impressed to receive such a lengthy list of all the special things that had taken place. They also accepted the annual as concrete evidence of "the basics" the children had learned. Along with reading, writing, spelling, math, and science, children had obviously learned the important skills of collaborating, organizing, planning, arranging work, and problem solving.

To produce their Book of Memorable Events, children did the layout and illustrations after their messages had been edited, proofread, and typed. The year-end project consolidated learning, added new skills, and produced tangible evidence that making strides forward is both enjoyable and productive.

VISIONS OF THE YEAR AHEAD

The lively discussions of all the memorable events of the year just naturally led into thoughts about the year to come. The warm feelings of "debriefing in a big way" encouraged speculation about new activities, new skills, new friends, and new teachers: "Next year I want to learn to read." "I'm going to publish a book." "I want to do a lot more drawing with my writing." "Emily is going to be in my class." " I'm going to miss the kindergarten kids when I move into Miss _____'s class." "I wonder who the new teacher will be?"

APPRECIATING THE TEACHER

Entering into these speculations, the teacher asked the children to think about what they would like to see in their new teacher. After some brainstorming and a bit of prompting, the children came up with quite a comprehensive list, including "has a soft voice," "likes to sing," "reads lots of stories," and "goes on lots of field trips" – all qualities they had learned to appreciate in their own teacher.

Students become totally absorbed as they collaborate to create their "Wanted" poster.

With that kind of looking ahead, it became easy to initiate the next project simply by wondering aloud, "Maybe it would be fun to create a job description for the new teacher." That idea was picked up with alacrity, and since a visiting team of teachers was observing in the classroom at the time, they followed the lead of the children and produced a Wanted poster of their own, describing the superkids they were looking for in their next teaching year. Imagination and fun once again joined solid learning as everyone planned, thought, wrote, and collaborated.

Kirsty

WANTED: TEACHER.

#1 Rosie cheeks

#2 Lots of songs

#3 Quiet Soft and Sweet voice

#4 Kind

#5 Let us have gym every day

#6 Computer Lab every day

#7 Show and Tell every day

#8 Read everyday for

Mrs. J.R. Kevins call:

156-2274

The finished poster lists many of the qualities children have enjoyed in their current teacher.

READING EXPANDS AND SUPPORTS THE YEAR-END DEBRIEFING

To enrich and round out the process of looking back, looking ahead, the teacher introduced children to a number of books that dealt with school and teaching. For many children, it had been their first year of school, and hearing stories about school added a new dimension of awareness to that experience. Delightful stories about children, teachers, and even the principal created openings to invite the children to speculate, to connect the stories to their own lives, and to gain a deeper appreciation and understanding of their social and learning interactions in school.

They entered into the spirit of the readings and brought in their own books, like *The First Day of School*, to enhance the collection of books their teacher was drawing on to bring "the school experience" to life. (See page 336 in the bibliography for a full list of the titles used.) Exploring the readings in depth became as absorbing for the teacher as the children. As they entered into the spirit of *What Mary Jo Shared*, they agreed that they too had been apprehensive about what would be all right to share in school, about being the first one to share, and being unsure of themselves in the class. Many feelings and thoughts surfaced as the teacher interrupted her reading to ask in a hushed voice, "When did *you* last feel afraid to share? What was that like?" or "Here's Mary Jo bringing in her dad to share. I wonder if you ever thought about sharing someone?"

The teacher's tone of voice, body language, and quiet manner as she waited for children to reflect clearly conveyed that questions like these are not intended for fact gathering but are invitations to become involved with the story and to look back over the year to relive experiences and clarify feelings. Given time to reflect and encouraged to talk about themselves, the children revealed their deep concerns and often quite profound understanding of their own hesitations, hopes, and anxieties.

And so reading, as well as writing, gained extra depth right at the end of the year as children became totally absorbed in the collection of school-experience books. Instead of simply reading for fun or facts, they related the stories to their own school experience, their thoughts and feelings about school, and their visions for the year ahead. Because the readings were accompanied by in-depth discussions and their own looking back, looking ahead, children expanded their reading skills to analysis, synthesis, and personal application. They maintained their interest and enthusiasm and proudly took home their class annuals as the concrete manifestation of the personal growth and effective work they had accomplished throughout the year. The project generated many wonderful ideas as children made new connections and explored their memories in their own ways.

Pulling it all together

For the teacher too, closure becomes a way of pulling it all together. As you join the students in reviewing the high points of the past year, you pull together memories of the ways in which you and the children worked together most successfully. The warm glow of positive feelings makes you eager to move ahead, to consolidate the successes, to let go of failures, and to let new ideas emerge. The class annual becomes a metaphor for your own positive ways of learning and growing, for your vision of new work yet to be done.

A JOURNEY INTO THE PAST— A VISION OF THE FUTURE

For us, writing this book has been a way of pulling together what we have learned and evolved during twenty years of partnership. As we talked and reflected, insights surfaced – "As a teacher I not only trust but am the recipient of trust in return. What a way to put me on my mettle!" It gave voice to the many subtle, intuitive ways in which Margaret worked with children, ways that gave rise to the myth that "she isn't doing anything." Often the power of her interactions revealed themselves in her voice as she recalled instances of teaching/learning in hushed tones or in a voice brimming with excitement and laughter. Together we teased out "the teachers' ways" of helping children become aware of their knowledge and strengths, of setting the scene for their having of wonderful ideas.

We examined our beliefs about learning to clarify more fully what it means to acknowledge the power of teaching children in ways that build on their learning. And we gloried in the rich research evidence that continues to emerge to point the way to still better, more congruent ways of teaching/learning. As Margaret says:

> For me, thinking about the book has been a journey back into my years of teaching and involvement with children. It has also been a letting go of past failures and unhappy times when my teaching did not go as I wished. It is a celebration of my years of working with children and parents and an affirmation of my oneness with teachers I met along the way who believed in the uniqueness of children and

their potential. Reflecting on my work has also left me with a vision of things left undone and the need to continue my efforts on behalf of children and teachers.

We hope this book becomes an invitation to you to review your own successes and to reflect on the subtle ways in which you are influencing children to create their own learning. Like Margaret – and the children creating their annuals – you will learn to let regrets fade into the background. They are the past. Your vision of the future arises from the energy of discovery you and the children share and the knowledge that you are making a difference in their lives.

MAKING IT ALL WORTHWHILE

As you pull together the threads of your insights and memories, there will be high points that tell you more surely than any accolade that your hard work has been worthwhile. They are the gifts you receive from your children, their parents, or from colleagues. Even when they take the form of small gifts – a look of trust or a card of thanks – they are the catalysts that keep your energy high until the last day of teaching. Treasure them, share them, and keep them around.

Here are a few gifts we have collected and want to share with you:

There are many warm fuzzies I remember about dealing with children, but one stands out in my mind above all others. I was teaching at Fairburn School, and as we were leaving the gym after an assembly, I walked alongside my children as they filed out in line – as all Fairburn children used to do. As I moved toward our classroom, I felt a warm little hand slip into mine and I looked down into a little

To a nice teacher like you

Most of the best rewards come from the children. Margaret received this card at the end of the year from a group of children who had really enjoyed their year with her.

Dear Mrs. Reinhard,

We would like to give this to you becuse we like you.

We like you so much that we want you to teach us for grade seven!

From

Jeannie
Jenny
and
alayne

face looking up at me with the most beautiful smile. Love, trust, "everything's all right with the world as long as you are there" shone out of those smiling eyes. The moment has stayed with me. I can still feel that little trusting hand slip into mine and experience the warmth and trust it imparted. (*Margaret Reinhard*)

I can think of many incidents that leave me with a warm glow, but the one that springs to mind is the time Colleen, an eight-year-old girl who was just beginning to read, included the following entry in her self-evaluation: "I've been told that I'm blossoming!" She had remembered my comment that her reading was now blossoming forth. (*Karen Abel*)

At the end of the school year, a mother sent me a crystal bowl as a present of thanks. With it she included an even more precious gift, a note that said, "All year long you have made rainbows for my child. Here is a way of making rainbows for you." (*Anne Peterson*)

The day before Thanksgiving the children and I were talking about all the things we were thankful for. I noticed how well the day went even though my teaching assistant was absent and I had no help with my special-needs children. So I made it a point to comment on the joy of being in class, and I singled out Tommy – who can be a real handful – for a special comment of thanks: "I am really grateful for the way you have worked today, Tommy, and all without extra help!" Tommy beamed but made no response at the time. Later, as the children were busy in the hall getting their coats on, Tommy rushed back into the classroom to give me a big hug. To the amazement of mothers who knew his sometimes quite rough ways, he told me, "I'm thankful I have you for a teacher, Mrs. Cowden!" (*Diane Cowden*)

I don't have a single event that stands out from the many. But I know that a gleam of understanding, the big smile of "I got it!" that lights up children's faces as I teach them are the most precious to me. (*Linda Picciotto*)

I was ready to retire and thought of doing so early. Then you showed me a new way of teaching and interacting with the children. So I hung in there. Those last six years of teaching kindergarten have been the best of all my years of teaching. I am retiring on a wave of good feelings and wonderful memories. (*Port Angeles teacher talking to Margaret at a workshop*)

Looking back over our years of collaboration, we share feelings of gratitude for our joint work. Many times as we worked late into the night on our research and writing, we would look at each other and wonder if it was all worthwhile. Then, the next day, as we worked with children and teachers once again, there would no longer be any doubt. Seeing the children happily at work and watching their break-throughs and their keen interest in learning gave us instant energy. The knowledge that our work was indeed worthwhile gave us a warm glow of satisfaction.

Then after *The Learners' Way* was published, there were teachers who told us, "Your book has been a lifesaver," or "Once I read *The Learners' Way*, I knew I could survive!" On one occasion a woman tapped Margaret's shoulder at a conference to tell her, "Your book has become my teaching bible." Hearing comments like these assures us that our efforts *are* worthwhile. But our greatest reward is seeing classrooms in which teachers have implemented their own climates of delight. They and the children in their classes radiate excitement about learning. From them we draw new energy and enthusiasm as we carry on working with teachers and children.

Bibliography

PROFESSIONAL REFERENCES

Ashcroft, Leslie. "Defusing 'Empowering': The What and the Why," *Language Arts* 64:2 (February 1987): 142–156.

Ashton–Warner, Sylvia. *Teacher.* New York: Bantam Books, 1971.

Baskwill, Jane. *Connections: A Child's Natural Learning Tool.* Toronto: Scholastic, 1990.

Bean, Wendy, and Chrystine Bouffler. *Spell by Writing.* Rozelle, NSW: Primary English Teaching Association, 1987.

Bialostok, Steven. *Raising Readers: Helping Your Child to Literacy.* Winnipeg, MB: Peguis, 1992.

Boomer, Garth, ed. *Negotiating the Curriculum: A Teacher-Student Partnership.* Gosford, NSW: Ashton Scholastic, 1982.

Braun, Carl. *Looking, Listening, and Learning: Observing and Assessing Young Readers.* Winnipeg, MB: Peguis, 1993.

Bruner, J. S. *On Knowing: Essays for the Left Hand.* New York: Basic Books, 1957.

Byham, William C. *Zapp! in Education: How Empowerment Can Improve the Quality of Instruction and Student and Teacher Satisfaction.* New York: Fawcett Columbine, 1992.

Caine, Renate Numella, and Geoffrey Caine. *Making Connections: Teaching and the Human Brain.* Alexandria, VA: Association for Supervision and Curriculum Development, 1991.

Cambourne, Brian, and Jan Turbill. *Coping with Chaos.* Rozelle, NSW: Primary English Teaching Association, 1987.

Chenfield, Mimi Brodsky. Keynote address presented at the annual meeting of the BC Primary Teachers' Association, Victoria, BC, 1993.

Davies, Anne, Caren Cameron, Colleen Politano, and Kathleen Gregory. *Together Is Better: Collaborative Assessment, Evaluation, and Reporting.* Winnipeg, MB: Peguis, 1992.

Diamond, Marian Cleeves. "Education in the Decades Ahead." In Dee Dickinson, ed. *Creating the Future: Perspectives on Educational Change.* Aston Clinton, U.K.: Accelerated Learning Systems, 1991.

Doake, David B. "Learning to Read: It Starts in the Home." In Duane R. Tovey and James E. Kerber, eds. *Roles in Literacy Learning.* Newark, DE: International Reading Association, 1986.

Duckworth, Eleanor. *"The Having of Wonderful Ideas" and Other Essays on Teaching and Learning.* New York: Teachers' College Press, 1987.

Ferguson, C. A., and D. A. Slobin, eds. *Studies in Child Language Development.* New York: Holt, Rinehart and Winston, 1973.

Forester, Anne D. "The Acquisition of Reading." Master's thesis. Victoria, BC: University of Victoria, 1975.

Forester, Anne D., and Margaret Reinhard. *The Learners' Way.* Winnipeg, MB: Peguis, 1989.

_____. *On the Move: Teaching the Learners' Way in Grades 4–7.* Winnipeg, MB: Peguis, 1991.

Gamberg, Ruth, Winnifred Kwak, Meredith Hutchings, and Judy Altheim with Gail Edwards. *Learning and Loving It: Theme Studies in the Classroom.* Portsmouth, NH: Heinemann, 1988.

Gardner, Howard. *Frames of Mind.* New York: Basic Books, 1985.

_____. *The Unschooled Mind: How Children Think and How Schools Should Teach.* New York: Basic Books, 1991.

Gentry, Richard R. *SPEL . . . Is a Four-Letter Word.* New York: Scholastic, 1987.

Glasser, William. *Control Theory in the Classroom.* New York: Harper and Row, 1986.

_____. "The Quality School." *Phi Delta Kappan* 71, no. 6 (1990) 424–435.

Goodlad, John I., and Robert H. Anderson. *The Non-Graded Elementary School.* New York: Teachers' College Press, 1987.

Goodman, Ken S. *What's Whole in Whole Language?* Toronto: Scholastic, 1986.

Goodman, Ken S., and Yetta M. Goodman. "Learning to Read Is Natural." In L. B. Resnick and P. A. Weaver, eds. *Theory and Practice of Early Reading,* vol. 2. Hillsdale, NJ: Erlbaum, 1979.

Graves, Donald H. *Writing: Teachers and Children at Work.* Exeter, NH.: Heinemann, 1983.

Graves, Donald, and Virginia Stuart. *Write from the Start: Tapping Your Child's Natural Writing Ability.* New York: Signet, 1985.

Gunderson, Lee, and Jon Shapiro. "Whole language instruction: Writing in the 1st grade." *Reading Teacher* 41:4 (January 1988).

Harste, Jerome C., Virginia A. Woodward, and Carolyn L. Burke. *Language Stories and Literacy Lessons*. Portsmouth, NH: Heinemann, 1984.

Hassard, Jack. "Synergy: People Power for the Classroom." *Science Teacher* 44 (1977): 18–21.

Healy, Jane M. *Endangered Minds: Why Our Children Don't Think*. New York: Simon and Schuster, 1990.

Holdaway, Don. *The Foundations of Literacy*. Gosford, NSW: Ashton Scholastic, 1979.

_____. *Independence in Reading*. Gosford, NSW: Ashton Scholastic, 1980.

Huey, E. B. *The Psychology and Pedagogy of Reading*. Cambridge, MA: M.I.T. Press, 1968.

Johnson, David W., and Roger T. Johnson. *Circles of Learning: Cooperation in the Classroom*. Alexandria, VA: Association for Supervision and Curriculum Development, 1984.

Kamii, Constance, and Louise Derman. "Comments on Engelmann's paper" in D. R. Green, M. P. Ford, and G. P. Flamer, eds. *Measurement and Piaget*. New York: McGraw–Hill. (Quoted in Duckworth's *The Having of Wonderful Ideas*. New York: Teachers' College Press, 1987.)

Lampert, M. "How Teachers Manage to Teach." Ph.D. diss., Harvard University, 1981. (Quoted in Duckworth's *The Having of Wonderful Ideas*. New York: Teachers' College Press, 1987.)

Lozanov, Georgi. *Suggestology and Outlines of Suggestopedy*. New York: Gordon and Breach, 1978.

Macrorie, Ken. *Uptaught*. Rochelle Park, NJ: Hayden Book Co., 1970.

Miller, Jenny. "Flowers Are Red: A Comparison of Educational Experiences." University paper prepared by a former kindergarten student of Margaret's, 1993.

Moerk, E. L. *Pragmatic and Semantic Aspects of Early Language Development*. Baltimore, MD: University Press, 1977.

Peetoom, Adrian. *Reflexions: Professional Reflections and Connections*. Toronto: Scholastic, 1992.

Peterson, Ralph. *Life in a Crowded Place: Making a Learning Community*. Toronto: Scholastic, 1992.

Phenix, Jo, and Doreen Scott Dunn. *Spelling Instruction That Makes Sense.* Markham, ON: Pembroke Publishers, 1991.

Picciotto, Linda Pierce. *Evaluation: A Team Effort.* Toronto: Scholastic, 1992.

_____. *Learning Together: A Whole Year in a Primary Classroom.* Toronto: Scholastic, 1993.

Preece, Alison, and Diane Cowden. *Young Writers in the Making: Sharing the Process with Parents.* Portsmouth, NH: Heinemann, 1993.

Sarason, Seymour B. *The Case for Change: Rethinking the Preparation of Educators.* San Francisco: Jossey–Bass, 1993.

Schonell, F. J. *The Psychology and Teaching of Reading.* 4th Ed. New York: Philosophical Library, 1961.

Shapiro, Jon, and Lee Gunderson. "A Comparison of Vocabulary Generated by Grade 1 Students in Whole Language Classrooms and Basal Reader Vocabulary". *Reading Research on Instruction* 27:2 (1988).

Smart, Steve, Lorraine Taylor, Sonja Johinke, Rob Seidel, Christine Davis, and Mary Jane Michael. "Using Mathematics Books Backwards." In Garth Boomer, ed. *Negotiating the Curriculum.* Gosford, NSW: 1982.

Sternberg, Robert J. *The Triarchic Mind: A New Theory of Human Intelligence.* New York: Viking, 1988.

Tarasoff, Mary. *Spelling Strategies You Can Teach.* Victoria, BC: Active Learning Institute, 1990.

_____. *A Guide to Children's Spelling Development for Parents and Teachers.* Victoria, BC: Active Learning Institute, 1992.

Tovey, Duane R., and James E. Kerber, eds. *Roles in Literacy Learning.* Newark, DE: International Reading Association, 1986.

Van Manen, Max. *The Tone of Teaching.* Toronto: Scholastic, 1986.

Wells, Gordon. *Learning Through Interaction: The Study of Language Development.* Cambridge, UK: Cambridge University Press, 1981.

White, Connie. *Jevon Doesn't Sit at the Back Anymore.* Richmond Hill, ON: Scholastic Tab, 1990.

CHILDREN'S BOOKS

Ahlberg, Janet, and Allen Ahlberg. *Each Peach Pear Plum.* New York: Viking, 1985.

Allard, Harry. *The Stupids Step Out.* Boston, MA: Houghton Mifflin, 1974.

Barchas, Sarah F. *I Was Walking Down the Road.* Toronto: Scholastic. 1975.

Barnes, Mark. *Setting Wonder Free.* Toronto: Annick Press, 1993

Bonne, Rose. *I Know an Old Lady.* New York: Scholastic, 1961.

Chase, Edith Newlin. *Waters.* Richmond Hill, ON: North Wind Press, 1993.

Cumming, Peter. *A Horse Called Farmer.* Toronto: Annick Press, 1987.

_____. *Out on the Ice in the Middle of the Bay.* Toronto: Annick Press, 1993.

Freeman, Don. *Space Witch.* New York: Penguin, 1987.

Gilman, Phoebe. *The Balloon Tree.* Toronto: Scholastic, 1984.

Hawkins, Colin, and Jacqui Hawkins. *I Know an Old Lady Who Swallowed a Fly.* London, UK: Methuen, 1987.

Herriot, James. *The Christmas Day Kitten.* London, UK: Pan Books, 1986.

Karlin, Nurit. *The Tooth Witch.* New York: Lippincott Junior Books, 1985.

Kellogg, Steven. *Chicken Little.* Boston, MA: Houghton Mifflin, 1985.

Kent, Jack. *The Fat Cat.* Toronto: Scholastic, 1971.

Krauss, Ruth. *The Carrot Seed.* New York: Scholastic, 1945.

Lioni, Leo. *Alexander and the Wind-up Mouse.* Boston, MA: Houghton Mifflin, 1969.

Littledale, Freyda. *The Magic Fish: The Fisherman and his Wife.* Toronto: Scholastic, 1967.

Luppens, Michel. *What Do the Fairies Do With All Those Teeth?* Toronto: Scholastic, 1989.

Mahy, Margaret. *17 Kings and 42 Elephants.* London: Dent, 1987.

Martin, Jr., Bill. *Brown Bear, Brown Bear, What Do You See?* New York: Holt, Rinehart and Winston, 1970.

Mayer, Mercer. *Just Me and my Friend.* Wisconsin: Western Publishing, 1988.

_____. *What Do You Do with a Kangaroo?* New York: Scholastic, 1987.

Morgan, Allen. *Matthew and the Midnight Tow Truck.* Toronto: Annick Press, 1986.

Munsch, Robert. *Something Good.* Toronto: Annick Press, 1986.

Nelson, JoAnne. *There's a Dragon in My Wagon.* Cleveland, OH: Modern Curriculum Press, 1989.

Nurit, Karlin. *The Tooth Witch.* New York: Lippincott Junior Books, 1985.

Rey, H. A. *Curious George Rides a Bike*. Boston, MA: Houghton Mifflin, 1952.

Richards, Nancy Wilcox. *Farmer Joe's Hot Day*. New York: Scholastic, 1987.

Sendak, Maurice. *Where the Wild Things Are*. New York: Scholastic, 1963.

Shaw, Nancy. *Sheep on a Ship*. Boston, MA: Houghton Mifflin, 1989.

Slobodkina, Esphyr. *Caps for Sale*. Toronto: Scholastic, 1975.

Steig, William. *Sylvester and the Magic Pebble*. Boston, MA: Houghton Mifflin, 1989.

Waber, Bernard. *Ira Slept Over*. Toronto: Scholastic, 1972.

White, E. B. *Charlotte's Web*. New York: Harper and Row, 1952.

Wilder, Laura Ingalls. *Little House on the Prairie*. New York: Harper and Row, 1953.

SCHOOL-EXPERIENCE BOOKS

Calmenson, Stephanie. *The Principal's New Clothes*. Toronto: Scholastic, 1989.

Hoban, Russell. *Bread and Jam for Frances*. Toronto: Scholastic, 1964.

Marshall, James. *Miss Nelson Is Missing*. Toronto: Scholastic, 1977.

_____. *Miss Nelson Is Back*. Toronto: Scholastic, 1982.

Parish, Peggy. *Teach Us, Amelia Bedelia*. Toronto: Scholastic, 1977.

Seliman, Lynn. *Warner, Don't Forget*. Toronto: Scholastic, 1989.

Thaler, Mike. *The Teacher from the Black Lagoon*. Toronto: Scholastic, 1989.

Udry, Mary. *What Mary Jo Shared*. Toronto: Scholastic, 1966.

BOOKS FOR CHICK-HATCHING PROJECT

Back, Christine, and Jens Olesen. *Chicken & Egg*. London: A and C Black Ltd., 1990.

Bourgeois, Paulette. *Too Many Chickens*. Toronto: Kids Can Press, 1990.

Garelick, May. *What's Inside?* Toronto: Scholastic, 1968.

Ginsburg, Mirra. *Good Morning, Chick*. Toronto: Scholastic, 1980.

Heller, Ruth. *Chickens Aren't the Only Ones*. Toronto: Scholastic, 1981.

Krauss, Ruth. *The Happy Egg*. Toronto: Scholastic, 1967.

Selsam, Millicent E. *Egg to Chick*. New York: Harper and Row, 1970.